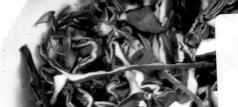

You lead a busy life and it can be tough to find the time and energy to make nourishing, flavorful meals every morning, afternoon, and night. Maybe you tried meal prepping and it zapped all the joy out of eating. Was it the rigidity? The repetitive meals day after day? The hours of work? Don't give up: *The Feel-Good Meal Plan* has a fresh, flexible, and unfussy solution to get you ready for the week—with less than two hours of prep and meals on the table every night in 30 minutes or less.

With Registered Dietitian and mom of two Lindsay Pleskot as your guide, take the next steps on your meal-planning journey with:

- **A Four-Week Meal Plan:** Dive into a month of lunches and dinners designed to save time, minimize food waste, and maximize taste and nutrition. Follow ready-made grocery lists and step-by-step meal prep instructions to simplify the process.

- **Affordable, Accessible Cooking:** No fancy ingredients required— just everyday staples you likely already have on hand. These recipes and shopping tips will keep your grocery bill and food waste to a minimum.

- **100+ Family-Friendly Recipes:** Try breakfasts like One-Pan Green Goddess Hash and Tiramisu Overnight Oats, snacks like Chocolate Chip Cookie Dough Energy Bites and Mexican Street Corn–Inspired Guacamole, and heaps of mains, like Korean-Inspired Beef and Rice Bowls with Pickled Cukes, Sheet Pan Margarita Shrimp Fajitas, Best-Ever Veggie Bolognese, and Juicy Spinach and Feta Turkey Burgers.

- **Healthful, Intuitive Eating:** Drawing on her certification as an Intuitive Eating Counselor, Lindsay has crafted meal plans and recipes that foster a balanced and joyful relationship with food, nurturing body, mind, and soul.

Ideal for busy families looking to alleviate the daily cooking grind, *The Feel-Good Meal Plan* gives you the freedom to enjoy mealtimes with ease!

The
Feel-Good
Meal Plan

A Fresh Take on
Meal Prep with Over
100 Nourishing Recipes
to Feed Your Family
with Ease

The Feel-Good Meal Plan

Lindsay Pleskot, RD

appetite
by RANDOM HOUSE

CREATOR OF **MAKE FOOD FEEL GOOD**

Appetite by Random House® and colophon are registered trademarks of Penguin Random House LLC.

Library and Archives Canada Cataloguing in Publication is available upon request.
ISBN: 978-0-525-61232-2
eBook ISBN: 978-0-525-61233-9

Book design: Matthew Flute
Interior photography: Janis Nicolay
Food styling: Lindsay Pleskot and Sophia MacKenzie
Typesetting: Daniella Zanchetta

The content of this book is for education purposes only and is not meant to replace medical advice. For recommendations that meet your specific health needs, contact your physician, registered dietitian, or other healthcare professional.

Printed in China

Published in Canada by Appetite by Random House®,
a division of Penguin Random House Canada Limited.

www.penguinrandomhouse.ca

10 9 8 7 6 5 4 3 2 1

For Wylder, Indie, and
our star in the sky, Theo.
My forever inspiration and
greatest teachers. I love you
to the moon and stars and back
and forth and back and forth.

Contents

Introduction

To tell you the truth, there was a time I was adamantly against meal prep. The rigidity, the repetitive meals, and the work it appeared to need just seemed to take all of the enjoyment out of eating. But day in and day out, I was hearing the same frustrations from my clients and community about getting meals on the table that I was feeling in my own home—burnout from the endless decisions about what to cook every night, never mind actually getting around to chopping and slicing and cooking. The overwhelm of it all left me feeling resentful of having to start yet another meal from scratch each night. So while I had initially been resistant to the idea of meal prep for both myself and my clients, I knew I needed to find a solution to the exhaustion— but on my own terms.

What if I could come up with a method that would have you prepped for the entire week in under two hours, with meals on the table in just fifteen to thirty minutes every night of the week? I'm talking a variety of flavorful, nutrition-packed dishes that leave you craving them time and time again. So that's exactly what I did: I created my own method that will save you hours of time and frustration without sacrificing the flavor, variety, and nourishment we all crave from our food.

It's my experience that food enriches every aspect of our lives. The kitchen has always been a point of connection in our family, from gathering around the dinner table each night, chopsticks in hand for one of my dad's famous stir-fries as we shared our adventures from the playground, to setting the table for one of my mom's hug-in-a-bowl soups to mend a broken heart. Some of my fondest memories with my grandparents are also connected to food: folding wontons with my ma-ma at the kitchen table, back when my feet wouldn't even touch the ground, the smell of rosemary and roasting garlic wafting through the air as we walked through the door to my granny's. I even made my first (questionable) cookbook at a young age (featuring delicacies like crackers and cheese topped with white vinegar and hot chocolate powder) and served my very first full meal with my sister, Kristi, at the age of six, accidentally mixing up the measurements for soy sauce and chicken stock for one incredibly salty fried rice. (Before you close this book right here, I promise you I've worked on my cooking skills since then, and am confident that the fried rice on page 205 is 1000% better than our original creation.) So while my skills weren't always the most refined, out of the encouragement to be creative, having space to fail and try again, and discovering the power of a home-cooked meal to bring your loved ones together (regardless of whether it was five-star-worthy), we all did our part to get these family meals on the table and connect over food. It's a tradition that my husband, Meik, and I have maintained as our own little family has grown to fill these four seats at the table.

> What if I could come up with a method that would have you prepped for the entire week in under two hours, with meals on the table in just fifteen to thirty minutes every night of the week?

With all that said, I know mealtimes can bring about a lot of stress. Sometimes it's from lack of time, and sometimes it's the pressure to get the perfect "healthy," balanced meal on the table. As a dietitian and someone who struggled with my own relationship with food in the past, I understand how all-consuming these pressures can be. In these pages, I want to share what I've learned through my formal education and personal experience to help you find ease in the kitchen and pleasure in all aspects of food. In fact, meal planning has been a way to create that space for connection, by freeing up more time for what matters most: time with loved ones.

My "Make Food Feel Good" Philosophy

It's true what they say: from our biggest challenges stem our greatest growth. While my years spent struggling in my relationship with food were incredibly challenging, they brought me to where I am today. To have landed in a place of peace and freedom with food—no guilt, no food rules hovering over me—I am grateful to now be in a position to share this with others.

The power food has to energize, heal, and nourish is woven into everything I create as a dietitian. But food is about so much more than just nutrition. Food is love, it is community, it is connection to our past, and it has the ability to draw us into the present. And while the opportunity to write this book (and make the dream of the little girl in me a reality) was born from my career as a dietitian, what you'll find in these pages is a result of an intricacy of experiences (many around food) that make up the fabric of who I am.

I want to help you see food through a lens of more, not less. Instead of focusing on what we should cut out of our diets, why not focus on what we want more of? More color, more flavor, more nourishment, more enjoyment, and more pleasure. For this reason, you won't find any hard-and-fast food rules, as it is my belief that all foods are nourishing in their own way, and that all foods can fit within the flow of your daily nourishment. What you *will* find are dishes brimming with colorful, antioxidant- and fiber-rich vegetables and an abundance of nutrients that can support us in optimizing our well-being. Each recipe is packed with flavor that will leave you satisfied, and a little dose of TLC as I pull from family-favorite recipes that have stood the test of time.

While I discourage strict regimens and restrictive food rules, by sticking to the philosophy of "more," what I recommend for pretty much everyone is eating *more* regularly throughout the day (hence my love of snacks—find my favorites in the snacks chapter, page 125) and leaning into *more* balanced meals, which these recipes are designed to provide. When possible, I aim to fill half of my plate with colorful vegetables or fruits that provide the micronutrients (vitamins and minerals) that help our bodies thrive, as well as gut-loving fiber that keeps us full longer and keeps blood sugars stable. Next up, around a quarter of the plate gets fiber-rich carbohydrates. Yes, carbohydrates—after all, they are our body's favorite way to get and use energy, not to mention the B vitamins that support energy metabolism, among other things. The final quarter of the plate, I aim to fill with protein, which helps rebuild and repair muscles and plays an integral role in the many chemical reactions going on in our body at any given time. Protein also keeps us full and fueled longer after eating. And last but not least,

> Instead of focusing on what we should cut out of our diets, why not focus on what we want more of?

I always look to finish with fat—this could be a drizzle of sauce or dressing, a sprinkle of nuts, seeds, or cheese, or the cooking oil used to get that chicken or tofu nice and crispy. Fat is essential for the absorption of vitamins A, D, E, and K and provides that satiety factor that leaves us not only full, but satisfied after eating (us nutrition nerds literally call it "the satiety factor" of a meal), lending a unique mouthfeel and carrying the flavor molecules of your favorite dishes!

That said, not every meal needs to look like this! At the end of the day, my goal is for you to enjoy what you're eating and to help you get those meals on the table more easily, so you can connect with the people and experiences around you. When it comes to flavor and nutrition, it doesn't have to be one or the other. It is my belief, not only personally but also professionally, as an intuitive eating dietitian, that all foods have their place, and that heart-, soul-, and body-nourishing meals can be one and the same. Through letting go of the rules and following what feels good, we are able to get out of our heads and into our bodies and be more connected to ourselves and others. Whether I'm wearing my hat as a mom, daughter, friend, or dietitian, my philosophy remains the same. I just want to make food feel good.

Why Meal Prep and Meal Planning Are the Answer

The concept of making food feel good sounds appealing, but I get it: you're busy. So how do we achieve this from a practical sense? That's where meal prep and meal planning fit in.

You might be wondering how someone who has fallen in love with the creative process of getting delicious, nourishing meals on the table and is passionate about intuitive eating and letting your body be your guide also became passionate about something as seemingly meticulous as meal prep. (I know, right—who's passionate about meal prep?) Doesn't that seem like the opposite?

I wanted to create a system that was organized, yet flexible, where the benefits of meal prep shone, without having to eat the same bland, boring meals every night. If you've been a part of my community for a while, you may remember my 3-2-1 Method, the very first meal plans I created, which were based on ingredient prep. This system involved prepping three vegetables, two proteins, and one carbohydrate each week to mix and match into a variety of balanced meals throughout the week. This method took off and brought a lot of ease into many kitchens. But it had its limits and had me reconsidering a pillar of my core values—letting go of the rules.

As time went on and my household grew, my style of meal prep naturally evolved. While I still pull a ton of inspiration from that initial 3-2-1 Method (you'll see that ingredient prep is the core method I follow), I also include batch prep (including freezer-friendly meals) and quick-cooking dishes that can be whipped up from scratch in under 30 minutes. You'll get a taste of all of these in the four weeks of meal plans starting on page 36 (complete with grocery lists and weekly prep instructions) and will also be able to put together your own meal plans with the recipes and methods in this book, guided by a step-by-step template that begins on page 29.

My goal is for you to enjoy what you're eating and to help you get those meals on the table a little more easily, so you can connect with the people and experiences around you.

> Having the fore-thought to plan ahead and give a bit of structure to this daily task—the very acts of meal planning and prep—actually allows for more flexibility and ease.

Through my years of trial and error, I have discovered that having the forethought to plan ahead and give a bit of structure to this daily task—the very acts of meal planning and prep—actually allows for more flexibility and ease, not only in the kitchen but in the rest of our lives, as they free up our time and mental space.

This book is a reflection of the decade-plus I've been meal prepping and meal planning in one form or another. I've literally tried and tested it all. I've made mistakes, I've spent way too much time in the kitchen, and now I've put my learnings together for you here, in what I believe is truly the best of all worlds: nutrition-packed, heart- and soul-nourishing, delicious, and vibrant meals that come together with ease. Because you deserve great food, even on a Tuesday.

Thank you for sharing a little slice of your kitchen and your life with me through these pages. It is truly an honor to get to share this with you.

xo *lindsay*

How to Use This Book

This book is here to make life easier. We've got enough going on, but we do need to eat. Every day. Multiple times a day. I want food to feel like an exciting yet grounding part of your day, whether it's sitting down for a moment to yourself in the middle of the day, or re-centering at the end with those you love most.

There are two main components to this book: 1) guidance on how to meal plan and prep with ease (including four weeks of meal plans to get you started), and 2) the recipes themselves.

The Meal Plans

The meal plans are where this book really shines. Now, I didn't just slap together a calendar with five random recipes from the book for each week; every ingredient, cooking method, and meal prep opportunity was specifically considered to give you the smoothest week possible. Complete with organized grocery lists, meal calendars, and streamlined prep instructions to carry you through the week with energy and ease, these meal plans will also help reduce food waste and save money on your grocery bill!

If you're looking to take the guesswork out of mealtimes, I suggest starting off with the premade weekly meal plans, beginning on page 36. They provide dinner for four people and lunches for two. I've found that this gives flexibility (in case anyone's not too keen on leftovers, you're not stuck with servings that go uneaten) and takes care of the more challenging and time-consuming meals of the day while being mindful of food waste and fridge storage space.

As you master the meal plans and gain confidence with meal prep, you may choose to build on them by adding a batch-prep breakfast to the week or a snack or two to fill the gaps. You'll find a ton of meal prep–friendly recipes in every chapter, and a couple of suggestions from me that are best suited to each plan.

> These meal plans will also help reduce food waste and save money on your grocery bill!

If you're just dipping
your toes into meal
prep and the idea of
doing a full week feels
overwhelming, start
where you're at!

Alternatively, if you're just dipping your toes into meal prep and the idea of doing a full week feels overwhelming, start where you're at! Ask yourself, "What feels like the easiest win or most impactful meal to begin with?" Maybe pick one to three foundational recipes, so you know you'll always have a delicious and nutritious base, or batch prep a few meals for the week and go from there. You'll find what works for your life.

The Recipes

Although you can use this cookbook like any other (by cooking any recipe that pops out at you), actually reading through all of the elements in it will help you take things to the next meal prep level—and feel like you've got it all together. (Don't worry, none of us really do, but this will help!)

The book is organized by recipe type, including breakfasts, snacks, soups and salads, and mains of noodles and rice, handhelds like sandwiches, tacos, and pizzas, and nourishing family comforts like chili, stir-fries, and curries—along with a chapter on foundational recipes and flavor hacks.

The foundational recipes teach the fundamentals of meal prep. They are some of my favorite staples that follow the ingredient prep method. They will help you master some basic meal prep recipes and give you building blocks that can be mixed and matched into different meals throughout the week, to save you time without sacrificing flavor and variety.

The flavor hacks are sauces, spreads, and toppings that level-up your meal in just about ten minutes or less. A drizzle of this and a dollop of that can take a totally average meal to restaurant-worthy with minimal extra effort! These are my best little tricks to create crave-worthy sauces and lick-the-plate-clean flavor with minimal ingredients.

Many of the recipes are included in the four weeks of meal plans I've provided for you, but there are over fifty more, to give you even more variety in your mealtimes. They are designed to work well when you're building your own meal plan (page 29) by using similar ingredients and meal prep methods.

All of the book's recipes come together quickly and easily and are full of flavor. While each one can be made as a standalone dish to be eaten fresh, they were all created with the intention of saving you time—whether they're batch-prep meals to set you up for the week (maybe even freezer-friendly to save you down the line) or have larger yields to purposefully provide leftovers. I go into detail of the different types of meal prep and what to look for in this book with Meal Prep 101 on page 11.

Identifying Meal Prep Styles and Dietary Types

When you're putting your week together, it's helpful to be able to identify at a glance which meal prep style a recipe uses. I've identified whether each recipe is one or more of the following (read more about each on page 11):

INGREDIENT PREP	BATCH PREP	SUPER-QUICK	FREEZER-FRIENDLY

Whether you're following certain dietary restrictions or you're just looking to incorporate more plant-based meals into your week, these dietary tags are super handy to help you sift through the recipes:

VEGETARIAN | VEGAN | DAIRY-FREE | GLUTEN-FREE | NUT-FREE

My Top Cooking Tips

Regardless of whether you start with a single recipe or full-on meal plan, I always recommend two steps before you start cooking, to save time and frustration: 1) Read through the entire recipe before starting, and 2) set up your mise en place (see the sidebar on page 12).

My top tip once you actually start cooking is this: when it says don't stir, don't stir! Yes, this deserves its own note. You'll notice many of the recipes state to cook without stirring. Seriously, DO NOT STIR! It's the key to 1) lazy cooking, but more importantly, 2) more flavor. Browning and searing build flavor.

Recipes Are a Template

While these recipes are designed the way that I eat or like them best, you can look at them as a template. You can often swap like for like to mix things up, or use any ingredients you have on hand. By "like for like," I mean swap grains for grains (for example, try quinoa instead of rice in the Sweet and Spicy Soy-Glazed Salmon Bowls, page 201), protein for protein (swap chicken for the shrimp in the Sheet Pan Margarita Shrimp Fajitas, page 219), or veg for veg (got some broccoli wilting in the fridge? Swap it for the peppers in Mila's Sticky Orange Chicken, page 194). This approach will not only help you save a ton of food waste, but will allow you to tailor pretty much any recipe to your liking and prevent the frustration of going to three grocery stores to find a missing ingredient. You might just create your own favorite version of a recipe!

> Swapping ingredients like for like will not only help you save a ton of food waste, but will allow you to tailor pretty much any recipe to your liking.

Meal Prep 101

Meal Prep Styles

There are different styles of meal prep, and though we can often feel like we need to commit to only one method, through years of trial and error I have landed on using a combination of ingredient prep and batch prep, as well as leaving some nights open in my meal plan for super-quick meals that come together so quickly, they don't need any advance prep. These types of things aren't black or white: it's about making life easier! Forget the rules and do what feels good!

INGREDIENT PREP

This is the method I gravitate towards, and the one you'll see most in my meal plans. It's what really got me into meal prep, as I love the variety it provides! The idea is that instead of fully prepping five to seven meals for the week, you prep only the components or individual core ingredients—cutting up veggies, cooking ground meat, batch prepping grains, and preparing sauces and dressings—so they're ready to throw into various dishes. That way, you can get a home-cooked dinner on the table in a fraction of the time.

WHEN TO DO IT: When you want quick and easy meals throughout the week, but also want variety in what you're eating.

BATCH PREP

Batch prep is when you either make an entire dish in advance, then store it for later in the week, or make a large serving of a dish with the purpose of having leftovers. I used to be somewhat opposed to making large-batch meals, not wanting to eat the same thing again and again, but over time, I have found that throwing a batch-prep meal or two into the mix can really come in handy!

Freezer-Friendly
Many batch-prep meals are freezer-friendly so I consider freezer meals to be a subcategory of batch-prep meals. These are full dishes that can be frozen and stored as is for up to a few months, ready to pull out when you need them most!

WHEN TO DO IT: If you want to set yourself up for future meals that are ready to rock, batch-prep meals are the way to go! With the prep and cleanup done, all you have to do when it comes time to eat is reheat and enjoy! I often incorporate one batch-prepped meal into my weekly rotation, like the Best-Ever Veggie Bolognese (page 237), the Save-the-Day Freezer Enchiladas (page 254), A Vegan Chili the Meat Lovers Will Beg For (page 270), or the Skillet Turkey Nacho Bake (page 258).

Freshen It Up!

When you're going the batch-prep route, I recommend adding a touch of something fresh when serving. It could be a sprig of herbs, a squeeze of citrus, diced avocado, or your favorite pickled veg. This is especially helpful if you're not a huge fan of leftovers—it's an easy way to get that just-prepared feeling. A little freshness goes a long way! This is also a great hack for store-bought frozen meals!

SUPER-QUICK

These are freshly made meals that come together from scratch, from prep to plating, in 30 minutes or less. Leftover protein and grains are a lifesaver when pulling together a super-quick dish! I've tagged recipes that use pre-cooked ingredients with a Super-Quick Option.

WHEN TO DO IT: When you want a super fresh meal and need it to come together ASAP (like on those Friday nights in the meal plans I've left open), a super-quick meal will be your best friend. If you've got ingredients on hand that you want to use up, it may also be worth exploring these recipes to see what you can whip up!

Mise en Place

Mise en place is a French culinary phrase that translates to "everything in place," which refers to having your ingredients organized and ready to go before you start cooking. For example, having a bowl of minced garlic and onion so they're ready to add to the pan as soon as the oil gets hot, or having bell peppers or broccoli washed, chopped, and at your side when the time comes to add them to the dish. If you've ever worked in a professional kitchen, you know this is how the pros stay organized and efficient—and there's a good reason for that! While it may feel like more work up front, it actually saves you time and a lot of chaos while cooking. It also makes cleaning up much easier. It took me far too long to adopt this practice, so here's me, strongly encouraging you to save yourself the years of frustration and do your mise en place!

"Fast Foods"

- Cajun seasoning
- Capers
- Coconut milk
- Couscous
- Curry paste
- Enchilada sauce
- Greek seasoning blend
- Italian seasoning blend
- Legumes (chickpeas, beans, and lentils)
- Nut butters
- Oats
- Olives
- Pesto (regular and sun-dried tomato)
- Roasted red peppers
- Tomatoes (diced, crushed, and oil-packed sun-dried)
- Tomato paste
- Tomato sauce

Stocking Up for Meal Prep Success

Having a well-stocked pantry is the key to successful meal prep. That doesn't mean you need to go out and buy anything and everything you can fit in your cupboards (or fridge or freezer); instead, keep a few well-thought-out, commonly used items on hand. Some of these staples are also what I call "fast foods," my dietitian go-to's that are exactly that: foods that are ready to go or require very little prep to complete a meal. I've pulled these out into sidebars to inspire you on those days when you just aren't able to dedicate much time to chopping and prepping ingredients—maybe another week you'll have more time and energy. Buying certain ingredients already prepped is one of my greatest time-saving kitchen hacks. As a dietitian and busy mom, I encourage you to take any shortcut you can find. Let it be easy!

Meal Prep Pantry

OILS

Don't be afraid of oil! For many of us who grew up through the eighties and nineties, when fat was demonized, it can be hard to shake the idea that less fat is better. But when it comes to cooking *flavorful* meals, you need fat—especially with plant-based proteins that have little to no natural fat, a (generous) splash in the pan will do wonders for the flavor of the dish! Fat carries flavor molecules, it helps us absorb vitamins A, D, E, and K, and many cooking oils support brain and heart health. Need I say more? These are my favorite oils for everyday cooking:

> **EXTRA VIRGIN OLIVE OIL:** Extra virgin olive oil is unrefined and typically made without heat or chemicals. This allows it to retain more of its flavor and nutritional properties. Olive oil contains polyphenols, known to have antioxidants and to be anti-inflammatory. Because of its delicate nature, extra virgin olive oil has a medium smoke point of 350°F (180°C), so it's good for medium-heat cooking or baking, but is not great for high-heat cooking, like stir-frying, barbecuing, or roasting at high temperatures.

AVOCADO OIL: Refined avocado oil is my favorite oil for high-heat cooking, with a smoke point around 500°F (260°C). With a similar nutrition profile to olive oil, it carries many of the same benefits, without it breaking down at higher heats. Its flavor is quite neutral, making it very versatile. Just make sure not to buy unfiltered avocado oil; it has a strong flavor that doesn't make it appropriate for cooking. (I've made that mistake!)

SESAME OIL: I love the flavor that sesame oil adds to certain dishes, like Better-than-Takeout Tender Beef and Broccoli Udon (page 190) and Ma-Ma's Wontons (page 266). It also has a high smoke point, between 400°F and 450°F (200°C and 230°C), making it great for stir-fries and other high-heat cooking. I almost always go for toasted sesame oil, which has a richer flavor, but it can be hard to find. You can replace it with regular pure sesame oil, but the flavor won't be quite as deep.

GRAINS

Before we go any further, can we all just agree to leave the low-carb era in the past? The myth that carbs are "bad" drives me crazy. Not only are carbo-hydrates our bodies' (and brains') preferred source of fuel (a.k.a. energy!), they are also packed with B vitamins to support our metabolism and energy production, fiber to keep us full, and so much more. Here are my go-to's:

COUSCOUS: If you want fast, couscous is your best friend. Combine it with boiling water, cover, and it cooks itself while you prep the rest of your meal. I usually opt for whole wheat couscous. I don't find there's much difference in taste or texture compared to regular couscous, and I appreciate the extra fiber and minerals!

OATS: Oats are so versatile! I love them as a base for quick and delicious breakfasts or an extra boost of fiber and minerals in baked goods (whole or ground into flour). I can't wait for you to try them in my 15-Minute Savory Oat "Risotto" with Asparagus and Peas (page 122)! *Note:* While oats don't contain gluten, they can be susceptible to cross-contamination. If you want to ensure your oats have not come into contact with gluten, be sure to opt for oats clearly labeled "gluten-free."

QUINOA: Light and fluffy, this protein-forward grain is perfect to add to salad or to soak up the sauce and dressing in a bowl. It cooks faster than rice, making it a great option when you need a meal to come together quickly!

RICE: I like to mix things up. Often I go for brown rice, but some days (and with certain dishes) white rice just tastes better! And here is your official permission from a dietitian: it's totally okay! If you're trying to incorporate more brown rice into your meals, you can mix it half and half with white rice for the best of both worlds. In some recipes, I've suggested my preferred rice, but to keep your prep simple, use one rice for the week's meals.

While the grains above are my absolute staples, I love to mix things up with barley, farro, kamut, and wheat berries. Remember, you can swap different grains into your favorite recipes if they're already prepped or if you just want to try something new!

"Fast Food" Grains

These are perfect to keep stocked in the pantry and cook up in minutes when you need an almost-instant option!

Microwavable grain pouches
I keep one or two pouches on hand for nights when even making rice feels too hard. You can find great variety in stores now, including quinoa and grain blends.

Gnocchi
These little potato dumplings cook quickly and taste delish.

Tortillas, wraps, and bread
I like to have these on hand as a no-cook grain option for meals.

CANNED AND JARRED GOODS

I love having a few staple canned foods on hand at all times. Here are some of my favorites that are used in the book. They can help you pull an easy meal together with whatever you have available, without sacrificing flavor!

- Capers
- Coconut milk (full-fat)
- Curry paste
- Enchilada sauce
- Legumes (my favorites are chickpeas, lentils, cannellini/white kidney beans, and mixed beans)
- Olives
- Pesto (regular and sun-dried tomato)
- Roasted red peppers
- Tomatoes (diced, crushed, and oil-packed sun-dried)
- Tomato paste
- Tomato sauce

SPICES, SEASONINGS, AND FLAVORINGS

I love a well-stocked spice stash—and a good shortcut! Most spice blends are simply that—a bunch of spices already blended for you, so don't be afraid of them! If you're conscious of sodium, take a quick peek at the ingredient list and make sure it contains only dried spices and no added salt. While I prefer to cook with fresh garlic, onion, and ginger, I do keep the powder forms on hand in case I run out or need a quick substitute.

The spices used in this book are:

- Black pepper
- Bouillon or stock powder (I like mixing Better Than Bouillon paste with water to make stock)
- Cajun seasoning
- Cayenne pepper
- Chili powder
- Cinnamon (ground)
- Cumin (ground)
- Flaky salt (for finishing dishes, I love Maldon)
- Garlic powder (½ tsp ground = 1 clove)
- Ginger powder (¼ tsp ground = 1 tsp minced fresh)
- Nutritional yeast
- Onion powder (1 tsp powder = 1 onion)
- Oregano (1 tsp dried = 1 Tbsp fresh)
- Red pepper flakes
- Table salt
- Turmeric (ground)

NUTS AND SEEDS

These are truly little nutrition powerhouses and are so versatile. Whether you're looking for a little crunch to finish a meal, some extra protein or fiber, or a way to up the antioxidant and anti-inflammatory properties of a meal, here are the nuts and seeds (and their butters) that I always keep stocked:

- Almonds and almond butter
- Chia seeds
- Flax seeds
- Hemp hearts
- Peanut butter
- Pecans
- Pumpkin seeds (shelled)
- Sesame seeds (toasted and raw)
- Sunflower seeds (shelled)
- Tahini
- Walnuts

Others I often keep in my pantry include:

- Cashew butter
- Pine nuts (these little guys are pricey, but a little goes a long way!)
- Salted roasted peanuts
- Sunflower seed butter

Hot Tip, Frozen Dough!

This one is a game changer. Many bakeries, grocery store freezer aisles, and even pizza shops sell premade frozen dough. It's just like homemade, but ready to go when you are!

Meal Prep Fridge and Freezer

So many fridge and freezer items are already "fast foods"—ready to go and amp up your meal.

CHEESES

FETA CHEESE: This is another staple in our house—you'll rarely find a salad without it. It's also great with eggs, in wraps, and for dips!

SHREDDED CHEESE: I don't know what it is, but grating cheese has to be one of my least favorite kitchen tasks. I used to always get Meik to do it, but then we discovered the magic of pre-shredded cheese. Now we always have a bag of it in our fridge, perfect to throw into scrambled eggs or to top casseroles, tacos, or pastas. It's one item I find well worth the extra money for the time and frustration it saves! If you prefer to shred your own, use your food processor to grate a whole block at once and store in a sealable storage bag.

EGGS

Eggs are such a convenient source of protein (not to mention iron, vitamin B_{12}, and choline, and one of the best dietary sources for vitamin D), and they are not just for breakfast! Fry them up to throw on a salad or pasta, poach them to add protein to a risotto, or make the Perfectly Prepped Jammy Eggs (page 71) for soups and bowls!

GREEK YOGURT

I always have Greek yogurt on hand. Not only does it provide the best creamy texture, but it is also packed with protein, at around 18 grams per ¾-cup serving. That's almost as much as a serving of meat or fish! Plain yogurt is especially versatile for anything from aiolis to cream sauces or dressings to dips and, of course, smoothies. I use vanilla yogurt when I want a little extra sweetness in a smoothie or for a snack, like the PB&J Greek Yogurt Snacking Bark on page 144. You don't need to go fat-free; having some fat actually keeps us full and satisfied longer, plus I find the texture creamier, with a less bitter taste. I usually buy yogurt with between 2% and 5% milk fat.

MILK

We generally keep 2% milk in our fridge as a nice middle-of-the-road option that works in pretty much any dish. If you're looking for a creamier consistency, opt for 3.25% or higher. I don't typically recommend skim/non-fat milk, as I find it is generally too watery. An exception would be for smoothies, where it works just fine!

Plant-based milks are another option. Nutritionally, soy milk is the most similar to cow's milk and, along with oat milk, tends to have the creamiest consistency. Opt for unflavored plant-based milks for savory dishes, but I do enjoy unsweetened vanilla options in things like smoothies, overnight oats, or chia pudding.

Pro Tip

Did you know cheese can be frozen? Stock up when it's on sale or freeze any extra before it goes bad, to pull out as needed.

Nutrition Hack

If you're using flavored yogurt and want to reduce the amount of sugar, either replace half of the flavored yogurt with plain or opt for a reduced-sugar version. These are different from the artificially sweetened or "diet" varieties; they simply have less sugar added, which may be clearly noted on the label as, for example, "30% less sugar" or "lower sugar."

ROTISSERIE CHICKEN

Grocery store rotisserie chickens are a lifesaver on busy weeks. Cut them up for an instant protein to add to salads or wraps, or to speed up many of the recipes in this book.

VEGETABLES

BINS OF GREENS: Avoid washing and cutting up all those greens! These pre-washed greens are great in smoothies and for quick salads. Pro tip and even bigger time-saving hack: You know those nights when you don't care about the presentation and would do anything to save a dish? Make the salad right in the bin! If you don't finish it all, just close it up and store it in the fridge—no extra container needed!

PRE-CUT CAULIFLOWER AND BROCCOLI: Avoid the mess and save yourself time on busy weeks.

SHREDDED CARROTS: If you don't feel like pulling out the box grater or food processor, pre-shredded carrots are a time saver for dishes like Best-Ever Veggie Bolognese (page 237) and Korean-Inspired Beef and Rice Bowls with Pickled Cukes (page 198)

SLAW MIXES: I love adding these to bins of greens for super-quick salads or to replace cabbage in recipes like Charlie's Lo Mein (page 189) or tacos!

SALAD KITS: These are an instant way to get that half plate of vegetables.

SNAP PEAS, TOMATOES, AND BABY CARROTS: These no-prep veggies are another instant way to get more vegetables on your plate. They make great sides for pizzas and burgers, and are a quick way to balance out your meal with minimal effort.

FROZEN FRUITS AND VEGETABLES

FRUITS: Frozen fruits like berries, pineapple, or mango work great in smoothies and yogurt bowls. As they thaw, they will even produce a natural "sauce" with their juices!

VEGETABLES: Frozen broccoli, cauliflower, corn, peas, and corn/pea/carrot mix can be used in cooked dishes like stir-fries, fried rice, soups, or pasta sauces. They won't be quite as crisp as fresh vegetables, but play around and see what works for you!

RICED CAULIFLOWER: You can make your own, but I often buy it ready to go. Add it to chilis, pasta sauces, mac 'n' cheese, and so many other dishes. It's a great way to add a dose of veggies and antioxidants that is also kid-approved!

Fridge and Freezer "Fast Foods"

- Shredded carrots and baby carrots
- Pre-cut cauliflower and broccoli
- Cherry tomatoes
- Edamame beans
- Snap peas
- Bins of greens
- Slaw mixes
- Salad kits
- Burger patties
- Rotisserie chicken
- Scallops
- Shrimp

Tip

Use your processor for
everything from thinly slicing
cabbage or mushrooms to
grating carrots, celery, and
cheese. You can even mince
garlic and ginger! It's also the
perfect tool for sauces like
the Chimichurri on page 81
and the Green Goddess
Dressing on page 75.

Setting Up Your Kitchen for Meal Prep Success

I'm not one for buying every kitchen gizmo and gadget just because. But there are a few that, without a doubt, make cooking and meal prep much more enjoyable (read: quicker, easier, and more efficient).

Tools and Supplies

BLENDER

High-speed blenders can be an investment, but they are totally worth it if you can swing it. I'm a Vitamix gal, but there are many others on the market that will do the trick. Blend up smoothies and ice pop mixes, purée soups (like the Creamy Roasted Tomato and White Bean Soup on page 253) to the perfect creamy consistency, or make your own homemade oat flour in under a minute. A traditional blender will also work for most recipes but may not provide as smooth a consistency.

CUTTING BOARDS

I recommend having one or two plastic cutting boards in various sizes and at least one large wooden cutting board or butcher block. While meal prepping, you can easily stick to one board and wash between uses, but I often have two out: one for raw meat and one for veggies. This helps keep your kitchen food-safe, preventing cross-contamination.

FOOD PROCESSOR

This is my absolute favorite time-saving kitchen tool. I can slice, grate, and chop in a fraction of the time, which makes all the difference in place of long, laborious meal prep. Make sure to get a food processor with slicing/shredding disc attachment(s). Some have multiple discs with varying sizes and thicknesses. As long as you have at least one slicing and one grating option, you should be fine, but it never hurts to have more!

(GOOD) KNIVES
Good knives are an investment, but nothing is worse (or more unsafe) than cutting with dull knives. On that note, you don't have to buy the most expensive knives, but you do want them sharp and of good quality. *Pro Tip:* Keep an eye out for sales! Knives and even whole knife blocks often go on sale.

MIXING BOWLS
I have mixing bowls in three different sizes that I use for whipping up doughs and batters, making things like burger patties, or putting together meal prep recipes. I recommend getting stackable bowls, to save space.

MEASURING CUPS AND SPOONS
As time goes on, you may find that you're able to eyeball certain measurements, which can speed up the cooking process (especially for things like sauce ingredients that can be poured right into the pan and adjusted to taste), but I always recommend measuring the first time or two you make any recipe. For baking, it's important to always measure your ingredients, as small changes can really impact the outcome of a recipe.

MICROWAVE-SAFE GLASS MEASURING CUP
This can be used not only to measure ingredients but also to quickly melt chocolate sauces or to warm sauces without dirtying more dishes. I recommend buying one that can hold at least 3 cups of liquid and that has a spout for easy pouring.

MICROPLANE
This small but mighty kitchen tool gets used daily in my kitchen, most frequently for grating garlic. Grated garlic has a more vibrant flavor than chopped, and with a Microplane you can grate up a whole week's worth in minutes. I also use it to zest citrus and finely grate Parmesan cheese.

PARCHMENT PAPER
Parchment paper is the ultimate item to prevent losing half of your meal from sticking to the bottom of the pan, and makes cleaning up so much quicker and easier.

RAMEKINS OR PREP BOWLS
Ramekins or small prep bowls are so handy for mise en place (see page 12). They take up minimal space, saving counter and dishwasher space, and just make cooking easier.

RUBBER SPATULAS
Spatulas are magic for getting every last drip and drop into a recipe. I recommend having one to two large spatulas and one to two small spatulas in the rotation.

SILICONE WHISK
Whisks are great for incorporating ingredients well and preventing lumps in sauces. Silicone whisks ensure you don't scratch the bottom of any nonstick surfaces.

WOODEN SPOONS AND SPATULAS

Wooden spoons are great for stirring recipes in nonstick pans to make sure you don't scrape and damage the bottom. I also love a wooden spoon or spatula to really get that crispy crust off the bottom of the pan (like in Jangs' Famous Fried Rice, page 205)—especially when using a wok or cast-iron pan.

Cookware

BAKING SHEETS

Baking sheets, also known as sheet pans, are a must. For meal prep, it's best to have two or three to maximize efficiency and be able to roast multiple things at once. Pretty much any basic baking sheet will do the trick, so don't worry about breaking the bank or getting anything fancy here!

BAKING PANS AND DISHES

For the recipes in this book, you'll need a metal 8-inch square baking pan and 9 × 5-inch loaf pan, a ceramic 8½ × 11-inch baking dish, and a glass 9 × 13-inch baking dish. Note that metal heats faster than ceramic or glass, so if you're substituting in metal pans, you'll need to adjust cooking time accordingly.

MUFFIN TINS

These are pretty self-explanatory! If you have little ones in the house, or like a smaller snack size yourself, add mini muffin tins to your collection.

RICE COOKER

I grew up using a rice cooker, so I've never really known any other way. If you've got the space, I definitely recommend one! They don't need to be monitored; you simply push the On button and wait to open the lid to perfectly cooked grains. (They're not just for rice!) You don't have to worry about overflowing pots or burnt grains sticking to the pan. Especially during meal prep, with multiple things going on at once, rice cookers save time and effort.

Meal Prep Containers

STORAGE CONTAINERS

It's a must to have storage containers in various sizes for meal prep! We have a variety of shapes and sizes of glass, plastic, and bamboo containers (more on each below) that we've collected over the years. If you're starting from scratch, I'd go with a set of glass containers, as they're likely designed to stack together and fit in a fridge best, then add a few plastic or bamboo containers to your collection for a lighter option when you don't need an airtight seal. I recommend having a range of the following microwave- and freezer-safe containers:

- Two to four large (8 to 10 cups)
- Six to ten medium-large (3 to 4 cups)
- Four to six medium (1 to 2 cups)
- Five to ten small (¼ to ½ cup); jars work great for this (see page 24)

GLASS: Snap-top glass containers are my favorite, as they seal best and are durable. That said, they can be heavy and run the risk of chipping and breaking (especially if you've got little ones around), but if you're careful, they can last a long time.

PLASTIC: Plastic containers are lighter and more flexible, but often don't have a tight seal, so avoid them for saucier dishes. Most are microwave-, freezer-, and dishwasher-safe, but be sure to double-check and opt for BPA-free options.

BAMBOO: Bamboo containers have become increasingly popular and are more environmentally friendly than plastic, but can be pricier.

GLASS JARS

Jars are great for storing sauces, salad dressings, and pickled vegetables. They provide a tight seal and offer additional storage without taking up a ton of space in your storage area or fridge. I like to have a variety of sizes, including:

- 4 oz (125 ml) for minced ginger, garlic, or small-volume sauces
- 8 oz (250 ml) for salad dressings, aiolis, and sauces
- 16 oz (500 ml) for pickled onions, larger-volume sauces, and salad dressings
- 24 oz (750 ml) to 32 oz (1 L) for pickled cabbage, jar soups, and batch-prep salads

SEALABLE STORAGE BAGS

I love using sealable silicone or plastic bags to store things like cooked grains, shredded cabbage, and prepped greens or vegetables. They also work great for thicker liquid recipes like curries, pasta sauce, or soups. They stack well, to optimize space, and are low-cost, easy-to-store meal prep containers if you have limited space. You can buy them in various sizes and easily wash and reuse them. For freezing leftovers, be sure to buy freezer-safe bags, which are more likely to prevent freezer burn and are more durable.

STORAGE WRAP

Having some type of storage wrap on hand is essential for meal prep! Plastic wrap and foil are common options. My favorite is beeswax wraps, for a more environmentally friendly option—as a bonus, they smell really nice!

The "Nice-to-Haves"

These items aren't absolute musts, but if you have the space and the means, they're super handy!

KITCHEN SCISSORS

I use them to cut up fresh herbs, open packages, and sometimes even cut ingredients. It's just nice not to have to mix them with the arts and crafts scissors, ya know?

Pro Tip

Save jars from pasta sauces and jam to add to your meal prep container collection!

INSTANT-READ THERMOMETER

This helps ensure meat and poultry are cooked through without having to cut in (letting the protein rest after cooking allows for a juicier, more tender product).

SLOTTED SPOON

A slotted spoon allows you to remove food from a pot of boiling water easily. I use mine when making poached eggs or Perfectly Prepped Jammy Eggs (page 71) and Ma-Ma's 100 Wontons (page 266).

WOK

I grew up eating a ton of stir-fries, so a wok was a kitchen staple. They definitely take up their fair share of space, so if you just can't swing it, don't sweat: a regular large frying pan will do the trick for any of these dishes!

CAST-IRON PAN

These are perfect for searing and getting perfect blackened crust on fish. They are also oven-safe, so are great for dishes you want to start on the stove and transfer to the oven to finish!

How to Create Your Own Meal Plan

There are many recipes in this book that aren't included in the premade meal plans (pages 36–55), so I've put together this step-by-step guide on how to build your own plan, complete with a ready-to-fill-in template! Whether you want to play around with swapping a few recipes into the existing plans or create all-new plans for more variety, I want you to have all the tools you need to feel like a true meal planning and prepping master!

Must-Know Meal Prep Tips

If you're like me, you may be tempted to skip over this part and just dive in. PLEASE DO NOT SKIP THIS SECTION!

CONSISTENCY IS KEY

Meal prep gets quicker and easier the more practice you get. When you do it consistently, you'll learn all sorts of time savers, like how to prep rollover items for the following week, such as minced ginger or onion, shredded cabbage, extra pickled vegetables, or salad dressings—or even full servings of meals to stock your freezer! Stick with meal prepping; it is so worth it!

GROUPING TASKS IS THE ULTIMATE TIME SAVER

Whether it's prepping meals or answering emails, grouping similar tasks and tackling them all at once saves you time, plain and simple. Prepping all of your veggies on one day means pulling out your cutting board and knives only once. Browning enough ground turkey for the week means only washing those dishes once. You multiply the output without requiring much extra input. Kind of genius, right?

Grocery Shopping Tips

Write Your Grocery List
I highly recommend sorting your grocery list by section of the grocery store to save yourself time and frustration. You'll notice I've organized mine this way in the meal plans, so you can use those as a template.

Shop Your Home First
DO NOT SKIP THIS STEP! Before you head out to grocery shop, grab your list and do a quick inventory of what you already have on hand. This will save you time, money, and storage space. I bet you'll be surprised to see what you've already got!

Remember, Recipes Are a Template
While you take your kitchen inventory, remember that you can usually swap like for like. Found hot dog buns or English muffins in the freezer? Use those for burger buns! Have some leftover asparagus kicking around? Swap it in for green beans or snow peas. Got leftover quinoa from last week's prep in the freezer? Save yourself time and swap it for rice to switch things up. You may even discover a new favorite recipe variation while you're at it!

Save on Your Grocery Bill
My meal plans should help trim your grocery spending, as they are designed to use up as much of the purchased items as possible. The first week your bill may be higher as you buy items like oils and spices, but remember, you won't need to buy these every week!

Order Groceries Online
Online grocery shopping has been nothing short of life-changing for me. I know that sounds extreme, but seriously, it saves so much time, whether you order for pickup or delivery! For those with young kids, it has also saved many an in-store meltdown or frustrated momma trying to wrangle kids from every which way. Consider this time in the bank that you can put towards meal prep! If you enjoy grocery shopping, though, carry on, and take comfort knowing the heavy lifting of meal planning and grocery list writing is done!

Shop and Prep on Different Days
If possible, get your groceries on a different day than you prep. This breaks things up and makes them feel a lot more manageable!

Don't Grocery Shop Hungry!
You know what happens. Overbuying, overspending, and ending up with things you don't want or need.

CLEAR YOUR WORKSPACE BEFORE YOU START
Trust me, taking the extra five minutes to start with a clean slate makes all the difference!

TIDY AS YOU GO
I usually leave big dishes for the end (or pull in my husband, Meik, partway through!), but I recommend clearing anything you're done with as you go, even if it is just moving it into the sink. Put containers in the fridge once an ingredient is prepped, and do anything else you can to keep a tidy and organized workspace.

HAVE A SCRAP BIN OR BOWL
Get your compost bin out or, if you don't have one, designate a large bowl for food scraps so you can easily discard onion peels, carrot tops, and bell pepper seeds and keep your counter space cleaner. It may seem insignificant, but not having to open the cupboard to discard an item each time can make a big difference in the end!

PACK LUNCHES WHILE YOU CLEAN UP DINNER
While everything is already out, pack up the next day's lunch. It won't really add to cleaning time, since you've got to pack things up anyway, and you will be so happy when the morning rolls around and this task is already done!

Creating Your Meal Plan

CONSIDER YOUR CALENDAR
How many nights will you actually be home for dinner? Start here to make sure you don't overbuy. Nothing is more frustrating than throwing out a bunch of food at the end of the week! If you're following the meal plans on page 36–55 and won't be needing every meal, simply cut one or two out OR follow through with all of the prep and stock your freezer with a few homemade freezer meals— your future self will thank you!

PICK YOUR RECIPES
When choosing recipes for the week, you'll want to be strategic. Here's what I recommend:

> **Look for recipes with the Ingredient Prep tag, then select recipes with similar prep ahead ingredients.** These will become your ingredient prep items that can be mixed and matched with other "fast foods" (see pages 14 to 19) to create a variety of quick and easy meals throughout the week.

> **Consider including one big batch-prep meal.** That way, you'll have multiple meals at the ready without any extra cooking.

> **Streamline.** Selecting recipes with similar ingredients and/or preparing a big batch-prep recipe will help you limit the number of items on your grocery list, eliminate food waste because you'll be more likely to use up what you've bought, and simplify your weekly meal prep.

> **Consider cost.** If you have a pricier ingredient, like tuna or salmon, in one meal, consider balancing it with a plant-based recipe, which tend to include low-cost proteins.

WRITE OUT YOUR MENU FOR THE WEEK

You can use my meal plan template (see page 34). Consider your proteins and their best-before dates; I recommend putting recipes with fresh seafood at the beginning of the week, recipes with poultry, pork, or beef at the middle, and vegetarian recipes at the end.

GET READY TO GROCERY SHOP

Grocery shopping is an art in itself, so be sure to read through my tips on page 30.

PREP WITH PURPOSE

This is the key to a successful and stress-free week of FAST meals. My method stands apart from others in the way I've designed it to save as much time as possible, without sacrificing flavor or variety in your meals.

Consider cook time. Start with either set-and-forget items like grains (get them cooking on the stove and then leave them be until they're done) or items with the longest cooking time. You can fill in the time by prepping veggies, sauces, and quick-cooking meats.

Consider cooking methods. Look for ways to cook different ingredients simultaneously: on the stovetop, in the oven, or on the barbecue or an indoor grill. Your time won't be used as efficiently if you have multiple oven-baked items on your prep list (unless they require a similar baking temperature and can fit in the oven at the same time).

Try batching by kitchen tool. Prep all food processor ingredients one after another before moving on to the cutting board—leaving aromatics like garlic and onion for last, so as not to impact the flavor of the other vegetables.

Minimize dishes. Prep all of your raw meat at once, so you only need to wash your cutting board once.

Mastering Meal Prep Day

Scan this QR code to download a blank template to build your own meal plan.

Here are the steps I take when planning out my prep day, which you might find useful if you start putting together your own meal plans. The order has been carefully constructed to keep prep time to a minimum. Start with cooking grains and protein so that you can use their cooking time to prep your veggies and sauces. For further efficiency, stick to one "station" before moving on to the next (for example, do everything you need to with the food processor before going to the cutting board). Lastly, always end with aromatic and raw ingredients to minimize dishes, since you need to wash aromatics' strong smell and lingering flavor off the tools after using and raw ingredients' bacteria that could cross-contaminate.

BEFORE YOU START PREPPING

1 **GET YOUR PREP CONTAINERS READY:** This will vary depending on what you're prepping this week, but here's what I typically use:

- Two to three bowls (for batch prepping salads, bowls, or big-batch recipes like pasta sauce)
- One to three medium to large glass jars (for sauces, dressings, or pickled vegetables)
- One to three extra-small glass jars or airtight containers (for garlic or ginger)
- Eight to twelve airtight containers or sealable storage bags; I like a mix of two to three large, four to six medium, two small or extra-small (for veggies, batch-cooked grains, batch-prepped bowls, or salads and other various ingredients)

2 **GET YOUR EQUIPMENT READY:** Preheat the oven, barbecue, or grill, if needed. Set up your food processor and rice cooker, if you have these appliances, and lay out all the pots, frying pans, cutting boards, knives, measuring cups and spoons, and any other tools you will need for your prep. *Pro Tip:* If the oven temperatures for your recipes are off by 25°F or so you can still cook them at the same time and adjust the cooking time accordingly (checking sooner if at a higher temperature than the original recipe and cooking longer if at a lower temperature than the recipe).

COOK THE GRAINS

Since grains can cook away essentially unattended, start with them and use their cook time to prep your other ingredients. See page 58 for How to Meal Prep Grains.

PREP AND COOK MEAT/VEGGIES (OVEN)

If your meal plan has both veggies and meat that need to be cooked in the oven, do so at this stage. If the meat and veggies are prepped but not cooked, complete those tasks **in the food processor** or **on the cutting board** (see those steps below). Prep your veggies first, and then the meat (so you won't have to wash your knife and cutting board in between, saving time).

Depending on the size of your oven, you can prepare two to four baking sheets or pans of meat and veggies if they cook at a similar temperature. Switch the pans' positions in the oven halfway through the cooking time to evenly distribute the heat. Cooking time may be impacted by how much is in the oven. The more there is, the longer they'll take to cook. For meat, use a thermometer to determine doneness. For veggies, they are done when fork-tender and starting to brown around the edges.

MAKE SAUCE/DRESSING FOR BATCH-PREP LUNCHES

If your DIY meal plan includes a batch-prep lunch, like the Greek Chickpea Salad (page 175) or the Taco Salad in a Jar (page 160), whisk together the sauce or dressing ingredients in one of your bowls.

IN THE FOOD PROCESSOR

To save time, prep the ingredients that require the same blade attachments first. If prepping aromatics like ginger, garlic, and onion, do these last to prevent their taste and smell from transferring to the other vegetables.

ON THE CUTTING BOARD

Cut your veggies (or any that have not already gone in the oven). Transfer those for your batch-prep lunch into their bowl—this will save counter space.

MAKE YOUR BATCH LUNCH

Add the remaining ingredients for your batch lunch to their bowl, toss to coat, and transfer to an airtight container. If you are layering your salads/bowls, add the ingredients one at a time, finishing with anything that could wilt or get soggy (like leafy greens) on top. If you are making your recipe in one large container, add leafy greens fresh on the day you will be eating them.

OPTIONAL PREP

If you have some extra time and fridge space, make your sauces for the week. Otherwise, these come together quickly the day of.

Four-Week Meal Plan

First and foremost, these meal plans are designed to save you a ton of time and ease the mental energy of planning your weekly meals. From picking out recipes to writing your grocery list to cooking everything from scratch each night—it's a lot. I see you. These meal plans are my gift to you. Here are some important tips and tricks to help you get the most out of them.

What's Included

These meal plans are designed to feed four people as follows (though this may vary depending on your household's appetites, which *you* know best, so feel free to scale them up or down as you see fit): four servings for dinner and two servings for lunch.

Lunches

My meal plans are designed to cover dinner for four and lunches for two. Why? It's a fine balance between covering everyone's needs. I know leftovers aren't for everyone but not letting any food go to waste is one of the foundations of this book. Whether they need to be adapted for young family members who don't eat full servings, selective eaters, business lunches, or those who prefer a "snacky lunch," I designed these plans to consider the realistic dance of different needs and preferences under one roof. But don't worry! I've got you covered with quick options to fill the needs of all family members—see Quick Lunch Ideas on page 37.

What to Know

1. **PREP TIME:** The weekly prep will take around one and a half to two hours, depending on your experience, and comfort level in the kitchen, and distractions (hi, kids!). Plus, of course, any of the optional prep you decide to do.

2. **GIVE IT A CHANCE:** Meal prep gets exponentially easier each week you do it! The first time you do anything is the hardest and most time-consuming, especially when you're learning a new system. Allow for extra time the first week so you don't feel rushed. Throw on some tunes, pour your favorite drink, and don't be afraid to delegate some of the tasks! I promise you will build confidence and efficiency each week!

Quick Lunch Ideas

Here are options to fill out your meal plans with nourishing and balanced lunches, if desired, that either come together quickly in a build-your-own adventure style or are grab-and-go freezer meals right from the pages of this book!

Build Your Own Lunchables (protein + carb + fat + fruit/veg)
· **Protein Box:** Deli meat (I like turkey or chicken) + whole-grain crackers or pita + cheese + grapes and cucumber
· **Cracker-Stacks:** Hard-cooked eggs + fiber-rich crackers (I like Ryvita, Wasa, or Finn Crisps) + sliced avocado + sliced tomato and cucumber
· **"Banana Sushi":** Tortilla + peanut butter or nut-free seed butter + a sprinkle of hemp hearts + a banana laid lengthwise; roll up and slice crosswise (like sushi) and serve with veggie sticks
· **Sandwich and Veggies:** Tuna salad sandwich with veggie sticks and dip
· **Breakfast-for-Lunch Bowls:** Greek yogurt or cottage cheese + granola + nuts or seeds + fresh fruit (berries, apples, banana)
· **Pita Pizza:** Whole-grain pita with tomato sauce + leftover meat, deli meat, sliced smoked tofu, or beans + cheese + veggies (I like mushrooms, peppers, or chopped spinach); assemble and serve cold, or broil for 2 to 4 minutes, cut into pieces, let cool, and store in an airtight container; heat in the microwave or oven when ready to eat

Quick Store-Bought Options
· Canned soup (I like Italian wedding soup, bean soup, chicken gumbo, or chicken and rice; they all provide a decent amount of protein)
· Canned chili
· Individual frozen meals, like stir-fries or bowls

Past Meal Prep
· Plan for leftovers when you cook and throw the extra servings in the freezer. Consider freezing in individual servings. My favorite freezer-friendly recipes are tagged throughout the book and listed on page 276.

3. **BUY ONLY WHAT YOU NEED:** The grocery lists include exact measurements because I recommend shopping your pantry first, and having the exact measurement of what you'll need allows you to quickly identify whether you need more, even if you have an item on hand. It also helps you determine which size of bottle or package you need to buy.

4. **READ THROUGH EVERYTHING (SERIOUSLY):** Before you start chopping, read through the week's prep instructions in their entirety. Having a broad overview and knowing what's coming next will have you feeling more confident as you move through the prep, and will save time in the end.

5. **DON'T FORGET TO ADJUST:** If you're building on the meal plans to include additional batch meals, adjust the grocery lists and prep amounts as needed.

6. **THE JOYS OF INGREDIENT PREP:** One of the things that makes these meal plans unique is that you're not just batch prepping and eating the same thing day in and day out. Many of the recipes benefit from the ingredient prep done at the beginning of the week to mix and match and cook up a delicious variety of meals that come together in 15 to 30 minutes on the night of.

Adapting Recipes to Plant-Based

If you're looking to incorporate more plant-based meals, many recipes can be easily adapted to do so. Remember, recipes are a template! I find these swaps often work well, but play around with them. You might just be surprised to find a new favorite recipe variation!

CHICKEN, PORK, OR BEEF
Sub in tofu or tempeh, cut as described in the recipe (cubed, sliced, etc.).

GROUND MEAT
Try veggie ground round, crumbled tofu, lentils, or pulsed/mashed beans. Burgers or wontons can also be replaced with your favorite store-bought varieties.

FISH AND SEAFOOD
Substitutions for these will vary depending on the recipe. For something like the Seared Salmon Burgers with the Easiest Tartar Sauce Ever (page 215), falafel or bean-based patties may work best. For a recipe like the Waikiki Tuna Poke Bowls (page 202) or 15-Minute Cajun Fish Tacos with Quick Pickled Cabbage (page 216), cubed tofu, cubed tempeh, or cannellini (white kidney) beans can work well.

Note: Although the cooking method will remain mostly the same, keep in mind that you may need to add a bit more cooking oil with plant-based proteins and that the cooking time may need to be adjusted.

Week 1

Welcome to Week 1 of the meal plans! I can't wait for you to experience the ease (and deliciousness) to come this week! By spending just one and a half to two hours to complete this week's prep (not to mention the time and mental energy you've already saved by having your meal planning done for you and your grocery list written), you'll be miles ahead heading into the week! To kick it off on Sunday night, the **Best-Ever Veggie Bolognese** is a satisfying and vegetable-filled dinner that is just as delicious when reheated for dinner on Wednesday. The **Waikiki Tuna Poke Bowls** are a refreshing taste of Hawaii and a delicious way to add nutrient-packed fish to your meals. The **Greek Chickpea Salad** is full of fresh, antioxidant-rich veggies and the fiber-fueled plant protein of chickpeas, making it one of the ultimate batch-prep recipes; the version in this meal plan saves time, dishes, and counter space, but you can also enjoy it as a layered jar salad. The **Korean-Inspired Beef and Rice Bowls with Pickled Cukes** pack a punch with colorful, antioxidant-rich veggies (made even easier if you buy pre-shredded carrots and cabbage). To round off the week, the **Sheet Pan Margarita Shrimp Fajitas** are a balanced meal, with lots of vitamin C, that's light on cleanup.

Scan this QR code to download the grocery list.

Recipes You're Making This Week

- Best-Ever Veggie Bolognese (page 237)
- Greek Chickpea Salad (page 175)
- Waikiki Tuna Poke Bowls (page 202)
- Korean-Inspired Beef and Rice Bowls with Pickled Cukes (page 198)
- Sheet Pan Margarita Shrimp Fajitas (page 219)

	LUNCH	DINNER
SUNDAY	Meal Prep Day	Best-Ever Veggie Bolognese
MONDAY	Greek Chickpea Salad	Waikiki Tuna Poke Bowls
TUESDAY	Waikiki Tuna Poke Bowls	Korean-Inspired Beef and Rice Bowls with Pickled Cukes
WEDNESDAY	Korean-Inspired Beef and Rice Bowls with Pickled Cukes	Best-Ever Veggie Bolognese
THURSDAY	Greek Chickpea Salad	Sheet Pan Margarita Shrimp Fajitas
FRIDAY	Sheet Pan Margarita Shrimp Fajitas	Enjoy leftovers or a "super-quick" meal, or order in!

Grocery List

PRODUCE

- 1 lemon
- 1 lime
- 2 mangos (or 2 cups frozen mango)
- 2 small avocados
- 1 pint cherry tomatoes
- 10½ oz (300 g) cremini mushrooms (or mushrooms of your choice)
- 5 large carrots (or 5 cups pre-shredded carrots)
- 3 stalks celery
- 11 mini cucumbers
- 6 bell peppers (yellow, orange, or red)
- 1 jalapeño
- ½ purple cabbage (or 6½ cups pre-shredded cabbage; some will be used to make pickled cabbage for Week 2)
- 1 head romaine lettuce
- ½ cup fresh basil
- Fresh flat-leaf parsley
- Fresh cilantro
- 1 bunch green onions
- 1 small red onion (some of the onion will be used to make pickled red onion for Week 2)
- 2 white onions (1 small, 1 medium)
- 2 bulbs garlic (16 cloves)
- 4-inch knob ginger

MEAT & ALTERNATIVES

- 1½ lb (680 g) extra-lean ground beef
- 1½ lb (680 g) sushi-grade tuna (or sub sushi-grade salmon)
- 1½ lb (680 g) veggie ground round

REFRIGERATED

- Plain Greek yogurt (¼ cup)
- Sour cream or plain yogurt
- Feta cheese (1 cup)
- Shredded cheese (I like marble cheese or Tex-Mex mix)
- Parmesan cheese (for garnish)
- Guacamole (for topping)

FREEZER

- 1½ lb (680 g) raw peeled shrimp (or sub chicken, tofu, or tempeh)
- Shelled edamame beans (1½ cups)

BAKERY

- Twelve 6-inch tortillas

GRAINS & STARCHES

- Rice (3¼ cups) (I like short-grain brown or white or brown jasmine)
- Whole wheat couscous (⅔ cup)
- 1 lb (450 g) pasta (I like pappardelle, spaghetti, or rotini)

OILS & CONDIMENTS

- Avocado oil or other high-heat cooking oil (1 Tbsp)
- Extra virgin olive oil (1 cup)
- Toasted sesame oil (½ cup) (or sub pure sesame oil)
- Red wine vinegar (⅓ cup)
- Unseasoned rice vinegar (2 Tbsp)
- White vinegar (4½ cups) (for 2 weeks' worth of Quick Pickles)
- Mayonnaise (¼ cup)
- Dijon mustard (2 tsp)
- Soy sauce (1 cup)
- Sriracha (2 tsp)
- Hot sauce (for topping)
- Salsa (for topping)
- Pickled ginger (for garnish)
- Wasabi (for garnish)

SPICES, SEASONINGS & FLAVORINGS

- Chili powder (1 Tbsp)
- Ground cumin (1 Tbsp)
- Black pepper
- Red pepper flakes (2 tsp)
- Salt
- Dried oregano (4 tsp)
- Roasted sesame seeds (2 to 3 Tbsp)
- Nutritional yeast (¼ cup)

PANTRY STAPLES

- 1 can (19 oz/540 ml) chickpeas
- 1 can (28 oz/796 ml) crushed tomatoes
- Tomato paste (1 Tbsp) (buy a resealable tube to prevent waste)
- Pitted sun-dried or regular kalamata olives (½ cup)
- Granulated sugar (9 Tbsp) (for 2 weeks' worth of Quick Pickles)
- Packed brown sugar (⅔ cup)

OTHER

- Red wine (½ cup) (or 1 Tbsp balsamic vinegar)
- Parchment paper

Reminder

Remember to shop your house first. With all the spices, condiments, and pantry staples you already have on hand, you will likely be able to trim down your grocery list.

On Meal Prep Day

EQUIPMENT
2 medium pots (or 1 rice cooker and 1 pot)
Food processor (or grater and knife or mandoline)
1 large frying pan
1 to 2 cutting boards
Chef's knife
Measuring cups and spoons

CONTAINERS
1 large bowl, 1 medium bowl, 1 small bowl
3 glass jars (one 32 oz/1 L, two 16 oz/500 ml)
12 airtight containers or sealable storage bags (5 large, 4 medium, 2 small)

COOK THE GRAINS

1   **RICE:** Cook **3¼ cups rice** in **5 cups water** (for white rice) or **6½ cups water** (for brown rice) as directed on page 58 or according to package directions. This will yield about 9½ cups of cooked rice. Let cool, then store in a large container in the fridge for the poke bowls and the beef and rice bowls.

2   **COUSCOUS:** Cook **⅔ cup couscous in 1 cup water** as directed on page 58 or according to package directions. This will yield 2 cups of cooked couscous. Let cool, then add to the large bowl for the chickpea salad, started below.

MAKE THE DRESSING FOR YOUR BATCH-PREP LUNCH

1   Meanwhile, in a large bowl, whisk together **½ cup extra virgin olive oil, ⅓ cup red wine vinegar, juice of 1 lemon, 2 tsp Dijon mustard, 2 tsp dried oregano, 1 tsp salt,** and **freshly ground black pepper** until well combined for the chickpea salad.

IN THE FOOD PROCESSOR

1   **CARROTS:** Using the shredding disc attachment, and with the inside blade removed, grate the **5 carrots**. Store 2 cups in a medium container in the fridge for the beef bowls. Leave the rest in the food processor.

2   **CELERY:** Using the same shredding disc, grate the **3 celery stalks** into the food processor with the carrots. Transfer the carrots and celery to a medium bowl for the Bolognese sauce.

3   **MUSHROOMS:** Swap the shredding disc for the blade attachment. Chop the **mushrooms (10½ oz/300 g)** into pea-sized pieces and add to the medium bowl for the Bolognese sauce. Note: You may need to chop the mushrooms in batches if they are becoming too fine or watery.

4   **GINGER:** Peel the **4-inch knob ginger**. Rinse the food processor and blade and wipe dry. Using the same blade attachment, mince the whole knob. Store in a small container in the fridge.

5   **PURPLE CABBAGE:** Swap the blade for the slicing disc. Thinly slice the **½ purple cabbage**. Put 3½ cups in the 32 oz (1 L) glass jar, for pickled cabbage. Wrap the remainder in a paper towel and store in a medium container or storage bag in the fridge, for the beef bowls.

6   **WHITE ONIONS:**
   • Rinse the food processor and slicing disc. Using the same slicing disc attachment, slice **1 medium onion** and store in a medium container in the fridge for the shrimp fajitas.

   • Remove the slicing disc and insert the blade attachment. Dice **1 small onion** by pulsing a few times, then set aside in a small bowl for the Bolognese sauce.

7   **RED ONION:** Using the same slicing disc, slice **1 small red onion**. Add one-eighth of the onion to the bowl for the chickpea salad. Put the remainder in a 16 oz (500 ml) glass jar for pickled red onion.

ON THE CUTTING BOARD (VEGGIES)

① **BELL PEPPERS:**

- Meanwhile, thinly slice **5 bell peppers**. Wrap them in a paper towel and store in a large container in the fridge, for the fajitas.

- Cut the **remaining 1 pepper** into 1-inch squares and add to the bowl for chickpea salad.

② **CUCUMBERS:**

- Thinly slice **7 mini cucumbers**. Store 2 cups in a medium container in the fridge for the tuna poke bowls. Put the remainder in a 16 oz (500 ml) glass jar for pickled cucumbers.

- Dice the remaining **4 mini cucumbers** and add to the bowl for the chickpea salad.

③ **CHERRY TOMATOES:** Quarter **1 cup cherry tomatoes**. Add to the bowl for the chickpea salad.

④ **ROMAINE LETTUCE:** Roughly chop **1 head romaine lettuce** and spin or pat dry. Wrap in a paper towel and store in a large storage bag in the fridge for the chickpea salad. *Note:* Wait until just before eating to add it to the salad; otherwise, the leaves will get slimy.

⑤ **GARLIC:** Press, mince, or use a Microplane to grate **16 cloves garlic**. Set aside 1½ tsp in the small bowl with the onion for the Bolognese sauce. Store the remainder in a small container in the fridge.

PREP AND COOK MEAT/VEGGIES (STOVETOP)

① **BOLOGNESE SAUCE:** Follow steps 2 to 4 on page 237 to make the sauce. For this you'll need: **3 Tbsp extra virgin olive oil, the prepped white onion and 1½ tsp garlic** (set aside in a small bowl), **1½ lb veggie ground round, the prepped carrots, celery, and mushrooms** (set aside in a medium bowl), **½ cup red wine, 1 can (28 oz/796 ml) crushed tomatoes, ¼ cup nutritional yeast, 1 Tbsp tomato paste, 2 tsp dried oregano, salt,** and **pepper**. Let cool and store in a large container in the fridge.

MAKE YOUR QUICK PICKLES

① In a large pitcher, combine **4½ cups boiling water, 4½ cups white vinegar, 9 Tbsp sugar,** and **4 Tbsp salt**, stirring until the salt and sugar dissolve. Pour this brine over the **cabbage in the 32 oz/1 L jar, the cucumbers in the 16 oz/500 ml jar,** and **the red onion in the 16 oz/500 ml jar**. Make sure to completely cover the vegetables and discard any remaining brine. Let cool, cover tightly, and store in the fridge. (The pickled cabbage and onions will also be used for Week 2's fish tacos.)

MAKE YOUR BATCH LUNCH

① To the bowl for the chickpea salad, add **1 can (19 oz/540 ml) drained and rinsed chickpeas, ½ cup pitted sun-dried or regular kalamata olives,** and **1 cup crumbled feta cheese**, tossing to coat all the ingredients in dressing. Transfer to a large container and refrigerate.

Optional Prep

Still have energy and fridge space on Meal Prep Day? Continue with these items! If not, whip them up while your other ingredients cook on the day of eating.

Sauce It Up

In each of four small glass jars, make and store one of these sauces: Tuna Poke Sauce (page 202), Sriracha Aioli (page 77), Korean-Inspired Beef Sauce (page 198), and the marinade for the Sheet Pan Margarita Shrimp Fajitas (page 219).

You're All Set!

Now that you're all prepped, mealtimes will be a cinch! When you're ready to serve, go to each recipe in the book and pick up where it says **IF YOU'RE FOLLOWING THE MEAL PLAN** and get ready for a week of quick, easy, delicious, and nourishing meals.

Week 2

Week 2, here we go! With one week under your belt, you will notice things already feel easier as you get the hang of meal prepping! This week highlights the plant power of cruciferous kale in the **Famous Kale Caesar** (with crispy chickpeas for an extra boost of filling protein and fiber). The **Creamy Roasted Vegetable Sheet Pan Gnocchi**, featuring antioxidant-rich peppers and plump, crispy gnocchi, comes together in record time but makes a meal worthy of your favorite restaurant. **Better-than-Takeout Tender Beef and Broccoli Udon** will be on the table quicker than an Uber Eats driver can get there and will have even the most selective eaters piling the saucy broccoli onto their plates! We've also got flavor-packed **Juicy Spinach and Feta Turkey Burgers** (a great source of iron) because . . . well, burgers. And the **Taco Salad in a Jar**, batch-prepped for an instant lunch you'll crave time and time again, is quite possibly the most fun way to get that daily dose of greens! The version here saves time, dishes, and counter space, but you can also enjoy it as a layered jar salad. You will love the variety of flavors and colors in the nutrition-packed meals that come together with ease this week, thanks to your meal prep!

Scan this QR code to download the grocery list.

Recipes You're Making This Week

- Juicy Spinach and Feta Turkey Burgers (page 228) with an optional side of Easiest Arugula Salad (page 168)
- Taco Salad in a Jar (page 160)
- Better-than-Takeout Tender Beef and Broccoli Udon (page 190)
- 15-Minute Cajun Fish Tacos with Quick Pickled Cabbage (page 216)
- Famous Kale Caesar with Creamy Greek Yogurt Dressing and Crispy Chickpeas and Capers (page 159)
- Creamy Roasted Vegetable Sheet Pan Gnocchi (page 245)

	LUNCH	DINNER
SUNDAY	Meal Prep Day	Juicy Spinach and Feta Turkey Burgers with an optional side of Easiest Arugula Salad
MONDAY	Taco Salad in a Jar	15-Minute Cajun Fish Tacos with Quick Pickled Cabbage
TUESDAY	Taco Salad in a Jar	Better-than-Takeout Tender Beef and Broccoli Udon
WEDNESDAY	Better-than-Takeout Tender Beef and Broccoli Udon	Famous Kale Caesar with Creamy Greek Yogurt Dressing and Crispy Chickpeas and Capers
THURSDAY	Famous Kale Caesar with Creamy Greek Yogurt Dressing and Crispy Chickpeas and Capers	Creamy Roasted Vegetable Sheet Pan Gnocchi
FRIDAY	Creamy Roasted Vegetable Sheet Pan Gnocchi	Enjoy leftovers or a "super-quick" meal, or order in!

Grocery List

PRODUCE

- 2 lemons
- 5 limes
- 1 mango (or 1 cup frozen mango)
- 1 large + 1 small avocado
- 3 pints cherry tomatoes
- 1 tomato
- 2 crowns broccoli (or buy pre-cut florets; you'll need about 6 to 7 cups)
- 1 mini cucumber
- 2 bell peppers (red, orange, or yellow)
- 2 bins (5 oz/142 g) baby arugula (or 8 oz/225 g of loose arugula; if you buy the bin you'll have extra to use)
- 3 large bunches curly kale
- 1 head lettuce
- 1 bin (5 oz/142 g) spinach (or 2½ oz/75 g loose spinach; if you buy the bin you'll have extra to use)
- 1 bin (5 oz/142 g) mixed greens (or 2½ oz/75 g loose greens; if you buy the bin you'll have extra to use)
- 1 bunch fresh basil
- 1 small bunch fresh cilantro
- 1 bunch green onion
- 3 to 4 small red onions (only buy 3 if opting for pickled red onion in the taco salad)
- 1 small white onion
- 2 bulbs garlic (about 16 cloves)
- 3-inch knob ginger

MEAT & ALTERNATIVES

- 1½ lb (680 g) flank steak or skirt steak
- 1 lb (450 g) mild Italian sausage or vegetarian sausage
- 3 lb (1.4 kg) ground turkey
- 1 lb (450 g) white fish (I like cod, halibut, or tilapia)

REFRIGERATED

- Eggs (2)
- Plain Greek yogurt (1¾ cups)
- Feta cheese (1⅔ cups)
- Cheese (for topping burgers, I liked aged white Cheddar)
- Grated Parmesan cheese (1 cup)
- Tzatziki (½ cup)

FREEZER

- Corn kernels (1 cup) (or canned)

BAKERY

- 4 burger buns (I like brioche)
- Twelve 6-inch flour tortillas (or gluten free if needed)

GRAINS & STARCHES

- Quinoa (⅔ cup)
- 1¾ lb (800 g) udon noodles (you can buy four 7 oz/200 g packages)
- 1 lb (450 g) gnocchi

OILS & CONDIMENTS

- Avocado oil or other high-heat cooking oil (⅓ cup)
- Extra virgin olive oil (1 cup)
- Toasted sesame oil (3 Tbsp)
- Unseasoned rice vinegar (1 Tbsp)
- Soy sauce (3 Tbsp)
- Oyster sauce (1½ Tbsp)
- Hot sauce (for topping)
- Black bean paste (1 Tbsp) (or sub black bean sauce)

SPICES, SEASONINGS & FLAVORINGS

- Cajun seasoning (1 Tbsp)
- Chili powder (1 Tbsp)
- Ground cumin (1 tsp)
- Black pepper
- Red pepper flakes (¼ tsp)
- Salt and flaky salt
- Sesame seeds (for garnish)
- Chicken stock (¾ cup)

PANTRY STAPLES

- 2 cans (each 19 oz/540 ml) chickpeas
- 1 can (14 oz/398 ml) black beans (a 19 oz/540 ml can will also work)
- Capers (½ cup)
- Nacho chips or tortilla chips (2 cups)
- Panko bread crumbs (2 Tbsp)

OTHER

- Parchment paper

ALREADY PREPPED

- Pickled red onion (1 cup) (If not prepped in Week 1, add to your list: 1 small red onion, ¾ cup white vinegar, and 1½ Tbsp granulated sugar)
- Pickled cabbage (2 cups) (If not prepped in Week 1, add to your list: ¼ purple cabbage, 1½ cups white vinegar, and 3 Tbsp granulated sugar)

Reminder

Remember to shop your house first. With all the spices, condiments, and pantry staples you already have on hand, you will likely be able to trim down your grocery list.

On Meal Prep Day

EQUIPMENT
1 medium pot
Food processor (or knife and mandoline)
1 large frying pan
1 to 2 cutting boards
Chef's knife
Measuring cups and spoons

CONTAINERS
2 large bowls
2 glass jars (one 32 oz/1 L, one 16 oz/500 ml) (optional, if making Quick Pickles)
7 airtight containers or sealable storage bags (3 large, 3 medium-large, 1 small)

COOK THE GRAINS

1. **QUINOA:** Cook **⅔ cup quinoa** in **1 cup water** as directed on page 58 or according to package directions. This will yield **2 cups of cooked quinoa**. Let cool, then add to the bowl for the taco salad with the salad dressing made below.

MAKE THE DRESSING FOR YOUR BATCH-PREP LUNCH

1. Meanwhile, in a large bowl, whisk together **⅓ cup extra virgin olive oil, juice of 3 limes,** and **½ tsp salt** for the taco salad. Adjust to taste with salt and more lime juice as desired.

IN THE FOOD PROCESSOR

1. **GINGER:** Peel the **3-inch knob ginger**. Using the blade attachment, mince the whole knob. Transfer to a medium-large container for the steak marinade (see below).

2. **PURPLE CABBAGE (OPTIONAL):** If you don't have pickled cabbage on hand from Week 1, shred the **¼ purple cabbage** now. Place in the 32 oz (1 L) glass jar.

3. **WHITE ONION:** Rinse the food processor. Use the slicing disc attachment to slice **1 small white onion**. Wrap in paper towel and place in a large container or storage bag in the fridge for the beef and broccoli udon.

4. **RED ONIONS:**

   - If you don't have pickled onion on hand from Week 1, using the same slicing disc attachment, slice **1 small red onion** and add to a 16 oz/500 ml jar.

   - Removing the slicing disc and replacing it for the blade attachment, dice another **2 small red onions**. Put half in a large bowl for the turkey burgers and the other half in a large container for the sheet pan gnocchi.

   - If using raw onion in the taco salad, dice another **½ small red onion** and add to the bowl for the taco salad.

ON THE CUTTING BOARD

1. **CHERRY TOMATOES:** Quarter **1 cup cherry tomatoes** and add to the bowl for the taco salad.

2. **BROCCOLI:** Cut **2 crowns broccoli** into bite-size florets and add to the container with the white onion for the beef and broccoli udon.

3. **KALE:** Remove the kale leaves from the stems of the **3 large bunches** and cut or tear into bite-size pieces. Spin or pat dry. Wrap in a reusable cloth or paper towel and store in a large storage bag, squeezing out as much air as possible. Store in the fridge for the kale Caesar.

4. **SPINACH:** Finely chop **4 cups spinach** and add to the bowl for the turkey burgers.

5. **BELL PEPPERS:** Cut **2 bell peppers** into 1-inch squares. Wrap in a paper towel and store in the large container in the fridge for the sheet pan gnocchi.

6 **GARLIC:** Press, mince, or use a Microplane to grate **16 cloves garlic**. Add 1 Tbsp to the container for the steak marinade. Add 1 tsp to the bowl for the turkey burgers. Store the remainder in a small container in the fridge.

MAKE YOUR QUICK PICKLES (OPTIONAL IF NOT ON HAND FROM WEEK 1)

1 In a large pitcher, combine 2¼ cups boiling water, 2¼ cups white vinegar, 4¼ Tbsp sugar, and 6 tsp salt, stirring until the salt and sugar dissolve. Pour this brine over the cabbage in the 32 oz/1 L jar and the red onion in the 16 oz/500 ml jar. Make sure to completely cover the vegetables and discard any remaining brine. Let cool, cover tightly, and store in the fridge.

PREP AND COOK MEAT

1 **GROUND TURKEY FOR THE TACO SALAD:** Cook **1 lb (450 g) ground turkey** as directed in step 2 on page 160. For this you'll also need: **1 Tbsp avocado oil, 1 Tbsp chili powder, 1 tsp ground cumin,** and **½ tsp salt**. Let cool, then add to the bowl for the taco salad.

2 **STEAK MARINADE FOR THE BEEF AND BROCCOLI UDON:** Add **1½ Tbsp soy sauce, 1 Tbsp rice vinegar,** and **salt** and **pepper** to taste to the container with the ginger and garlic, stirring to combine. Thinly slice **1½ lb (680 g) flank or skirt steak** against the grain, cutting the slices in half if needed to make strips about 2 inches long and ¼ inch thick. Add to the container and toss to coat. Seal the container and store in the fridge.

3 **GROUND TURKEY FOR THE BURGERS:** To the bowl for the turkey burgers, add the remaining **2 lb (900 g) uncooked ground turkey, 2 eggs, ⅔ cup feta cheese, ½ tsp salt,** and **½ tsp pepper**. Combine and form into patties as directed in steps 1 and 2 on page 228. Store four patties in a medium-large container in the fridge and four patties in a medium-large storage bag in the freezer.

MAKE YOUR BATCH LUNCH

1 If using **pickled red onion**, add **½ cup** to the bowl for the taco salad, along with the **1 can (14 oz/398 ml) drained and rinsed black beans** and **1 cup corn kernels (thawed if frozen)**. Toss to coat the ingredients in the dressing. Seal the bowl and refrigerate. *Note:* Do not add the taco chips or mixed greens until just before eating.

You're All Set!

Now that you're all prepped, mealtimes will be a cinch! When you're ready to serve, go to each recipe in the book and pick up where it says **IF YOU'RE FOLLOWING THE MEAL PLAN** and get ready for a week of quick, easy, delicious, and nourishing meals.

Optional Prep

Still have energy and fridge space on Meal Prep Day? Continue with these items! If not, whip them up while your other ingredients cook on the day of eating.

Sauce It Up

In each of three small glass jars, make and store the ingredients for one of these sauces: Lime Crema (page 84), Famous Kale Caesar dressing (page 159), and Beef and Broccoli Sauce (page 190). Additionally, if you'd like to make and store your own tzatziki for the turkey burgers, see page 82 and add those ingredients to your grocery list.

Spice It Up

If you'd like to make and store your own Cajun seasoning, see page 76 and add those ingredients to your grocery list.

Week 3

Week 3 is here to show you that the nutrition powerhouse tofu can be crave-worthy, in the batch-prepped lunch of the week, **Coconut Thai Green Curry Noodle Soup in a Jar**, adjusted for this meal plan to save time, dishes, and counter space. As always, your ingredient prep creates incredible variety, with juicy, protein-rich chicken breasts turned into **10-Minute Chicken, Fig, and Brie Sourdough Sandwiches** and then totally revamped into tasty **Chicken, Corn, and Feta Quesadillas** the whole family will love (these freeze and reheat super well too)! One of my favorite cruciferous vegetables—purple cabbage—adds the perfect crunch to **Peanutty Soba Noodle Bowls** and complements the rich and creamy peanut dressing. The **Sheet Pan Chimichurri Salmon with Crispy Roasted Potatoes and Green Beans** is loaded with brain- and heart-healthy omega-3s—and you get to enjoy it again with built-in leftovers (you'll be looking for any excuse to enjoy more of the fresh, vibrant, anti-oxidant-rich chimichurri). As with every week, each recipe is dietitian-designed to provide a balanced, nourishing, and satisfying meal, to help you feel your best. Now that you're at Week 3, I have to ask: How nice is it to no longer have to ask (or hear) "What's for dinner?" Know that I am over here, giving you a high five, and soak in the glory of how much better this week will be with this prep under your belt. Enjoy!

Scan this QR code to download the grocery list.

Recipes You're Making This Week

- Sheet Pan Chimichurri Salmon with Crispy Roasted Potatoes and Green Beans (page 257)
- 10-Minute Chicken, Fig, and Brie Sourdough Sandwiches (page 212) with an optional side salad
- Coconut Thai Green Curry Noodle Soup in a Jar (page 185)
- Peanutty Soba Noodle Bowls (page 193)
- Chicken, Corn, and Feta Quesadillas (page 232) with an optional side salad
- Creamy Parmesan Polenta with Tomato Cajun Shrimp (page 262)

	LUNCH	DINNER
SUNDAY	Meal Prep Day	Sheet Pan Chimichurri Salmon with Crispy Roasted Potatoes and Green Beans
MONDAY	Sheet Pan Chimichurri Salmon with Crispy Roasted Potatoes and Green Beans	10-Minute Chicken, Fig, and Brie Sourdough Sandwiches with an optional side (bagged) salad
TUESDAY	Coconut Thai Green Curry Noodle Soup in a Jar	Peanutty Soba Noodle Bowls
WEDNESDAY	Peanutty Soba Noodle Bowls	Chicken, Corn, and Feta Quesadillas with an optional side (bagged) salad
THURSDAY	Chicken, Corn, and Feta Quesadillas	Creamy Parmesan Polenta with Tomato Cajun Shrimp
FRIDAY	Coconut Thai Green Curry Noodle Soup in a Jar	Enjoy leftovers or a "super-quick" meal, or order in!

Grocery List

PRODUCE

- 3 large lemons
- 1 pint cherry tomatoes (mixed colors if available)
- 10½ oz (300 g) mixed mushrooms (I like cremini and shiitake, but you can sub in others)
- 1 bunch asparagus
- 1¼ lb (550 g) green beans (to save time, you can buy pre-washed and trimmed beans)
- 3½ oz (100 g) snap peas
- ¼ purple cabbage (or 3 cups pre-shredded cabbage)
- 1 large bunch lacinato kale (or sub curly kale)
- 1 bin (5 oz/142 g) spinach (or 4 oz/125 g loose spinach)
- 1 bunch fresh cilantro
- 1 bunch fresh oregano
- 1 bunch fresh parsley
- 1 bunch green onions
- 1 shallot
- 1 bulb garlic (about 7 cloves)
- 2¼ lb (1 kg) little gem potatoes
- 2 bagged salads (optional, to serve with sandwiches and quesadillas)

MEAT & ALTERNATIVES

- 3 lb (1.4 kg) boneless skinless chicken breasts (6 to 7 chicken breasts or use shredded meat from a store-bought rotisserie chicken)
- 1½ lb (680 g) skinless salmon
- 1 lb (450 g) medium-firm tofu

REFRIGERATED

- Milk (2 cups)
- Sour cream (for topping)
- Salted butter (3 Tbsp)
- 5 to 7 oz (150 to 200 g) Brie cheese
- Feta cheese (1 cup)
- Shredded cheese (2½ cups) (I like Monterey Jack)
- Grated Parmesan cheese (½ cup)
- Guacamole (for topping)

FREEZER

- Corn kernels (1½ cups) (or canned)
- 1 lb (450 g) raw peeled shrimp
- Shelled edamame beans (1½ cups)

BAKERY

- 1 loaf sourdough bread
- Six 10-inch flour tortillas (or gluten free if needed)

GRAINS & STARCHES

- 7 oz (200 g) rice vermicelli noodles
- 12 oz (350 g) soba noodles
- Ground yellow cornmeal (1 cup)

OILS & CONDIMENTS

- Avocado oil (2½ Tbsp)
- Extra virgin olive oil (¾ cup)
- Toasted sesame oil (2 Tbsp) (or sub pure sesame oil)
- Red wine vinegar (2 Tbsp)
- Unseasoned rice vinegar (2 Tbsp)
- Garlic aioli (¼ cup)
- Soy sauce (¼ cup)
- Fish sauce (1 Tbsp)
- Hoisin sauce (¼ cup)
- Sriracha (1 to 2 tsp)
- Salsa (for topping)
- Chimichurri or pesto (1 cup) (only buy if not making homemade chimichurri)
- Thai green curry paste (¼ cup)

SPICES, SEASONINGS & FLAVORINGS

- Cajun seasoning (1 Tbsp)
- Chili powder (for garnish)
- Black pepper
- Red pepper flakes (a pinch)
- Salt and flaky salt
- Roasted sesame seeds (for garnish)
- Chicken or vegetable stock (2 cups)
- Vegetable bouillon powder or paste (2 Tbsp) (I like Better than Bouillon)

PANTRY STAPLES

- 1 can (400 ml) full-fat coconut milk
- Creamy peanut butter (⅓ cup)
- Fig jam (6 Tbsp)

OTHER

- Parchment paper

Reminder

Remember to shop your house first. With all the spices, condiments, and pantry staples you already have on hand, you will likely be able to trim down your grocery list.

On Meal Prep Day

EQUIPMENT
2 baking sheets
Food processor
1 to 2 cutting boards
Chef's knife
Measuring cups and spoons

CONTAINERS
1 large bowl
Four 32 oz (1 L) glass jars
9 airtight containers or storage bags (2 large, 3 medium-large, 3 medium, 1 small)

GET YOUR EQUIPMENT READY

1. Preheat the oven to 400°F (200°C). Line a 9 × 13-inch baking dish with parchment paper as described on page 67.

PREP AND COOK MEAT

1. **CHICKEN:** Season and bake **3 lb (1.4 kg) boneless skinless chicken breasts** as directed on page 67. Let cool, then store 4 breasts in a medium-large container in the fridge for the sourdough sandwiches. Dice the remaining chicken and store in another medium-large container in the fridge for the quesadillas.

2. **SALMON:** If not already in fillets, cut **1½ lb (680 g) skinless salmon** into 6 fillets. Store in a medium-large container in the fridge for the chimichurri salmon.

BEFORE YOU START CHOPPING

1. In a large bowl, whisk together the **coconut milk (from 1 can/400 ml), ¼ cup curry paste, 2 Tbsp bouillon,** and **1 Tbsp fish sauce** until well combined, for the green curry noodle soup.

IN THE FOOD PROCESSOR

1. **PURPLE CABBAGE:** Using the thinnest slicing disc, and with the inside blade removed, slice **¼ purple cabbage** (this should yield 3 cups). Transfer to a medium container for the soba noodle bowls.

2. **MUSHROOMS:** Using the same slicing disc (or, if you have multiple slicing disc options, use a thicker one), slice the **mushrooms (10.5 oz/300 g)**. Transfer to a separate large container for the soba noodle bowls.

3. **CHIMICHURRI:** If you're using store-bought, skip this step. Pulse together **3 cloves garlic, 1 shallot, 1½ cups fresh parsley, 1 cup fresh cilantro, 2 Tbsp fresh oregano, ½ cup extra virgin olive oil, 2 Tbsp red wine vinegar, ½ tsp salt,** and **¼ tsp pepper,** following the method on page 81. Store in a medium container in the fridge for the chimichurri salmon. Note: You'll need ¼ cup parsley later in the week for the Cajun shrimp, so make sure not to use all the parsley in this sauce.

ON THE CUTTING BOARD

1. **TOFU:** Cut **1 lb (450 g) medium-firm tofu** into 1-inch cubes and add to the bowl for the soup.

2. **SNAP PEAS:** Trim the ends of **3.5 oz (100 g) snap peas** and add to the bowl for the soup.

3. **GREEN BEANS:** Trim the ends of **1¼ lb (525 g) green beans**. Wrap in a paper towel and store in a large container in the fridge for the chimichurri salmon.

④ **ASPARAGUS:** Trim and cut **1 bunch asparagus** into 1-inch pieces. Wrap in a paper towel and store in a medium container in the fridge for the quesadillas.

⑤ **LACINATO KALE:** Stem and thinly slice **1 bunch lacinato kale**. Wrap in paper towel and add to the large container with the mushrooms for the soba noodle bowls. Store in the fridge.

⑥ **GARLIC:** Press, mince, or use a Microplane to grate the remaining **4 cloves garlic**. Add 1 tsp to the bowl for the soup. Store the remainder in a small container in the fridge (unless using it immediately to do the optional Peanutty Soba Noodle Sauce prep).

MAKE YOUR BATCH LUNCH

① Roughly tear **4 cups spinach** and add to the bowl for the soup, along with **7 oz (200 g) rice vermicelli noodles**. Mix to combine, then divide between the four (32 oz/1 L) glass jars. Store in the fridge.

You're All Set!

Now that you're all prepped, mealtimes will be a cinch! When you're ready to serve, go to each recipe in the book and pick up where it says **IF YOU'RE FOLLOWING THE MEAL PLAN** and get ready for a week of quick, easy, delicious, and nourishing meals.

Optional Prep

Still have energy and fridge space on Meal Prep Day? Continue with these items! If not, whip them up while your other ingredients cook on the day of eating.

Sauce It Up
In a small glass jar, make and store the Peanutty Soba Noodle Sauce (page 193). Additionally, if you'd like to make your own garlic aioli for the 10-Minute Chicken, Fig, and Brie Sourdough Sandwiches, see page 77 and add those ingredients to your grocery list.

Spice It Up
If you'd like to use homemade Cajun seasoning for the Cajun shrimp, and you didn't make a batch last week, see page 76 and add those ingredients to your grocery list. Store in the pantry.

Week 4

Can you believe you're at Week 4?! This is one of my favorite weeks, with lots of Asian-inspired dishes similar to the ones we'd enjoy gathered around our kitchen table when I was growing up, from my grandpa's simple-yet-delicious **Charlie's Lo Mein** to our family's **Jangs' Famous Fried Rice** to another Jang essential: ramen noodles made even more body- and soul-nourishing in **20-Minute Miso Ramen with Jammy Eggs**. You'll be feeling a lot of love for your past self for prepping extra **Juicy Spinach and Feta Turkey Burgers** in Week 2, making for a super-speedy mid-week meal. To round things out, **Rainbow Power Bowls** will be just the midday lift you need: a ready-to-go lunch, packed with veggies and nourishing plant-powered fats to leave you satisfied throughout the afternoon. As you think back, reflect on how much ease you've brought into the last four weeks. I hope you've been able to enjoy more time with your family, a calmer vibe going into mealtimes, or anything else you've chosen to do with the time and mental space you've freed up!

Scan this QR code to download the grocery list.

Recipes You're Making This Week

- Charlie's Lo Mein (page 189)
- Mila's Sticky Orange Chicken (page 194)
- Juicy Spinach and Feta Turkey Burgers (page 228)
  with an optional side of Easiest Arugula Salad (page 168)
- Rainbow Power Bowls (page 179)
- Jangs' Famous Fried Rice (page 205)
- 20-Minute Miso Ramen with Jammy Eggs (page 186)

	LUNCH	DINNER
SUNDAY	Meal Prep Day	Charlie's Lo Mein
MONDAY	Charlie's Lo Mein	20-Minute Miso Ramen with Jammy Eggs
TUESDAY	Rainbow Power Bowls	Jangs' Famous Fried Rice
WEDNESDAY	Jangs' Famous Fried Rice	Mila's Sticky Orange Chicken
THURSDAY	Rainbow Power Bowls	Juicy Spinach and Feta Turkey Burgers with an optional side of Easiest Arugula Salad
FRIDAY	Mila's Sticky Orange Chicken	Enjoy leftovers or a "super-quick" meal, or order in!

Grocery List

PRODUCE

- 2 lemons
- 5 large navel oranges
  (or 1½ cups 100% orange juice)
- 3 avocados
- 1 tomato
- 3½ oz (100 g) shiitake mushrooms
  (or mushrooms of your choice)
- 8 baby bok choy
- 1 mini cucumber
- 3 bell peppers (red or orange)
- 1 bin (5 oz/142 g) arugula
- 1 green cabbage (or 10 cups
  pre-shredded cabbage)
- ¼ purple cabbage (or 1½ cups
  pre-shredded cabbage)
- 1 bin (5 oz/142 g) baby kale
- 1 head of lettuce
- 1 bin (5 oz/142 g) spinach
  (or 2½ oz/75 g loose spinach;
  if you buy the bin you'll have
  extra to use)
- 1 bunch green onions
- 2 shallots
- 1 large white onion
- 1 red onion
- 2 bulbs garlic (about 18 cloves)
- 1½-inch knob ginger
- 1 sweet potato

MEAT & ALTERNATIVES

- 2 lb (900 g) pork tenderloin
- 3½ lb (1.6 kg) boneless skinless
  chicken thighs (about 14 to
  16 thighs)
- 3 Chinese sausages (cured
  sausages found in the refrigerator
  section, near the pepperoni)

REFRIGERATED

- Eggs (13)
- Cheese (for topping burgers,
  I like aged white cheddar)
- Grated Parmesan cheese (¼ cup)
- Tzatziki (½ cup)
- White (shiro) miso paste (2 Tbsp)

FREEZER

- Corn, pea, and carrot mix
  (3½ cups)

BAKERY

- 4 burger buns (I like brioche)

GRAINS & STARCHES

- Rice, white or brown (3⅓ cups)
- Quinoa (⅔ cup)
- 8½ oz/240 g baked ramen
  noodles (also called instant
  noodles)
- 12 oz (350 g) lo mein noodles
  (or sub ramen noodles, egg
  noodles, linguini, or spaghetti)

OILS & CONDIMENTS

- Extra virgin olive oil (⅔ cup)
- Avocado oil (½ cup)
- Toasted sesame oil (⅓ cup)
  (or sub pure sesame oil)
- Chili crisp oil
- White vinegar (¾ cup)
- White wine vinegar (1 Tbsp)
- Soy sauce (¾ cup)
- Oyster sauce (1 to 2 Tbsp)
- Char siu sauce (6 Tbsp)
  (or sub hoisin sauce)
- Sriracha (for topping)
- Honey (¼ cup)

SPICES, SEASONINGS
& FLAVORINGS

- Ground turmeric (½ tsp)
- Black pepper
- Red pepper flakes (for garnish)
- Salt and flaky salt
- Roasted sesame seeds (2 Tbsp)
- Chicken or vegetable stock
  (6 cups)

PANTRY STAPLES

- Salted roasted sunflower seeds
  (¼ cup)
- Tahini (1 Tbsp)
- Panko bread crumbs (2 Tbsp)
- Cornstarch (⅔ cup)
- Granulated sugar (2 tsp)

OTHER

- Parchment paper

ALREADY PREPPED

- 4 turkey patties (If not prepped in
  Week 2, add the ingredients for
  Juicy Spinach and Feta Turkey
  Burger patties, page 228, to
  your grocery list or swap in your
  favorite store-bought patties)

Reminder

Remember to shop your
house first. With all the spices,
condiments, and pantry staples
you already have on hand, you
will likely be able to trim down
your grocery list.

On Meal Prep Day

EQUIPMENT
2 medium pots (or 2 pots and 1 rice cooker)
1 baking sheet
1 food processor (or mandoline and knife)
Barbecue or grill (or a 9 × 13-inch baking dish or a large frying pan)
1 to 2 cutting boards
Chef's knife
Measuring cups and spoons

CONTAINERS
1 large bowl, 1 small bowl
16 oz (500 ml) glass jar
15 airtight containers or sealable storage bags (5 large, 6 medium-large, 1 medium, 3 small)

GET YOUR EQUIPMENT READY

1. Preheat the oven to 425°F (220°C). Line a rimmed baking sheet with parchment paper.

2. If barbecuing the chicken for the power bowls and fried rice (my favorite method), preheat the barbecue to medium-high (this will take about 15 minutes).

COOK THE GRAINS

1. **RICE:** Cook **3⅓ cups rice** in **5 cups water** (for white rice) or **6⅔ cups water** (for brown rice) as directed on page 58 or according to package directions. This will yield about 10 cups of cooked rice. Let cool, then store in a large container in the fridge for the fried rice and the orange chicken.

2. **QUINOA:** Cook **⅔ cup quinoa** in **1 cup water** as directed on page 58 or according to package directions. This will yield about 2 cups of cooked quinoa. Let cool, then transfer to a large bowl for the power bowls.

COOK MEAT/VEGGIES (OVEN)

1. **SWEET POTATO:** Cut **1 sweet potato** into 1-inch cubes. Toss in **1 Tbsp avocado oil** and season generously with salt and pepper. Spread out in a single layer on the prepared baking sheet. Roast as directed on page 62. Let cool, then add to the bowl for the power bowls.

2. **CHICKEN:** Cook **8 chicken thighs** as directed on page 68. My favorite method is barbecuing, but if you prefer to keep it in the kitchen, follow the stovetop or oven cooking method. You can bake the chicken at the same time as the sweet potato. Slice 4 cooked thighs and store in a medium container in the fridge for the power bowls. Dice the remaining chicken and store in a medium-large container in the fridge for the fried rice.

IN THE FOOD PROCESSOR

1. **GREEN CABBAGE:** Using the slicing disc, and with the inside blade removed, thinly slice **1 head green cabbage**. Wrap in paper towel and store in a large container in the fridge for the lo mein.

2. **PURPLE CABBAGE:** Using the slicing disc, thinly slice **¼ purple cabbage** (this should yield about 1½ to 2 cups). Add to the bowl for the power bowls.

3. **WHITE ONION:** Rinse the food processor and slicing disc. Using the same slicing disc attachment, slice **1 large white onion**. Add to a large container for the orange chicken.

4. **RED ONION:** Using the same slicing disc attachment, slice 1 red onion, place in a 16 oz (500 ml) glass jar, and make 1 batch of pickled red onion (page 72). For this, you'll also need: **¾ cup boiling water, ¾ cup white vinegar, 2 tsp salt,** and **1½ Tbsp sugar**. Let sit for 30 minutes, then add ½ cup of drained pickled onion to the bowl for the power bowls.

5. **GINGER:** Peel **1½-inch knob ginger**. Using the blade attachment, mince the whole knob. Store in a small container in the fridge.

ON THE CUTTING BOARD

1. **MUSHROOMS:** Thinly slice **3½ oz (100 g) shiitakes**. Wrap in a paper towel and store in a large container in the fridge for the miso ramen.

2. **BABY BOK CHOY:** Trim off the root ends of **8 baby bok choy** and separate the leaves. Add to the container with the mushrooms for the miso ramen.

3. **BELL PEPPERS:** Cut **3 bell peppers** into 1-inch squares. Wrap in a paper towel and add to the container with the white onion for the orange chicken.

4. **SPINACH:** Chop **3 cups spinach**, wrap in a paper towel, and store with the cooked chicken in the medium-large container in the fridge for the fried rice.

5. **SHALLOTS:** Mince **2 shallots** and store in a small container in the fridge for the fried rice.

6. **GARLIC:** Mince or use a Microplane to grate **18 cloves garlic**. Add 1 Tbsp to the container with the shallots (for the fried rice) and store the remainder in another small container in the fridge.

7. **PORK TENDERLOIN:** Cut **2 lb (907 g) pork tenderloin** into ½-inch rounds, then cut each round into ¼-inch strips (about 2 inches long and ½ inch thick). Add to a large container, add **6 Tbsp char siu sauce** and **¼ tsp salt**, mix to combine, and marinate until ready to make the lo mein.

8. **CHICKEN:** Cut the **remaining uncooked chicken thighs (about 6 to 8)** into bite-size pieces. Store in a separate medium-large container or sealable storage bag in the fridge for the orange chicken.

MAKE YOUR BATCH LUNCH

1. In a small bowl, whisk together **¼ cup extra virgin olive oil, juice of 1 lemon, 1 Tbsp tahini, 1 Tbsp white wine vinegar, ½ tsp grated garlic** (already prepped), **¼ tsp ground turmeric, ¼ tsp salt**, and **a pinch of black pepper**.

2. To the bowl with the quinoa, sweet potatoes, cabbage, and pickled red onion, add the dressing and toss to combine, then divide between four medium-large containers. (Wait until the day you eat the bowls to add the chicken, avocado, kale, sunflower seeds, and sesame seeds, then toss once more before eating.)

You're All Set!

Now that you're all prepped, mealtimes will be a cinch! When you're ready to serve, go to each recipe in the book and pick up where it says **IF YOU'RE FOLLOWING THE MEAL PLAN** and get ready for a week of quick, easy, delicious, and nourishing meals.

Optional Prep

Still have energy and fridge space on Meal Prep Day? Continue with these items! If not, whip them up while your other ingredients cook on the day of eating.

Sauce It Up

In a small glass jar, make and store the Orange Sauce (page 194). Additionally, if you'd like to make your own tzatziki for the turkey burgers (see page 82) and chili crisp oil for the fried rice and miso ramen (see page 78), add those ingredients to your grocery list.

Reminder

On Wednesday night, don't forget to take the turkey burgers out of the freezer and thaw overnight for dinner on Thursday.

Foundational Recipes and Flavor Hacks

How to Meal Prep Grains

GRAIN MATH: Dry grains approximately triple when cooked. To increase the yield of any grain, just multiply the amount of water called for by the number of cups of grains being cooked (for example, for quinoa, multiply 1¾ cups water by the number of cups of quinoa). It's always a good idea to double-check the package instructions, if available, as water volume and cook time may vary slightly from brand to brand or for different varieties of grain. *Pro Tip:* To add more flavor to your grains, replace the water with chicken or vegetable stock.

Quinoa

MAKES ABOUT 3 CUPS

1 cup quinoa, rinsed

1¾ cups water

1. Add the quinoa and water to a medium pot, cover, and bring to a boil. Reduce the heat to a simmer and cook for about 15 minutes, until the water is absorbed.
2. Remove from the heat and let sit, covered, for 5 minutes. Fluff with a fork and enjoy right away, or let cool and store as directed.

White Rice

MAKES ABOUT 3 CUPS

1 cup short-, medium-, or long-grain white rice, rinsed

1½ cups water

1. Add the rice and water to a medium pot, cover, and bring to a boil. Reduce the heat to a simmer and cook for about 18 to 20 minutes, until the water is absorbed (long-grain will likely be on the shorter end of the time range, while short- and medium-grain will be on the longer end).
2. Remove from the heat and let sit, covered, for 10 minutes. Fluff with a fork and enjoy right away, or let cool and store as directed.

Brown Rice

MAKES ABOUT 3 CUPS

1 cup short-, medium-, or long-grain brown rice, rinsed

2 cups water

1. Add the rice and water to a medium pot, cover, and bring to a boil. Reduce heat to a simmer and cook for about 45 minutes for medium- and long-grain, and 45 to 50 minutes for short-grain, until the water is absorbed.
2. Remove from the heat and let sit, covered, for 10 minutes. Fluff with a fork and enjoy right away, or let cool and store as directed.

Couscous

MAKES ABOUT 3 CUPS

1½ cups water

1 cup couscous

1. Add water to a medium pot, cover, and bring to a boil (or simply add boiling water to the pot or a large bowl). Stir in the couscous.
2. Cover, remove from the heat, and let sit for 5 minutes. Fluff with a fork and enjoy right away, or let cool and store as directed.

STORAGE: Store cooled cooked grains in an airtight container in the fridge for up to 5 days or in a sealable freezer bag in the freezer for up to 3 months. If freezing, let the grains cool completely on a parchment-lined baking sheet (to ensure they don't stick together when frozen and decrease the risk of freezer burn), then place them in the bag, laying the grains flat and removing as much air as possible to make the bag easy to stack. For food safety, if you're preparing the grains ahead of time to use in a dish, make sure to consume them before their total suggested storage time.

REHEATING: Grains can be reheated in the microwave or on the stovetop. If microwaving, add the quantity of cooked grains you need, plus 1 to 2 tablespoons of water to a microwave-safe bowl. Cover and microwave on high in 30-second increments, stirring between each, until warmed through. The time will vary depending on the volume of grains being heated. For larger servings, start with longer increments.

If using the stovetop, add the quantity of grains you need, plus 1 to 2 tablespoons of water to a frying pan. Warm over low heat for 3 to 5 minutes, stirring occasionally, until warmed through. If the grain is going to cook with other ingredients (like in the Thai-Inspired Lettuce Wraps, page 223, there's no need to reheat it first; just add it when the recipe calls for it and let it heat through with the other ingredients.

Tip

My preferred method for cooking rice is with a rice cooker. It is so easy and cleans up quickly. The rice cooker method uses the same rice-to-water ratio as noted on page 58 and simply requires adding rice and water to the rice cooker and turning it on. Most rice cookers will turn off automatically once the rice is cooked, so there really isn't much of a "recipe" to this method.

How to Meal Prep Pasta

Like grains, pasta can be cooked in advance to save time on the day of eating. This is especially nice if you also have your sauce ready to go. Stored noodles will feel a bit hard but they soften up when heated with a bit of water or in sauce.

1 lb (450 g) pasta

1. Bring a large pot of salted water to a boil. Cook the pasta according to package directions until al dente (or, if al dente instructions are not given, 1 to 2 minutes before the full cooking time). Drain.

2. Toss the pasta in the sauce and enjoy right away, or let cool and store undressed pasta as directed.

Tip
Reserve ½ to 1 cup of the pasta cooking water to add when you combine the noodles with sauce. This will give a creamier and smoother texture to the sauce and will help the sauce cling to the noodles.

STORAGE: Toss the undressed pasta with a little olive oil to prevent sticking, and store in an airtight container in the fridge for up to 5 days or in a sealable freezer bag in the freezer for up to 3 months. If freezing, let the pasta cool completely on a parchment-lined baking sheet to ensure noodles don't stick together, then place them in the bag, laying the noodles flat and removing as much air as possible to make the bag easy to stack. For food safety, if you're preparing the pasta ahead of time to use in a dish, make sure to consume it before its total suggested storage time.

REHEATING: Pasta can be reheated in the microwave or on the stovetop. If it is sticking together after refrigeration, first place it in a colander and run hot water over it until the noodles separate. If microwaving, add the quantity of pasta you need to a microwave-safe bowl. Add 2 tablespoons of water or toss the pasta in sauce. Cover and microwave on high in 20- to 30-second increments, stirring between each, until warmed through.

How to Meal Prep Cooked Vegetables

Non-Starchy Vegetables

This recipe can be used for most non-starchy vegetables. I love to enjoy batch-prep roasted cauliflower, broccoli, and Brussels sprouts throughout the week. Roast, checking as directed, until they are beginning to brown and become tender, but are still crisp when pierced with a fork.

3 to 4 cups non-starchy vegetables, cut into bite-size pieces

2 Tbsp avocado oil or other high-heat cooking oil

Salt, freshly ground black pepper, and/or other desired seasonings, such as garlic powder, onion powder, nutritional yeast, or Greek seasoning blend

1. Preheat the oven to 425°F (220°C). Line two rimmed baking sheets with parchment paper.

2. Place the vegetables in a medium bowl, add the oil, sprinkle generously with the seasonings, and toss to coat. Spread the vegetables in a single layer on the prepared baking sheets, leaving room between pieces so they crisp up and don't steam.

3. Roast until golden brown and tender, but still crisp when pierced with a fork, about 35 to 45 minutes. The higher water content a vegetable has, the less time it will need to roast: first check and give a stir at 15 minutes, and then every 5 to 10 minutes thereafter.

4. Remove from the oven and enjoy right away, or let cool and store as directed.

STORAGE: Store cooked vegetables in an airtight container or sealable storage bag in the fridge for up to 5 days or in a sealable freezer bag for up to 1 month. If freezing, let the vegetables cool completely on a parchment-lined baking sheet to ensure they don't get icy or stick together when frozen, then place them in the bag, laying the vegetables flat and removing as much air as possible to make the bag easy to stack. For food safety, if you're preparing the vegetables ahead of time to use in a dish, make sure to consume them before their total suggested storage time.

REHEATING: Vegetables can be reheated in the microwave or on the stovetop. If microwaving, add the quantity of cooked vegetables you need to a microwave-safe bowl. Cover and microwave on high in 20- to 30-second increments, stirring between each, until warmed through. If using the stovetop and you find the vegetables are sticking to the bottom of the pan, try adding a drizzle of oil.

Starchy Vegetables

This recipe can be used for most starchy vegetables. I batch roast sweet potatoes, potatoes, and beets to enjoy through the week. Roasting times vary depending on the size of the vegetables. The smaller the pieces, the faster they cook. Roast until they are browned around the edges and fork-tender.

4 to 5 cups cubed starchy vegetables

2 to 3 Tbsp avocado oil or other high-heat cooking oil

Salt, freshly ground black pepper, and/ or other desired seasonings, such as garlic powder, onion powder, ground cinnamon, cumin, or Cajun seasoning

1. Preheat the oven to 425°F (220°C). Line two rimmed baking sheets with parchment paper.

2. Place the vegetables in a medium bowl, add the oil, sprinkle generously with the seasonings, and toss to coat. Spread the vegetables in a single layer on the prepared baking sheets, leaving room between pieces so they crisp up and don't steam.

3. Roast until browned around the edges and fork-tender, about 40 to 45 minutes, stirring after 20 minutes.

4. Remove from the oven and enjoy right away, or let cool and store as directed.

STORAGE: Store cooked vegetables in an airtight container or sealable storage bag in the fridge for up to 5 days or in a sealable freezer bag for up to 1 month. If freezing, let the vegetables cool completely on a parchment-lined baking sheet to ensure they don't get icy or stick together when frozen, then place them in the bag, laying the vegetables flat and removing as much air as possible to make the bag easy to stack. For food safety, if you're preparing the vegetables ahead of time to use in a dish, make sure to consume them before their total suggested storage time.

REHEATING: Vegetables can be reheated in the microwave or on the stovetop. If microwaving, add the quantity of cooked vegetables you need to a microwave-safe bowl. Cover and microwave on high in 20- to 30-second increments, stirring between each, until warmed through. If using the stovetop and you find the vegetables are sticking to the bottom of the pan, try adding a drizzle of oil.

How to Meal Prep Uncooked Vegetables

Having all your vegetables for the entire week washed and cut makes meals a breeze. Cut them according to the recipes you plan to make, or in the most common form. For quick and easy meals, I try to always have at least minced garlic and ginger and diced onion prepped, plus two to three other vegetables.

Leafy Greens

Prepped leafy greens bring salads together in minutes and make it easy to eat more veggies!

STORAGE: Wrap leafy greens in paper towel or a cloth (see tip). Binned greens can also be wrapped in paper towel or a cloth, and then returned to their bin. Store in sealable storage bags, laid flat in the fridge, for up to 1 week. Check throughout the week and discard any pieces that are getting slimy to save the remaining greens.

Beware that not all leafy greens are created equal! Yes, more fibrous greens (like kale and spinach) can be frozen to be used in cooked dishes like soups or stews: store them in a sealable freezer bag, removing as much air as possible, for up to 3 months. Freezing less fibrous greens with a higher water content (like mixed greens, romaine, or butter lettuce) doesn't work for cooked recipes, but they're still great in a juice or smoothie!

HOW TO USE: When using them straight from the fridge, leafy greens are ready to go as is! Add frozen leafy greens straight into a juice, smoothie, or cooked dish as directed in the recipe. Once thawed, they can't be used for salads.

Aromatic Root Vegetables
(SUCH AS ONIONS, GARLIC, AND GINGER)

STORAGE: Store cut aromatics in an airtight container in the fridge for up to 1 week or in a small sealable freezer bag, with as much air removed as possible, or in the freezer for up to 3 months. Alternatively, make Flavor Bombs (page 84).

HOW TO USE: Refrigerated aromatics are ready to go; simply use as directed in the recipe. Frozen aromatics must be thawed on the counter for 30 to 60 minutes or overnight in the fridge, depending on the amount. Pat thawed aromatics dry with a paper towel to remove any excess liquid, then use as directed.

Vegetables with a High Water Content

(SUCH AS CUCUMBERS AND TOMATOES)

STORAGE: You can cut the vegetables before storing, although I avoid cutting tomatoes when refrigerating them because the juices seep out and they become soggy. Store the vegetables in an airtight container in the fridge for up to 1 week or in a sealable freezer bag, with as much air removed as possible, in the freezer for up to 3 months.

HOW TO USE: Refrigerated cucumbers and tomatoes are ready to use as they are. Frozen tomatoes can be used as is in soups and pasta sauces (like Creamy Roasted Tomato and White Bean Soup, page 253). Frozen cucumbers are best in uncooked recipes, like smoothies or juices.

Other Non-Starchy Vegetables

(SUCH AS CORN, BELL PEPPERS, GREEN BEANS, ZUCCHINI, BROCCOLI, AND CAULIFLOWER)

STORAGE: Wrap the cut vegetables in paper towel or a cloth and store in an airtight container or sealable storage bag in the fridge for 1 to 2 weeks, depending on their water content. You may want to replace the paper towel every 5 to 7 days so they don't get slimy. If freezing, store in a sealable freezer bag, with as much air removed as possible, for up to 3 months.

HOW TO USE: Refrigerated non-starchy vegetables can be used as is, as directed in the recipe. Frozen non-starchy vegetables are best used in cooked or blended dishes, like pasta sauce, soup, stir-fries, or smoothies (I love doing this with zucchini or cauliflower). They will not hold up well when used raw in salads.

Starchy Vegetables

(SUCH AS BEETS AND SWEET POTATOES)

STORAGE: Store the cut vegetables in an airtight container in the fridge for up to 1 week, or in a sealable freezer bag, with as much air removed as possible, in the freezer for up to 3 months.

HOW TO USE: If refrigerated, they are ready to prepare according to the recipe. If frozen, add to a soup, stew, or chili (like A Vegan Chili the Meat Lovers Will Beg For, page 270). If boiling, cook according to the recipe, adding on a few extra minutes of cook time. If roasting, cook according to the recipe, noting that you will likely need to add 10 to 20 minutes to the cook time.

How to Meal Prep Proteins

Beautifully Browned Ground Meat or Meat Alternative

This recipe works for any type of ground meat or meat alternative, though the cooking time and amount of oil needed will vary depending on the protein source; for instance, compared to beef, lower-fat options like chicken, turkey, and veggie ground round require more oil. Start by adding 1 to 2 teaspoons more oil and adjust both oil and cooking time as needed, following the visual cues.

1 Tbsp oil of choice (see tip)

2 cloves garlic, grated or finely minced (about 1 tsp)

1 lb (450 g) ground meat or meat alternative

Salt, freshly ground black pepper, and/or other seasonings as desired

1. In a large frying pan, heat the oil over medium-high heat. Add the garlic and cook until fragrant, about 1 minute. Add the ground meat or meat alternative and season generously with salt and pepper, breaking the protein into a few large pieces. Without stirring, brown on one side, about 4 to 5 minutes. Flip and brown the other side, another 2 to 4 minutes, then break into smaller pieces and cook, stirring, until no pink remains.

2. Enjoy immediately, or let cool and store as directed.

STORAGE: Store cooked meat or meat alternative in an airtight container or sealable storage bag in the fridge for up to 4 days or in a sealable freezer bag in the freezer for up to 3 months. For food safety, if you're preparing the meat or meat alternative ahead of time to use in a dish, make sure to consume it before its total suggested storage time.

REHEATING: To use, thaw overnight (if needed), then reheat on the stovetop over medium-low heat or in the microwave on high in 20- to 30-second increments, stirring between each, until warmed through. If using the stove and the protein is sticking to the bottom of the pan, try adding a splash of oil.

Tips

I usually use avocado oil or sesame oil to brown meat, depending on the flavor profile of the dish I intend to use the protein in.

If you are planning to increase the amount of meat you're going to brown, it's important to do so in batches, to allow it to brown, rather than boil.

Seafood

I prefer to cook seafood the same day as eating it. Fish and shellfish are such quick-cooking proteins and taste so much better when made fresh. That said, I do love good leftovers the next day, so I usually cook extra of the recipe for a quick, stress-free future lunch or dinner.

Juicy Baked Chicken Breasts

There is nothing worse than dry chicken breasts. Because of their low fat content, it can be easy to overcook them and end up with a less-than-desirable result. This recipe is tried and true, and will ensure you get juicy chicken breasts every time!

2 lb (900 g) boneless skinless chicken breasts

1 Tbsp avocado oil or other high-heat cooking oil

Salt, freshly ground black pepper, and/or other seasonings as desired

Time Saver

Butterfly the chicken breasts before cooking: hold the chicken in place on a cutting board and slice horizontally into the middle of the thickest part of the breast until you've almost reached the other side but have not cut all the way through. Open the breast like a book and place in your lined baking dish with the inside facing down. Continue from step 2, decreasing the total cook time to 12 to 15 minutes or until the juices run clear.

1. Preheat the oven to 400°F (200°C). Line a 9 × 13-inch baking dish with parchment paper, ripping off double the amount you need to line the dish.

2. Brush all side of the chicken with the oil and season generously. Place the chicken, top side down, in the prepared dish. Fold the extra parchment paper over the chicken and tuck it underneath.

3. Bake until cooked through and the juices run clear when the thickest part of the breast is pierced with a knife, or an instant-read thermometer inserted in the thickest part of a breast registers 165°F (74°C), about 25 to 30 minutes. The cooking time will depend on the size and thickness of the chicken breasts; check after 20 minutes, then return to the oven for another 5 to 10 minutes (or longer) if needed.

4. Remove from the oven and let sit for 5 to 10 minutes before cutting, to allow the juices to settle, for a more tender end product. Enjoy immediately, or let cool and store as directed.

STORAGE: Store cooked chicken in an airtight container or sealable storage bag in the fridge for up to 4 days or in a sealable freezer bag in the freezer for up to 3 months. For food safety, if you're preparing the chicken ahead of time to use in a dish, make sure to consume it before its total suggested storage time.

REHEATING: To use, thaw overnight (if needed), then reheat on the stovetop over medium-low heat or in the microwave on high in 20- to 30-second increments, stirring between each, until warmed through. If using the stove and the protein is sticking to the bottom of the pan, try adding a splash of oil.

Perfectly Cooked Chicken Thighs

I love batch prepping chicken thighs to have on hand throughout the week. They are so easy to cook and are the perfect ready-to-go protein. Barbecuing is my method of choice, but if you prefer to keep things in the kitchen, feel free to bake or pan-fry. However you cook them, chicken thighs are done when the juices run clear when the thickest part of the thigh is pierced with a knife, or an instant-read thermometer inserted in the thickest part of the thigh registers 165°F (74°C). Try tossing them in your favorite sauce or marinade, or season with some Cajun Seasoning Mix (page 76).

2 lb (900 g) boneless skinless chicken thighs (about 8 to 10)

1 to 2 Tbsp avocado oil or other high-heat cooking oil

Salt and freshly ground black pepper

To Barbecue

1. Preheat the barbecue to medium-high.

2. In a medium bowl, toss the chicken in 2 tablespoons of oil and season generously with salt and pepper.

3. Reduce the heat to medium. Place the chicken on the grill, close the lid, and cook until the bottom side is slightly charred and evenly comes off the grill, about 5 minutes. Flip the chicken and continue cooking until done (see headnote), about 5 to 7 minutes.

To Bake

1. Preheat the oven to 425°F (220°C). Line a 9 × 13-inch baking dish (or two smaller dishes) with parchment paper.

2. In a medium bowl, toss the chicken in 2 tablespoons of oil and season generously with salt and pepper.

3. Arrange the chicken in a single layer in the prepared dish. Bake for 20 to 25 minutes, until done (see headnote).

To Pan-fry

1. Pat the chicken dry and season both sides with salt and pepper.

2. In a large frying pan, heat 1 tablespoon of oil over medium-high heat. Add the chicken; it should sizzle when it hits the pan. Cook for 4 to 6 minutes per side or until the edges are nicely browned and the chicken is done (see headnote).

To Store and Reheat

1. If cutting, let the cooked chicken rest for 5 to 10 minutes to allow the juices to settle, for a more tender end product. Let cool and store as directed.

STORAGE: Store cooked chicken in an airtight container or sealable storage bag in the fridge for up to 4 days or in a sealable freezer bag in the freezer for up to 3 months. For food safety, if you're preparing the chicken ahead of time to use in a dish, make sure to consume it before its total suggested storage time.

REHEATING: To use, thaw overnight (if needed), then reheat on the stove-top over medium-low heat or in the microwave on high in 20- to 30-second increments, stirring between each, until warmed through. If using the stove and the protein is sticking to the bottom of the pan, try adding a splash of oil.

Tips

I usually use avocado oil or sesame oil to brown meat, depending on the flavor profile of the dish I intend to use the protein in.

If you are planning to increase the amount of meat you're going to brown, it's important to do so in batches, to allow it to brown, rather than boil.

Perfectly Prepped Jammy Eggs

Jammy Eggs are the perfect quick protein addition to many dishes. I especially love them in soups, like the 20-Minute Miso Ramen with Jammy Eggs (page 186).

8 large eggs

1. Bring a large pot of water to a boil over medium-high heat. Using a slotted spoon, carefully lower the eggs into the water, one at a time. Cook for 6½ minutes.

2. Meanwhile, fill a medium bowl with ice and cold water. When the eggs are done, use the slotted spoon to transfer them to the ice bath. Chill until cooled, about 2 minutes.

3. You can either peel the eggs now, before storing as directed, or when you're ready to eat them. To do so, crack the eggs all over and peel.

STORAGE: Store the cooked eggs in an airtight container in the fridge for up to 7 days.

SERVING: When ready to eat, cut the peeled eggs in half lengthwise. Heat, if desired, in the microwave in 20- to 30-second increments and enjoy in soups, on toast, or as is for a quick snack. For food safety, if you're preparing the eggs ahead of time to use in a dish, make sure to consume them before their total suggested storage time.

Crispy Tofu

I love making tofu this way! It adds texture and soaks up sauces nicely. It's amazing tossed in buffalo sauce and served on the Famous Kale Caesar on page 159.

1 block (12 oz/350 g) pressed tofu
¼ cup cornstarch
Salt and freshly ground black pepper
3 Tbsp avocado oil or other high-heat cooking oil, divided

1. Cut the block of tofu in half crosswise, then into ½-inch cubes. Place the tofu in a large airtight container or sealable storage bag and add the cornstarch, salt, and pepper. Seal and shake to coat evenly.

2. In a large frying pan, heat 2 tablespoons of the oil over medium-high heat. Add the tofu in a single layer, shaking off any excess cornstarch, and cook without stirring until the first side is browned, 4 to 5 minutes. Drizzle the remaining 1 tablespoon of oil overtop the tofu, flip and brown the other side, again without stirring, another 3 to 5 minutes.

3. Enjoy right away as a snack or with your favorite dish, or cool and store as directed.

STORAGE: Store in an airtight container in the fridge for up to 5 days.

REHEATING: I love using a toaster oven: place the tofu on a piece of foil or parchment paper, or in an oven-safe dish. Run it through one toasting cycle (set to the darkest/longest setting), then flip and repeat until tofu is crispy. Alternatively, lay the tofu on a parchment-lined baking sheet and bake at 425°F (220°C) for 7 to 10 minutes, stirring halfway through. For food safety, if you're preparing the tofu ahead of time to use in a dish, make sure to consume it before its total suggested storage time.

Quick Pickles, Four Ways

VEGETARIAN | VEGAN | DAIRY-FREE | GLUTEN-FREE | NUT-FREE

Discovering quick pickling has been a game changer for me! These pickles give beautiful color and the perfect hit of flavor to bowls, salads, tacos . . . or are great just eaten alone. Here, I've done red onion, purple cabbage, and cucumber—all three of which are staples in our house—and yep, I also threw in avocado for good measure! Quick pickles are such a fun way to enjoy your favorite vegetables and the variety of vitamins, minerals, and antioxidants they provide. Add them to your favorite sandwiches or wraps to take them to the next level . . . and to impress your friends.

MAKES 1 CUP

¾ cup boiling water
¾ cup white vinegar
2 tsp salt
1½ Tbsp granulated sugar
1 cup sliced cucumber, thinly shredded purple cabbage, thinly sliced red onion, or sliced avocado (see tips)

1. In a large, spouted measuring cup, combine the boiling water, vinegar, salt, and sugar, stirring until the salt and sugar are dissolved.

2. Pack the vegetable you want to pickle into a 16-ounce (500 ml) glass jar. Pour the pickling liquid over the veggies, making sure to completely cover them.

3. If you want to use the pickles right away, let them sit for 30 minutes before using them in a recipe. Otherwise, let cool to room temperature without the lid on, then screw on the lids before placing them in the fridge. You'll notice that the flavor mellows (the vinegar becomes less pronounced) over the days as the brine absorbs into the vegetables.

STORAGE: Store the pickles in their jar in the fridge for up to 3 weeks.

Swaps & Subs

You can replace the white vinegar with another vinegar of your choice. I like apple cider vinegar, white wine vinegar, or unseasoned rice vinegar, depending on the flavor of the dishes I'm using the pickled vegetables for. You can also swap the granulated sugar for another sweetener, like honey or maple syrup, if preferred.

Tips

It's super easy to make a large batch of pickles for upcoming weeks; simply multiply the ingredients as needed. If making a larger batch, use a large pitcher to make the pickling liquid, and use a 32-ounce (1 L) glass jar (or two if needed).

Use avocado that is not very ripe—almost unripe, even. Ripe avocados can get too mushy and are difficult to remove from the jar.

Basic Balsamic Vinaigrette

VEGETARIAN | VEGAN | DAIRY-FREE | GLUTEN-FREE | NUT-FREE

Balsamic vinaigrette is a classic, a recipe everyone should have in their back pocket. It is so easy to make, and once you do, you'll never want to go back to store-bought again. I like mine on the tangier side, which is why there's more vinegar than oil. If it's too much for you, simply add a bit more oil, shake up, and enjoy!

MAKES ABOUT ½ CUP

1 clove garlic, grated or finely minced (about ½ tsp) (optional)

¼ cup balsamic vinegar

3 Tbsp extra virgin olive oil

2¼ tsp Dijon mustard

1½ tsp granulated sugar (optional)

Salt and freshly ground black pepper

1. To a 4-ounce (125 ml) jar or an airtight container that holds at least ½ cup, add the garlic, vinegar, oil, mustard, sugar, salt, and pepper. Cover tightly and shake until well combined.

STORAGE: Store the vinaigrette in the jar or container in the fridge for up to 2 weeks.

MEAL PREP TIP: This recipe is great to batch prep and have on hand for salads throughout the week; simply multiply the ingredients by the amount you need.

Tip
Use this recipe as a template for other flavor add-ins. Mash up some raspberries or blueberries for a berry vinaigrette, or add a squeeze of lemon for a brighter variation (one of my personal favorites).

Green Goddess Dressing

VEGETARIAN | GLUTEN-FREE | NUT-FREE

I could drink this dressing up! It is packed with flavorful herbs and is so bright and fresh! I've shared a couple of uses for it, like Green Goddess Pasta Salad (page 163) and One-Pan Green Goddess Hash (page 114), but feel free to drip and drizzle it on anything your heart desires. I definitely recommend doubling it to have extra. Taste it and you'll see why!

MAKES ABOUT ¾ CUP

1 cup spinach

⅓ cup extra virgin olive oil

⅓ cup plain Greek yogurt

2 Tbsp fresh basil

1 Tbsp fresh dill

1 Tbsp fresh chives

Juice of ¼ lemon (about 1 Tbsp)

½ tsp granulated sugar

Salt and freshly ground black pepper

1. In a food processor, combine the spinach, oil, yogurt, basil, dill, chives, lemon juice, and sugar. Pulse until well combined but still a bit chunky, 30 to 60 seconds. Season with salt and pepper to taste.

STORAGE: Store the dressing in a jar or another airtight container in the fridge for up to 5 days or in the freezer for up to 2 months.

Swaps & Subs
Although the flavor will change slightly, if you're having trouble finding one of the herbs listed, simply increase the amount of one of the others, or swap in another herb, like parsley or cilantro.

Cajun Seasoning Mix

VEGETARIAN | VEGAN | DAIRY-FREE | GLUTEN-FREE | NUT-FREE

Cajun spice is one of the seasonings I use most. While there is absolutely nothing wrong with buying a store-bought blend (I do this too), it's kind of cool to be able to whip up your own! I also find that store-bought blends have a huge variation in spiciness. Making your own allows you to control the amount of heat, finding the perfect combo that works for you and your family. The recipes in this book use this blend, so if using store-bought, you may want to start with a bit less, adding more to your desired spice preference.

MAKES ¾ CUP

1 to 3 tsp cayenne pepper

3 Tbsp paprika or smoked paprika

2 Tbsp salt

2 Tbsp garlic powder

1 Tbsp freshly ground black pepper

1 Tbsp onion powder

1 Tbsp dried oregano

1 Tbsp dried thyme

1. To a small spice jar or airtight container, add 1 teaspoon cayenne pepper, the paprika, salt, garlic powder, black pepper, onion powder, oregano, and thyme. Cover and shake to combine evenly. Taste and add more cayenne pepper until you've reached your desired heat level.

STORAGE: Store the seasoning mix in the jar or container in the pantry for up to 3 months.

Tip

Gently shake before using each time to combine all the spices evenly. The cayenne and salt tend to settle at the bottom, giving the mix an inconsistent flavor and heat level if not shaken.

Three 2-Minute Greek Yogurt Aiolis

VEGETARIAN | DAIRY-FREE OPTION | GLUTEN-FREE | NUT-FREE

As a dip for fries, the perfect sandwich spread, or the finishing touch to your favorite bowl, aioli adds major flavor with very little effort. I mix Greek yogurt with aioli's traditional mayo to make my go-to blends. I love the creamy texture Greek yogurt provides, and it also adds a boost of protein without sacrificing flavor! It's an ingredient we always have on hand in our house.

MAKES ½ CUP

GARLIC AIOLI

¼ cup mayonnaise

¼ cup plain Greek yogurt

1 clove garlic, grated or finely minced (about ½ tsp)

Pinch of salt

SRIRACHA AIOLI

¼ cup mayonnaise

¼ cup plain Greek yogurt

1 clove garlic, grated or finely minced (about ½ tsp)

2 tsp sriracha

Pinch of salt

WASABI AIOLI

¼ cup mayonnaise

¼ cup plain Greek yogurt

1 clove garlic, grated or finely minced (about ½ tsp)

1 tsp wasabi paste

Pinch of salt

1. In a small bowl or jar, whisk together the aioli ingredients. Season with more salt, sriracha, or wasabi to taste (depending on which aioli you're making). If you want to thin it out to a "drizzle" consistency, whisk in some water, 1 teaspoon at a time, until desired consistency is reached.

STORAGE: Store the aioli in a jar or an airtight container in the fridge for up to 1 week.

Tip
If you only have one or the other, these aiolis can be made with just mayonnaise or just Greek yogurt. If using just Greek yogurt, add a splash of olive oil to smooth it out.

Chili Crisp Oil

VEGETARIAN | VEGAN | DAIRY-FREE | GLUTEN-FREE | NUT-FREE

I grew up with chili oil as a regular condiment, but somehow forgot about it for a couple of years. When my husband, Meik, discovered it, it became a staple in our house once again. He puts this sh*t on everything: soups (it's delish on the wontons on page 268), pizzas, pastas—literally everything! Make a jar, store it in the fridge, and instantly level-up any savory meal!

MAKES ABOUT 1¾ CUPS

1½ cups avocado oil or other high-heat cooking oil

10 cloves garlic, grated or finely minced (about 5 tsp)

2 shallots, diced (about ¼ cup)

1 tsp Szechuan or black peppercorns

¼ cup red pepper flakes

1 tsp granulated sugar

1 tsp salt

1 tsp soy sauce, plus more as desired

1. In a small pot, combine the oil, garlic, shallots, and peppercorns over medium-low heat, bringing the oil to a simmer. Stirring occasionally, cook until the shallots and garlic begin to brown and crisp up, 20 to 25 minutes. Remove from the heat and let cool for 5 minutes.

2. Meanwhile, in a 16-ounce (500 ml) glass jar or an airtight glass container that holds at least 2 cups, combine the red pepper flakes, sugar, salt, and soy sauce. Pour the oil through a strainer into the jar, keeping the shallot and garlic bits in the strainer to cool (this will help them crisp up). Once cooled, after 20 to 30 minutes, add the shallots and garlic to the jar. Add more soy sauce to taste, if desired.

3. Enjoy right away, or refrigerate for later use. The flavors will intensify over time.

STORAGE: Store the oil in the jar or glass container in the fridge for up to 3 months.

Chimichurri

VEGETARIAN | VEGAN | DAIRY-FREE | GLUTEN-FREE | NUT-FREE

Chimichurri is an Argentinian sauce popular throughout South America. I first tried it on a trip to Colombia and have been hooked ever since. There are variations using different herbs, but this combination is the one that has stuck in our household. I like it spicy, but often make it on the milder side to suit the kiddos too, which is why I left the red pepper flakes as optional. If you like spice, feel free to throw in a jalapeño or add that generous sprinkle of red pepper flakes. Use this flavor-packed sauce to level-up everything from tofu to fish to your favorite meats. It also makes a great dipping sauce for potatoes and roasted vegetables!

MAKES ABOUT 1 CUP

3 cloves garlic

1 shallot

1½ cups fresh parsley

1 cup fresh cilantro

2 Tbsp fresh oregano

½ cup extra virgin olive oil

2 Tbsp red wine vinegar

½ tsp salt

¼ tsp freshly ground
   black pepper

Pinch of red pepper flakes
   (optional)

1. In a food processor, combine the garlic, shallot, parsley, cilantro, oregano, oil, vinegar, salt, and pepper. Pulse until well combined and a minced consistency forms, about 30 seconds. Season with more salt and pepper, to taste, then stir in the red pepper flakes, if using.

STORAGE: Store the sauce in a jar or an airtight container in the fridge for up to 2 weeks or in the freezer for up to 3 months. For easy individual servings, pour it into ice cube trays and freeze, then transfer the frozen cubes to a sealable freezer bag.

Tip
This sauce freezes well! I recommend doubling the recipe and storing half in the freezer for later use.

Berry Chia Compote

VEGETARIAN | VEGAN | DAIRY-FREE | GLUTEN-FREE | NUT-FREE

When I was growing up, whenever we'd have pancakes, my mom would whip up a thick and glossy blueberry compote to top them with. To this day, the two go hand in hand for me. One of my favorite kitchen hacks I've discovered over the years is chia seeds' ability to thicken sauces. It honestly feels like a little magic trick as you watch them do their work! As a bonus, they also provide omega-3s, fiber, and a good dose of calcium.

MAKES ABOUT 1 CUP

2 cups frozen berries (I like blueberries, raspberries, or blackberries)

2 Tbsp chia seeds

1. In a small pot, heat the frozen berries over medium-high heat for 5 to 6 minutes, stirring occasionally, until the berries are soft.

2. Mash the berries with the back of a fork, then stir in the chia seeds and reduce the heat to low. Cook for another 3 to 5 minutes, until the compote has thickened. If it's too thick or for a runnier sauce or jam, add water, 1 tablespoon at a time, until desired consistency is reached.

3. Remove from the heat and let sit for about 5 minutes. The compote will continue to thicken up as it sits.

STORAGE: Store the cooled compote in a jar or an airtight container in the fridge for up to 1 week or in the freezer for up to 3 months. If frozen, thaw in the microwave or overnight in the fridge. Enjoy cold or reheat on the stove or in the microwave.

Tzatziki

VEGETARIAN | GLUTEN-FREE | NUT-FREE

I'm always that person asking for more tzatziki at restaurants. Why do they serve it in such small ramekins?! I love making my own at home so I can dollop as much as I want onto my plate, and this Greek yogurt version also makes for a satisfying snack with added protein. Enjoy it on burgers or as a dip for pita, crackers, or veggies!

MAKES ABOUT 1½ CUPS

1 mini cucumber, finely shredded (about ½ cup)

2 cloves garlic, grated or finely minced (about 1 tsp)

2 Tbsp minced fresh dill

½ tsp salt

¼ tsp freshly ground black pepper

1 cup 5% plain Greek yogurt

Juice of ½ lemon (about 2 Tbsp)

½ Tbsp extra virgin olive oil

1. Wrap the shredded cucumber in a cloth or paper towel and squeeze out as much liquid as you can.

2. In a small bowl, whisk together the cucumber, garlic, dill, salt, pepper, yogurt, lemon juice, and oil.

STORAGE: Store the sauce in a jar or an airtight container in the fridge for up to 5 days.

Tip
The tzatziki will thicken up as it sets in the fridge.

Tip
For flavor variations, try adding vanilla extract or citrus zest. If you like a sweeter compote, sweeten with maple syrup to taste!

Flavor Bombs

VEGETARIAN | VEGAN OPTION | DAIRY-FREE OPTION | GLUTEN-FREE | NUT-FREE

How frustrating is it to end up with little bits of herbs wilting in the crisper? I speak from experience, having wasted far too much myself. Flavor Bombs to the rescue! Chop up leftover herbs and freeze them with butter or olive oil, to pull out anytime you need to add a little extra flavor to a dish! They also work great as a meal prep strategy for garlic and ginger, for those days you just don't want to have to mince!

MAKES 14 TO 16 BOMBS

PER TRAY

¾ cup roughly chopped fresh rosemary, thyme, or basil, or minced garlic or ginger

About 1 cup extra virgin olive oil or melted butter

1. Divide the herbs or aromatics among the slots of an ice cube tray. Add enough oil to fill each slot, about 1 tablespoon. Garlic and ginger can be frozen on their own, without the oil or butter, to allow more flexibility for future use. Freeze overnight before using.

STORAGE: Remove the cubes from the ice cube tray and store in a sealable freezer bag in the freezer for up to 6 months.

Lime Crema

VEGETARIAN | GLUTEN-FREE | NUT-FREE

Doesn't the name Lime Crema just make you feel fancy? This super-easy sauce makes the most delicious drizzle for tacos and nachos, while giving you that restaurant feel.

MAKES ABOUT ½ CUP

1 clove garlic, grated or finely minced (about ½ tsp)

⅓ cup plain Greek yogurt

Juice of ½ lime (about 1 Tbsp)

1 Tbsp warm water, plus more as needed

Pinch of salt

1. In a small bowl, whisk together the garlic, yogurt, lime juice, water, and salt. Season with more salt to taste. If necessary, add more water, 1 teaspoon at a time, to thin to the desired consistency.

STORAGE: Store the crema in a jar or an airtight container in the fridge for up to 5 days.

Breakfasts

Roasted Red Pepper and Gruyère Egg Bites

VEGETARIAN | GLUTEN-FREE | NUT-FREE

These little egg bites are a lifesaver on busy mornings, and are so satisfying! They also make for great snacks on the go. They've got my dietitian-favorite PFF combo—protein, fat, and fiber—to power you through the morning. The cottage cheese ups the protein factor and makes for the creamiest, fluffiest consistency. I love the combination of Gruyère and roasted red pepper for these, but you can truly make them your own by switching up the cheese and vegetables. Chopped kale, mushrooms, or broccoli all work great! You can also dice up some ham or bacon for an extra bit of salty, savory goodness. You really can't go wrong with any additions. They may just be the secret ingredient to a great day!

MAKES 12 EGG BITES

8 eggs
1 cup cottage cheese
1 cup shredded Gruyère or aged Cheddar cheese
¾ cup drained chopped roasted red peppers, patted dry

1. Preheat the oven to 350°F (180°C). Line a muffin tin with parchment paper baking cups or spray with cooking spray.

2. In a blender, blend the eggs and cottage cheese on high for 30 seconds.

3. Evenly divide ¾ cup of the Gruyère and the roasted red peppers between the cups of the muffin tin. Pour in the egg mixture until each cup is two-thirds full, and stir with a spoon to combine. Top with the remaining Gruyère.

4. Bake for 25 to 30 minutes, until the tops are set and the egg bites are cooked through. Let cool for 5 to 10 minutes before removing from the muffin tin.

STORAGE: Store the cooled egg bites in an airtight container in the fridge for up to 5 days or in the freezer for up to 3 months. To serve refrigerated or thawed egg bites, pop into the toaster oven or oven at 350°F (180°C) for 10 to 15 minutes or microwave on high for 20 to 60 seconds, until warmed through. Frozen egg bites can be reheated in the microwave on high for 60 to 90 seconds, until warmed through. If reheating in the microwave creates excess moisture, simply dab with a paper towel before eating.

Breakfast Banana Splits

VEGETARIAN | GLUTEN-FREE OPTION

Don't they say mornings set the tone for the day? Breakfast should be fun! And banana splits for breakfast are exactly that. Plus, they come together in 5 minutes flat. If you've got little ones in the house (and even if you don't), these can be especially helpful to get the good vibes flowing! I love setting up a little station with the toppings so that everyone can tailor their own split to their liking; my son loves this, plus it's less work for you!

SERVES 4

4 bananas

2 cups plain Greek yogurt, vanilla Greek yogurt, or cottage cheese

1 cup granola (page 93 or store-bought)

¼ cup almond butter

Fresh berries, for serving

OPTIONAL TOPPINGS

Hemp hearts

Chia seeds

Coconut flakes or shredded coconut

Swaps & Subs

To make these banana splits gluten-free, ensure that you've chosen gluten-free granola.

1. Peel the bananas and slice in half lengthwise, placing one banana on each of four plates.

2. Top each banana with yogurt and granola, dividing evenly. Drizzle with almond butter, top with fresh berries, and sprinkle with your favorite optional toppings. This is best enjoyed fresh.

Chunky Chocolate Coconut Superseed Granola

VEGETARIAN | DAIRY-FREE OPTION | GLUTEN-FREE

In my humble opinion, the key to a good granola is clusters. I've been making granola for years, and I think I have finally mastered the perfect texture with this recipe. Big, chunky pieces of toasted nuts, coconut, and a little bit of chocolate make this perfect to snack on as is or add to your favorite smoothie bowl. It's also the perfect opportunity to squeeze in all three of my favorite little superseeds—chia, flax, and hemp—as you start the day. These small but mighty seeds are brimming with nutritional benefits. There isn't enough room on the page to name them all, but for starters: heart- and brain-healthy omega-3s, gut-healthy fiber, and cell-protecting antioxidants. This is the perfect recipe to double, as it takes zero extra time to do so. You'll end up with an instant, nutrition-packed, delicious breakfast you can stash away in the freezer!

MAKES ABOUT 6 CUPS

½ cup honey

2 Tbsp virgin coconut oil

3 cups old-fashioned rolled oats

1 cup whole almonds,
    coarsely chopped

½ cup coconut flakes,
    coarsely chopped

¼ cup chia seeds

¼ cup hemp hearts

¼ cup whole flax seeds

½ tsp salt

⅓ cup chocolate chunks,
    roughly chopped

⅓ cup dried fruit (I like
    cranberries and/or apricots)
    (optional)

Swaps & Subs

To make the granola dairy-free, opt for dairy-free chocolate or leave it out altogether.

1. Preheat the oven to 350°F (180°C). Line a large rimmed baking sheet with parchment paper.

2. In a small saucepan, melt the honey and coconut oil over medium heat, about 1 minute, stirring to combine. (Or microwave on high for 30 seconds, until fully melted, stirring to combine.)

3. In a large bowl, combine the oats, almonds, coconut, chia seeds, hemp hearts, flax seeds, and salt. Stir in the honey mixture until well combined and small clusters start to form (I use my hands to make sure everything is well mixed).

4. Pour the mixture onto the prepared pan, ensuring it is evenly distributed, including around the edges, to prevent burning. Using your hands or the back of a wooden spoon or spatula, press down on the mix so it is tightly packed (this helps create clusters).

5. Bake for 20 to 25 minutes, without stirring, until granola is a nice golden brown. Let cool for 10 to 15 minutes before breaking it apart. Stir in the chocolate and dried fruit.

STORAGE: Store the granola in an airtight container or jar in a cool, dry place for up to 4 weeks or in a sealable freezer bag or airtight container in the freezer for up to 3 months. Enjoy frozen or thaw at room temperature for 30 to 60 minutes.

Crave-Worthy
Everyday Green Smoothie

VEGETARIAN | VEGAN OPTION | DAIRY-FREE OPTION | GLUTEN-FREE

This is THE green smoothie to turn any skeptic into a believer. It is cold, it is creamy, and the combo of frozen mango and fresh mint give it the most perfect sweetness, balancing out the flavor of all of those nourishing greens. With over four servings of fruits and vegetables in each serving, your cells and your taste buds will thank you!

SERVES 1

2 cups leafy greens (baby spinach and/or baby kale, see time saver)

¾ cup frozen mango

½ cup milk or plant-based milk

½ cup plain Greek yogurt or plant-based yogurt

¼ cup fresh mint

1 small orange, peeled

1 Tbsp almond butter

Juice of ¼ lemon (about 1 Tbsp)

1. In a high-speed blender, combine the leafy greens, mango, milk, yogurt, mint, orange, almond butter, and lemon juice. Blend on high until smooth, 30 to 60 seconds. Enjoy now or store and serve as directed below.

STORAGE: Pour the smoothie into a 16-ounce (500 ml) jar, leaving 1 to 2 inches at the top, as the liquid may expand. Store in the fridge for up to 3 days or in the freezer for up to 3 months. Alternatively, freeze in a muffin tin, then remove the pucks and store in a sealable freezer bag. To serve from refrigerated, give the smoothie a good shake to mix any ingredients that may have settled. To serve from frozen, thaw overnight in the fridge (in a cup or jar) and give it a good shake to mix any ingredients that may have settled.

Tip

Pour the smoothie into ice pop molds and freeze to make smoothie popsicles—a snack your kids will love!

Time Saver

Use bins of pre-washed baby spinach or kale.

Oranges and Cream Smoothie

VEGETARIAN | VEGAN OPTION | DAIRY-FREE OPTION | GLUTEN-FREE | NUT-FREE

Okay, I need you to promise me something before you look at the ingredients: just PROMISE ME you will try this recipe. Did you look? I know cauliflower in a smoothie might sound weird, but trust me on this one, it works. It makes the smoothie nice and creamy (no banana necessary), and you cannot taste it. Don't let its pale color fool you: this cruciferous vegetable is packed with vitamin C, blood-sugar-balancing fiber, and anti-inflammatory and antioxidant compounds! Now go keep your end of the bargain!

SERVES 1

1 large navel orange, or 2 to
  3 mandarin oranges, peeled

1 cup frozen riced cauliflower

¾ cup vanilla Greek yogurt or
  plant-based yogurt

½ cup unsweetened
  vanilla plant-based milk
  (I like almond milk)

1 Tbsp chia seeds

1. In a high-speed blender, combine the orange, cauliflower, yogurt, milk, and chia seeds. Blend on high until smooth, 30 to 60 seconds. Enjoy now or store and serve as directed below.

STORAGE: Pour the smoothie into a 16-ounce (500 ml) jar, leaving 1 to 2 inches at the top, as the liquid may expand. Store in the fridge for up to 3 days or in the freezer for up to 3 months. Alternatively, freeze in a muffin tin, then remove the pucks and store in a sealable freezer bag. To serve from refrigerated, give the smoothie a good shake to mix any ingredients that may have settled. To serve from frozen, thaw overnight in the fridge (in a cup or jar) and give it a good shake to mix any ingredients that may have settled.

Tips

For the yogurt, you can use whatever percentage of milk fat you prefer. I like to use 5% or higher, for added creaminess. If you like your smoothies a little sweeter, add another ¼ cup of vanilla yogurt. If you prefer it less sweet, and want an extra boost of fiber, add ½ cup more cauliflower.

The chia seeds thicken the smoothie as it sits, so if you prefer a more sippable consistency, drink it right away. If storing for later and you find it too thick, simply stir in a bit more milk until you reach the desired consistency.

Protein-Powered Chocolate Coffee Smoothie

VEGETARIAN | GLUTEN-FREE

If this doesn't get your day going, then I'm sorry, I can't help you. Packed with filling fiber, satiating proteins, and nourishing plant-rich fats, this is the ultimate blood-sugar-balancing (i.e., energizing and mood-boosting) smoothie. Oh, and did I mention coffee? You're welcome. This really is the perfect balanced breakfast and morning coffee all in one, so save yourself the extra dish!

SERVES 1

½ cup milk

2 tsp unsweetened cocoa powder

2 shots espresso (or ¼ cup strong-brewed coffee, or 1 to 2 tsp instant espresso powder)

½ cup 5% plain or vanilla Greek yogurt

1 Tbsp chia seeds

1 frozen banana

1 Tbsp peanut butter

1 cup frozen riced cauliflower

Pinch of salt

Splash of maple syrup, to taste

1. Place the ingredients in a high-speed blender in this order: milk, cocoa, espresso, yogurt, chia seeds, banana, peanut butter, cauliflower, salt, and maple syrup. Blend on high until completely smooth, 30 to 60 seconds. Enjoy now or store and serve as directed below.

STORAGE: Pour the smoothie into a 16-ounce (500 ml) jar, leaving 1 to 2 inches at the top, as the liquid may expand. Store in the fridge for up to 3 days or in the freezer for up to 3 months. Alternatively, freeze in a muffin tin, then remove the pucks and store in a sealable freezer bag. To serve from refrigerated, give the smoothie a good shake to mix any ingredients that may have settled. To serve from frozen, thaw overnight in the fridge (in a cup or jar) and give it a good shake to mix any ingredients that may have settled.

Tip

The chia seeds thicken the smoothie as it sits, so if you prefer a more sippable consistency, drink it right away. If storing for later and you find it too thick, simply stir in a bit more milk until you reach the desired consistency.

Meal Prep Tip

Like with all of my smoothie recipes, this can be multiplied to batch prep. Depending on the size of your blender, you could make three or four servings at a time.

Coffee Shop Double Chocolate Tahini Breakfast Cookies

VEGETARIAN | DAIRY-FREE OPTION | GLUTEN-FREE | NUT-FREE

I LOVE breakfast cookies. I mean, how can you be in a bad mood if you start your day off with chewy, chocolatey cookies that also happen to be packed with nutrition? Tahini is high in iron, great for supporting energy in the body, and oat flour makes the perfect base for a breakfast cookie, high in soluble fiber to keep blood sugars balanced and a mellow flavor that lets the chocolate flavor shine. Flax and hemp hearts add omega-3s to support that beautiful brain, and antioxidants and satiating fats keep you full and energized throughout the morning. Bonus: since these are nut-free, they make awesome lunch-box cookies your kids will devour!

MAKES 12 COOKIES

½ cup oat flour
½ cup quick oats
½ cup dark chocolate chips
¼ cup ground flax
¼ cup hemp hearts
¼ cup unsweetened
   cocoa powder
½ tsp baking soda
½ tsp salt
1 cup tahini
⅓ cup honey
¼ cup olive oil
1 egg
Sesame seeds (optional)

1. Preheat the oven to 350°F (180°C). Line two baking sheets with parchment paper.

2. In a medium bowl, whisk together the oat flour, oats, chocolate chips, ground flax, hemp hearts, cocoa, baking soda, and salt.

3. In another bowl, whisk together the tahini, honey, oil, and egg until a smooth paste forms.

4. Fold the tahini mixture into the flour mixture until completely combined and a dough forms.

5. Form the dough into twelve evenly sized balls and place on the prepared pans, evenly spread out. Flatten with the back of a spoon or fork. Sprinkle the tops of the cookies with the sesame seeds (if using).

6. Bake for 10 to 12 minutes, until crispy on the outside and soft on the inside. (The cookies will seem quite soft when they come out of the oven—this is key for those soft, chewy centers—but will harden as they cool.) Transfer the cookies to a wire rack and let cool for 7 to 10 minutes, then enjoy!

STORAGE: Store the cooled cookies in an airtight container at room temperature for up to 5 days (up to 3 days in warm weather or humid climates) or in the fridge for up to 7 days. Or store in a sealable freezer bag in the freezer for up to 3 months. Enjoy frozen, or thaw in the microwave for 20 to 30 seconds or at room temperature for 20 to 30 minutes.

Swaps & Subs
To make these cookies dairy-free, opt for dairy-free chocolate chips.

Nutrition Hack
For a boost of protein, swap the oat flour for ¾ cup almond flour and bake for 13 to 15 minutes.

Lemon Meringue Pie Chia Seed Pudding

VEGETARIAN | VEGAN OPTION | DAIRY-FREE OPTION | GLUTEN-FREE OPTION

Chia pudding upleveled. Lemon meringue pie has always been one of my favorite desserts. I just love that tangy and creamy combo, and this pudding delivers! Chia seeds are little nutrition powerhouses. Packed with fiber, omega-3 fatty acids, and a decent dose of calcium, they help balance blood sugars and keep you feeling full longer after eating. They also have an amazing ability to absorb water, making them the perfect ingredient for a smooth and satisfying pudding. Don't skip the super-easy graham crust: it provides heart- and brain-healthy walnuts and a crunch that rounds out this perfect little breakfast or snack.

SERVES 4

CHIA PUDDING

3 cups lemon yogurt or
   plant-based yogurt
1 can (5.4 oz/160 ml) full-fat
   coconut milk
¾ cup milk or plant-based milk
Grated zest and juice of 1 lemon
   (about ¼ cup juice)
½ cup chia seeds

GRAHAM CRUST

½ cup graham cracker crumbs
¼ cup crushed walnuts
2 Tbsp virgin coconut oil, melted
Pinch of salt

TOPPINGS

Greek yogurt (I like 5% plain or
   coconut whip) or plant-based
   yogurt
Fresh berries

1. **Make the chia pudding:** In a medium bowl, whisk together the yogurt, coconut milk, milk, lemon zest and juice, and chia seeds. Place in the fridge to set, about 1 to 2 hours.

2. Preheat the oven to 400°F (200°C). Line a rimmed baking sheet with parchment paper.

3. **Make the graham crust:** In a small bowl, mix together the graham crackers, walnuts, coconut oil, and salt until well combined, ensuring the dry ingredients are coated evenly with the coconut oil. Spread out the mixture evenly onto the baking sheet to ensure the edges don't burn.

4. Bake for 5 to 7 minutes, until golden brown, stirring once halfway through and watching carefully to ensure the nuts don't burn.

5. **To assemble:** Divide the crumbled graham cracker mixture between four bowls (or if storing immediately, between jars or other airtight containers). Spoon in the chia pudding. Top with Greek yogurt and berries.

STORAGE: Store the puddings, without the toppings, in the fridge for up to 5 days. Add the toppings right before serving.

> **Tip**
> Yogurts have different consistencies. If using a thicker yogurt, like Greek yogurt, you may need to add extra liquid. Thin out with a little milk or milk alternative, or reduce the amount of chia seeds.

Muesli Overnight Oats

VEGETARIAN | VEGAN OPTION | DAIRY-FREE OPTION | GLUTEN-FREE | NUT-FREE

I remember going to a little Swiss pastry shop (literally called the Swiss Pastry Shop) with my mom when I was little. They had her absolute favorite dessert to this day, raspberry torte . . . and they had muesli. I didn't think much of it as a kid, but as an adult and a dietitian, I now know muesli is a breakfast dream, packed with fiber, antioxidants, and, most of all, the perfect combo of creamy soaked oats, bursts of sweet and tart flavor from the cranberries, crisp apple, and superseeds to boot. Whip up a batch for the week in under 10 minutes, and have breakfasts waiting for you that will actually keep you full, satisfied, and fueled all morning.

SERVES 4

2 apples, diced (I like Gala)

2 cups quick oats

½ cup hemp hearts

¼ cup chia seeds

¼ cup shelled pumpkin seeds (pepitas)

¼ cup unsweetened shredded coconut

¼ cup unsweetened dried cranberries

½ to 1 tsp ground cinnamon

½ tsp salt

3 cups milk or plant-based milk

2 Tbsp maple syrup

2 tsp vanilla extract

1. In a large bowl, mix together the apples, oats, hemp hearts, chia seeds, pumpkin seeds, coconut, cranberries, ½ teaspoon cinnamon, salt, milk, maple syrup, and vanilla until well combined. Taste and mix in more cinnamon if desired.

2. Divide between four small airtight containers or glass jars (or keep in one large container and scoop out when ready to eat). Refrigerate for at least 2 hours, or overnight, to set.

STORAGE: Store the overnight oats in the fridge for up to 5 days.

Tiramisu Overnight Oats

VEGETARIAN | VEGAN OPTION | DAIRY-FREE OPTION | GLUTEN-FREE | NUT-FREE

Mmmmmm tiramisu. I could settle my whole argument for making this delicious breakfast right there, but I'll give you a few more reasons why you need this in your life: a little caffeine kick from the espresso, just the right amount of sweetness (and a hefty dose of protein and calcium) from the creamy yogurt, and, to get into the science of it all, soluble fiber from the oats, to keep your blood sugar stable throughout the morning, plus an antioxidant and omega-3 boost from the hemp hearts and chia seeds. Not to mention a sense of luxury as you dive into what feels like a decadent "dessert for breakfast" situation. Close your eyes and you might even forget that you've got places to go and people to feed.

SERVES 4

2 cups quick oats

½ cup hemp hearts

¼ cup chia seeds

2 tsp instant espresso powder

½ tsp salt

½ tsp ground cinnamon

3 cups milk or plant-based milk

2 Tbsp maple syrup

2 tsp vanilla extract

TOPPINGS

2 cups plain or vanilla Greek yogurt or plant-based yogurt

Unsweetened cocoa powder, for dusting

1. In a large bowl, mix together the oats, hemp hearts, chia seeds, espresso powder, salt, cinnamon, milk, maple syrup, and vanilla until well combined.

2. Divide half of the oat mixture between four small storage containers (with lids) or sealable glass jars. Dividing evenly, layer with half of the yogurt, then the remaining oat mixture, then the remaining yogurt. Dust with cocoa. Cover and refrigerate for at least 2 hours, or overnight, to set.

STORAGE: Store the overnight oats in the fridge for up to 5 days.

Bakery-Style Garden Muffins

VEGETARIAN | DAIRY-FREE OPTION | GLUTEN-FREE

If it weren't for Momma Jang, these muffins would not have made it into the book. Growing up there was always a batch of something delicious-smelling in the oven— Momma was known to wake up in the early hours and pop a batch of muffins in, to be fresh, soft, and fluffy when we arrived down to the kitchen. To this day she often brings a batch of her famous muffins, cookies, or scones to stock our freezer when she visits, and I credit many of these for getting me through my early postpartum days. I can feel her love through her baking, and the way she does it with so much love has had a huge impact on how I see food as more than just nutrition—it's also love, joy, and connection. She is truly the baking master, so I always call her in when I can't get my baked goods quite right. These are a variation of the super-popular zucchini banana muffins on my blog, but I wanted to pack them with even more colorful vegetables—but veggies are dense, so it was a bit of a science experiment to get the muffins to fluffy, delicious perfection! These babies are equally sought-after by kids and adults alike. My favorite way to enjoy them is halved and toasted, with a little swipe of butter. Mmmmm, perfection.

MAKES 12 MUFFINS

¾ cup finely shredded zucchini
¾ cup finely shredded carrots
¾ cup finely shredded beets
1 cup + 2 Tbsp oat flour
¾ cup old-fashioned rolled oats
3 Tbsp chia seeds
1 Tbsp baking powder
1½ tsp baking soda
¾ tsp ground cinnamon
½ tsp salt
3 ripe bananas, mashed
3 eggs
½ cup peanut butter
½ cup maple syrup
1 Tbsp vanilla extract
½ cup dark chocolate chips

Swaps & Subs

To make these muffins dairy-free, opt for dairy-free chocolate chips.

1. Preheat the oven to 350°F (180°C). Line a muffin tin with parchment paper baking cups.

2. Place the zucchini, carrots, and beets in a paper towel or cloth and wring out any extra moisture. Set aside.

3. In a bowl, whisk together the oat flour, oats, chia seeds, baking powder, baking soda, cinnamon, and salt.

4. In another bowl, using a fork or electric mixer, mix the bananas, eggs, peanut butter, maple syrup, and vanilla until well combined.

5. Add the banana mixture to the flour mixture, along with the zucchini mixture and chocolate chips. Gently fold until just combined, making sure not to overmix.

6. Scoop the batter into the prepared muffin tin, dividing evenly between the cups.

7. Bake for 25 to 28 minutes or until golden brown and a toothpick inserted in the middle of a muffin comes out clean. Place the muffin tin on a cooling rack to cool.

STORAGE: Store the cooled muffins in an airtight container at room temperature for up to 5 days (up to 3 days in warm weather or humid climates) or in the fridge for up to 7 days. Or store in a sealable freezer bag in the freezer for up to 3 months. Thaw frozen muffins in the microwave or at room temperature overnight. Enjoy as is or cut in half, pop in the toaster oven, and serve warm with butter.

Carrot Cake Breakfast Loaf with Greek Yogurt Cream Cheese Icing

VEGETARIAN | DAIRY-FREE OPTION

Sometimes you just want a nice thick slice of breakfast loaf to enjoy while curled up on the couch with a hot cup of coffee. This one is loaded with nutritious ingredients to nourish not only the soul but that beautiful body of yours too! Whole wheat flour and ground flax make a fiber-packed base, while the applesauce helps keep it moist (sorry— there's just no other word for it). The walnuts provide brain fuel, and, I mean, a little dose of veggies in your breakfast never hurt anyone! The icing provides a little boost of protein, but I also love to toast a slice bare and finish with a swipe of butter. Perfection.

MAKES 10 SLICES

LOAF

1¼ cups whole wheat flour

⅓ cup ground flax

¼ cup + 2 Tbsp sweetened shredded coconut, divided

1½ tsp baking soda

1 tsp ground cinnamon

¼ tsp salt

2 eggs

⅔ cup unsweetened applesauce

⅓ cup maple syrup

1 tsp vanilla extract

1 large carrot, grated (about 1 cup)

¼ cup walnuts, roughly chopped

⅓ cup raisins

ICING

½ cup vanilla Greek yogurt

½ cup plain cream cheese

Tips

For a dairy-free option, simply omit the icing.

To make these in muffin form, simply reduce the cooking time to 20 to 25 minutes.

1. Preheat the oven to 350°F (180°C). Line a 9 × 5-inch loaf pan with parchment paper.

2. **Make the loaf:** In a medium bowl, whisk together the flour, ground flax, ¼ cup coconut, baking soda, cinnamon, and salt.

3. In another medium bowl, whisk together the eggs, applesauce, maple syrup, and vanilla.

4. Add the egg mixture to the flour mixture, along with the carrots, walnuts, and raisins. Gently fold until just combined, making sure not to overmix.

5. Spoon the batter into the prepared pan and sprinkle with 2 tablespoons of coconut.

6. Bake for 45 to 50 minutes or until a toothpick inserted in the middle comes out clean. Let cool in the pan for 10 minutes.

7. **Make the icing:** In a small bowl, whisk together the yogurt and cream cheese until well combined. Spread over the loaf right before slicing and serving.

STORAGE: Store the loaf, without icing, in an airtight container in the fridge for up to 1 week or in a sealable freezer bag in the freezer for up to 3 months. Store the icing in a jar or other airtight container in the fridge for up to 1 week or in the freezer for up to 3 months. If refrigerated, enjoy the loaf cold or pop slices in the toaster oven to reheat before spreading with the chilled icing. If frozen, thaw the icing and loaf separately in the microwave, or thaw the icing overnight in the fridge and the loaf at room temperature for 1 to 3 hours.

Spinach, Feta, and Sun-Dried Tomato Breakfast Burritos

VEGETARIAN | GLUTEN-FREE OPTION | NUT-FREE

I've got to give credit where credit is due. When my son, Wylder, was born, I was warned there would be days when I wouldn't eat until 2 p.m. The dietitian in me thought, *No way! How is that even possible?* Lo and behold, along came the days when 2 p.m. rolled around and I was desperate for some fuel. Then my mom and sister would come to the rescue, stocking my freezer with delicious breakfast wraps. Having a quick one-hand option was so handy that here I am, four years later, rarely to be found without some variation of these in the freezer. Pop one in the oven or toaster oven while you shower, and voilà—a hot, delicious breakfast waiting for you. Now that's how you start the day feeling on top of things!

MAKES 12 BURRITOS

18 eggs
2 Tbsp milk
Salt and freshly ground
  black pepper
2 Tbsp extra virgin olive oil
2 red bell peppers, diced
  (about 2 cups)
5 cups spinach, chopped
2 cups crumbled feta cheese
1 cup drained oil-packed
  sun-dried tomatoes, chopped
Twelve 10-inch flour tortillas

1. In a bowl, whisk together the eggs and milk. Season generously with salt and pepper. Set aside.

2. In a large frying pan, heat the oil over medium-high heat. Add the peppers and cook, stirring, until tender-crisp, 3 to 4 minutes. Stir in the egg mixture and cook, stirring frequently in a circular motion, for 5 to 6 minutes until eggs are mostly cooked but still a bit wet.

3. Add the spinach and stir until wilted. Remove from the heat. The eggs should be mostly cooked but still slightly wet. Stir in the feta and sun-dried tomatoes until evenly distributed throughout. Season with more salt and pepper to taste.

4. On a clean large surface, lay out the tortillas. Divide the egg mixture evenly among the tortillas, leaving about 1½ inches of space on either end. Fold the shorter edges of each tortilla in, then fold one of the long edges over the filling and roll up.

Swaps & Subs

Don't have feta? Sub in shredded Cheddar or a cheese blend! To make these gluten-free, opt for gluten-free tortillas.

STORAGE: Store the cooled burritos in an airtight container in the fridge for up to 5 days. Or place in a single layer (or multiple layers separated by parchment paper) in an airtight container or sealable freezer bag and store in the freezer for up to 3 months. To serve refrigerated burritos, pop them in a 400°F (200°C) toaster oven or oven for 10 to 12 minutes, or microwave on high for 45 to 90 seconds, until warmed through. If frozen, increase the oven time to about 30 to 35 minutes, or thaw them in the microwave for 1 to 2 minutes first.

One-Pan Green Goddess Hash

VEGETARIAN | GLUTEN-FREE | NUT-FREE

You know when you eat something and just feel so satisfied on all fronts? That's how you'll feel about this vibrant breakfast. The flavor is next-level, with the fresh and herby dressing dolloped over crisp potatoes and perfectly roasted veggies. I'll never complain about getting three-plus servings of vegetables to start the day! This is also a great way to use up any leftover potatoes, and can really be made with any veggies you need to clear out of your fridge. It might just be your favorite new way to get your daily dose of greens!

SERVES 4

3 red-skinned potatoes, cubed (about 4 cups)

4 Tbsp avocado oil or other high-heat cooking oil, divided

1 bunch curly kale, stemmed and chopped (about 4 packed cups)

1 small crown broccoli, cut into bite-size florets (about 2 cups)

1 small onion, diced (about 1 cup)

6 stalks asparagus, cut into thirds (about ½ cup)

Salt and freshly ground black pepper

8 eggs

1 batch Green Goddess Dressing (page 75 or store-bought)

Green onion, thinly sliced, for garnish

PREP AHEAD: The kale, broccoli, onion, and asparagus can be cut and the dressing (if using homemade) made ahead of time.

1. Preheat the oven to 425°F (220°C). Line two rimmed baking sheets with parchment paper.

2. In a large bowl, toss the potatoes with 3 tablespoons of the oil. Divide them evenly between the prepared baking sheets, spreading them in a single layer. Roast for 20 minutes.

3. Meanwhile, in the same bowl, combine the kale, broccoli, onion, and asparagus. Add the remaining tablespoon of oil, tossing to coat evenly. Season generously with salt and pepper.

4. Remove the potatoes from the oven and evenly divide the vegetable mixture between the two baking sheets, spreading everything in a single layer. Roast for another 20 minutes.

5. Remove the baking sheets from the oven and create eight divots (four per baking sheet) in the vegetable mixture. Crack the eggs into the divots. Bake for 6 minutes, then check; if you prefer a firmer yolk, bake for another 2 to 4 minutes.

6. Divide the hash between four plates, drizzle with the dressing, and sprinkle with green onions. If desired, season with more salt and pepper.

STORAGE: Store the cooled hash in an airtight container in the fridge for up to 5 days. To serve, reheat in a frying pan over medium heat until warmed through, bake in a 350°F (180°C) oven or toaster oven for about 15 to 20 minutes, until warmed through, or microwave on high for 1 to 2 minutes. Reheating times will vary depending on how much of the hash you've stored.

Sheet Pan Pancakes with Blueberry Chia Compote

VEGETARIAN | NUT-FREE

Pancakes have never really been my specialty—until I discovered sheet pan pancakes. Now *these* are my jam. Simply combine the ingredients, pour the batter onto a parchment-lined baking sheet to eliminate cleanup, pop the pan in the oven, and enjoy one of the most beloved breakfast staples without the fuss of standing over the stove while everyone else in the family gets to play. It took a little extra testing to get the texture just right while using whole wheat flour for added fiber and Greek yogurt for a boost of protein and calcium, but we got the results we wanted: fluffy, nourishing, delicious pancakes the whole household will love! You will never want to make pancakes any other way. To simplify and mix things up, try them with Greek yogurt and fresh fruit, like sliced banana, strawberries, or peaches, instead of the compote. Then sit back and enjoy the praise!

MAKES 12 PANCAKES

1 cup unbleached all-purpose flour

1 cup whole wheat flour

2 Tbsp granulated sugar

2 tsp baking powder

1 tsp baking soda

½ tsp salt

2 eggs

2 cups milk

½ cup 2% plain Greek yogurt

¼ cup melted salted butter

2 tsp vanilla extract

2 cups frozen blueberries

Berry Chia Compote, made with blueberries (page 82), for serving (optional)

PREP AHEAD: The compote can be made ahead of time.

1. Preheat the oven to 425°F (220°C). Line a 13 × 18-inch rimmed baking sheet with parchment paper.

2. In a large bowl, whisk together the flours, sugar, baking powder, baking soda, and salt.

3. In a medium bowl, whisk together the eggs, milk, yogurt, butter, and vanilla.

4. Gently fold the egg mixture into the flour mixture until just combined. Fold in the blueberries.

5. Pour the batter into the prepared baking sheet, distributing it evenly. Lift the pan and tap it on the counter a couple of times to release any trapped air bubbles, making sure the batter is evenly distributed across the pan.

6. Bake for 18 to 20 minutes or until the top is golden brown and a toothpick inserted in the middle comes out clean.

7. Cut the pancakes into twelve pieces and serve topped with the compote (if using).

STORAGE: Layer the cooled pancakes between pieces of parchment paper, then store in an airtight container or sealable freezer bag in the fridge for up to 5 days or in the freezer for up to 3 months. To serve refrigerated pancakes, reheat them in the toaster oven or microwave until warmed through. If frozen, microwave or toast them until heated through, or transfer them to a parchment-lined baking sheet and bake in a 350°F (180°C) oven until warmed through, about 10 to 12 minutes.

Sheet Pan Turkey Sausage Breakfast Sammies

DAIRY-FREE OPTION | GLUTEN-FREE OPTION | NUT-FREE

My love for meal-prepped savory breakfasts started with breakfast burritos (page 113) and has only grown from there. I *love* a good breakfast sandwich—but why make them individually when you can whip up a dozen in the same amount of time? Some for now, and a stash in the freezer for a breakfast sammy that's just as quick as drive-through, but way more delicious, whenever the urge strikes! You're about to fall in love.

MAKES 12 SANDWICHES

1 Tbsp extra virgin olive oil

7 oz (200 g) breakfast turkey sausages (about 6 to 7), removed from casings and crumbled

2 cups spinach, chopped

12 eggs

2 Tbsp milk

½ tsp salt

12 English muffins

Butter and/or mayonnaise

12 slices cheese

Sliced avocado, for serving (optional)

Tomato slices, for serving (optional)

1. Preheat the oven to 325°F (160°C). Line two rimmed baking sheets with parchment paper and set aside.

2. In a large frying pan, heat the oil over medium-high heat. Add the turkey sausage and cook, without stirring, until the first side is golden brown, 3 to 4 minutes. Flip and cook the other side until golden brown, another 2 to 3 minutes. Add the spinach and cook, stirring and breaking up the meat, until the spinach is just wilted (the sausage doesn't have to be fully cooked through, as it will finish cooking in the oven). Let cool.

3. In a large bowl, whisk together the eggs, milk, and salt. Stir in the turkey mixture until well combined. Pour onto one of the prepared baking sheets, spreading evenly.

4. Bake for 15 to 20 minutes or until the eggs are set. Let cool for 10 minutes, then cut into twelve squares.

5. Meanwhile, cut the English muffins in half. Place them cut side up on the other prepared baking sheet. Toast in the oven for the last 10 to 12 minutes of the egg baking time.

6. Spread butter and/or mayo over both halves of the English muffins (I like mayo on one side and butter on the other). Lay a slice of cheese on one half of each English muffin, followed by a square of egg. If desired, top with avocado and tomatoes. Cover with the other half of the English muffin.

STORAGE: Store the cooled sandwiches, without avocado or tomato, in an airtight container in the fridge for up to 4 days, or wrap individually in storage wrap and store in a sealable freezer bag in the freezer for up to 3 months. If frozen, thaw in the fridge overnight or in the microwave. To serve, microwave until heated through, 30 to 60 seconds. For a crispier sandwich (my preferred style), toast it open-faced in a 350°F (180°C) oven for 8 to 12 minutes or toaster oven for 3 to 5 minutes. Top with avocado and tomato slices (if using).

Nutrition Hack

Starting the day with a balanced meal, including protein (eggs and sausage), carbohydrates (English muffin—choose whole-grain for a little extra fiber), fiber-rich veggies (spinach), and some satiating fat (cheese), helps to keep you full and energized longer and supports blood-sugar balance throughout the day.

Swaps & Subs

To make these sammies gluten-free, opt for gluten-free English muffins or buns. To make them dairy-free, choose plant-based milk and cheese.

Wylder's Avocado Toast-adas

VEGETARIAN | GLUTEN-FREE OPTION | NUT-FREE

My son asks for these morning, noon, and night. I think it was this exact dish that taught him, at three years old, to ask for "breakfast for dinn-o." That's "dinner" in Wylder talk. But honestly, I can't blame him. Crispy tortilla shells meet creamy, drippy egg yolks and all the fun fixings of tacos, mixed with the OG breakfast fave, avocado toast. You've just gotta try them for yourself. For an extra super-quick version, use a toaster oven (see time saver tip). Enjoy!

SERVES 4

1 Tbsp extra virgin olive oil
8 eggs
Salt and freshly ground
   black pepper
Eight 6-inch flour tortillas
2 avocados, sliced
1 cup corn and bean salsa
1 cup crumbled feta cheese
Chopped fresh cilantro, for
   garnish (optional)

1. Preheat the oven to 350°F (180°C).

2. In a large frying pan, heat the oil over medium heat. Crack the eggs into the pan and cook for 3 to 4 minutes, then season with salt and pepper. Turn off the heat and flip the eggs. Let them sit in the pan for about 1 minute, or longer if you prefer firmer yolks.

3. Meanwhile, lay the tortillas out on a baking sheet (it's okay if they overlap a bit). Bake for 3 to 5 minutes or until lightly browned and puffed up with air (they will deflate once removed from the oven).

4. To assemble, top the tortillas with the avocados, eggs, salsa, feta, and cilantro (if using). These toast-adas are best when fresh, so enjoy right away!

Swaps & Subs
To make the meal gluten-free, opt for gluten-free tortillas.

Time Saver
Bring down your preheating time by using a toaster oven. The tortillas will take just 30 to 60 seconds to toast.

15-Minute Savory Oat "Risotto" with Asparagus and Peas

VEGETARIAN | GLUTEN-FREE | NUT-FREE

I love risotto. Like, really, really love it. So much so that I needed to create an even easier version than the oven-baked blog favorite I've also shared in this book (see page 249). Making it with oats might seem weird, but trust me, it *works*! Oats already have a perfect creamy consistency (plus the added benefits of soluble fiber and iron), so when you use broth for the cooking liquid and throw in some Parmesan cheese and your favorite veggies, you've got "risotto" in minutes! Make it to bring a little excitement to breakfast, or for the ultimate breakfast for dinner!

SERVES 4

1 Tbsp avocado oil or other high-heat cooking oil

1 cup frozen or fresh peas

8 stalks asparagus, cut into 1-inch pieces (about 1 cup)

4 cups vegetable stock

1⅓ cups quick oats

1 tsp garlic powder

1 tsp onion powder

1 cup grated Parmesan cheese, plus more for garnish if desired

1 Tbsp unsalted butter

Salt and freshly ground black pepper

1 Tbsp white vinegar

8 eggs

1. Bring a large pot of water to a boil.

2. Meanwhile, in a large frying pan, heat the oil over medium-high heat. Sauté the peas and asparagus until tender-crisp and vibrant, 3 to 4 minutes. Transfer to a bowl and set aside.

3. In the same pan, combine the vegetable stock, oats, garlic powder, and onion powder. Reduce the heat to medium and bring to a simmer. Simmer until thickened and most of the stock is absorbed, 3 to 5 minutes. Stir in the Parmesan, butter, and salt and pepper to taste. Gently fold in the cooked peas and asparagus.

4. Add the vinegar to the boiling water (this will help keep the eggs together). Gently crack the eggs right into the water and cook until the desired yolk consistency is achieved, about 2 to 3 minutes for soft-poached, 4 minutes for medium-poached, and 5 to 6 minutes for hard-poached. Remove with a slotted spoon and place on a plate lined with a paper towel to absorb any extra moisture.

5. Divide the risotto between four bowls and top with the eggs. If desired, sprinkle with more Parmesan and pepper.

Swaps & Subs

No asparagus or peas? No problem! Swap in frozen corn, bell peppers, or sautéed mushrooms for an equally satisfying dish!

STORAGE: Store the risotto in an airtight container in the fridge for up to 5 days. To serve, heat the risotto in a frying pan over medium heat without the eggs, and cook, stirring, until heated through, 3 to 5 minutes. If the risotto is too dry, add 1 to 2 tablespoons of water or broth to loosen it up. Add the eggs, cover, and cook until warmed through, another 1 to 3 minutes. Alternatively, reheat risotto and eggs in the microwave.

Snacks, Dips, and a Quick Sip

Chocolate Chip Cookie Dough Energy Bites

VEGETARIAN | VEGAN OPTION | DAIRY-FREE OPTION | GLUTEN-FREE

What is it about cookie dough that is just so pleasurable? It feels a bit rebellious and has a texture nothing else compares to. Well, cookie dough lovers, I've got the perfect snack for you: these cookie dough energy bites. My secret ingredient is chickpeas—don't knock it till you try it! The dietitian in me wanted to create a version of this childhood favorite that was safe to eat raw (no raw eggs here), boosted with plant-powered protein, fiber, and antioxidants to keep you satiated, and every bit as delicious as you remember it. (PS—with credit to my recipe testing wiz Sammi for this tip, I highly recommend breaking up an energy bite or two and mixing into a bowl of vanilla ice cream!)

MAKES 16 BITES

1 can (14 oz/398 ml) chickpeas, drained, rinsed, and patted dry (about 1½ cups)

⅓ cup almond flour

¼ cup oat flour

⅓ cup creamy peanut butter

3 Tbsp maple syrup

2 tsp vanilla extract

¼ tsp salt

⅓ cup mini chocolate chips

1. In a food processor, combine the chickpeas, almond flour, oat flour, peanut butter, maple syrup, vanilla, and salt. Process to a smooth, dough-like consistency, scraping down the sides as needed.

2. Fold in the chocolate chips until combined.

3. Roll the dough into 1½-inch balls and place in an airtight container. Refrigerate until set, 1 to 2 hours.

STORAGE: Store the bites in an airtight container in the fridge for up to 1 week or in a sealable freezer bag in the freezer for up to 3 months. Enjoy frozen or thaw at room temperature or in the fridge.

Tip
These are super freezer-friendly! Double up the batch and stash some away for easy snacks and lunches down the road!

Swaps & Subs
To make these vegan and dairy-free, opt for dairy-free chocolate chips.

No-Bake Chocolate Tahini Granola Bars

VEGETARIAN | DAIRY-FREE OPTION | GLUTEN-FREE | NUT-FREE

Okay, these might just be my favorite snack I've ever created. And that is saying a lot. The flavor combo of creamy tahini, crunchy dark chocolate, and tart yet sweet cranberries is out of this world. Not to mention these bars are filled with nutrition-packed seeds: iron-rich pumpkin seeds, omega-3s from the chia seeds, and magnesium from the sunflower seeds. The oats make the perfect base for long-lasting energy. One of my favorite things about these bars is that there is no baking involved. Last but not least, they are nut-free and school-safe, making packing lunches just a little bit easier! They are truly the best of all worlds, and will make you a superstar in your household.

MAKES 16 BARS

1 cup tahini

½ cup honey

2 tsp vanilla extract

2½ cups old-fashioned rolled oats

½ cup unsweetened dried cranberries

¼ cup chia seeds

¼ cup salted roasted shelled pumpkin seeds

¼ cup raw sunflower seeds

Pinch of salt

⅓ cup dark chocolate chips

1½ tsp virgin coconut oil

1. Line an 8½ × 11-inch baking dish with parchment paper.

2. In a medium bowl, mix together the tahini, honey, and vanilla until well combined. Stir in the oats, cranberries, chia seeds, pumpkin seeds, sunflower seeds, and salt.

3. Spread the oat mixture evenly in the prepared pan, pressing it down very firmly with the base of a cup.

4. In a small saucepan, melt the chocolate chips and coconut oil over medium heat, about 1 minute, stirring to make sure the mixture doesn't burn. (Or place the chocolate and coconut oil in a microwave-safe bowl and microwave on high in 20-second increments until the mixture is completely melted and smooth.) Pour the chocolate mixture over the oat mixture, using a spatula or the back of a spoon to spread it out evenly over top.

5. Cover and freeze until hardened, 30 minutes, or refrigerate until hardened, 1 to 2 hours.

6. Remove from the pan. Cut in half lengthwise and then into eight strips, making sixteen bars.

STORAGE: Store the granola bars in an airtight container in the fridge for up to 1 week or in a sealable freezer bag in the freezer for up to 3 months. Enjoy frozen or thaw at room temperature or in the fridge.

Swaps & Subs

To make the bars dairy-free, opt for dairy-free chocolate chips. If you don't have tahini, you can substitute any nut or seed butter. The pumpkin seeds and sunflower seeds can be replaced with any nut or seed you like!

Soft and Crispy Peanut Butter, Apricot, and White Chocolate Snacking Cookies

VEGETARIAN | DAIRY-FREE OPTION | GLUTEN-FREE

These cookies were the best kind of accident. I was making a batch of my favorite crispy almond butter oat flour cookies from the blog, but was out of a bunch of the ingredients . . . and these INSANELY delish snacking cookies were born! Yes, I said snacking cookies. I often talk about the PFF combo (protein, fat, fiber) to keep you full and satiated, and these cookies have nutrition-packed versions of all three! Fiber-packed oat flour for slow-burning fuel, and creamy peanut butter for flavor and that touch of satiating fat and protein. You cannot go wrong stocking your freezer with these—if they make it that far!

MAKES 16 COOKIES

¾ cup quick oats

½ cup oat flour

⅓ cup unsweetened shredded coconut

1 tsp baking soda

½ tsp salt

1 egg

1 cup regular or natural peanut butter (see tip)

⅓ cup honey

¼ cup white chocolate chips

6 dried apricots, roughly chopped (about ¼ cup packed)

1. Preheat the oven to 350°F (180°C). Line two baking sheets with parchment paper.

2. In a medium bowl, whisk together the oats, oat flour, coconut, baking soda, and salt.

3. In a small bowl, whisk together the egg, peanut butter, and honey.

4. Add the egg mixture to the oat mixture, along with the chocolate chips and apricots, and mix together until well combined and a dough forms.

5. Form into sixteen cookies and place on the prepared pans, evenly spaced, flattening the tops with the back of a spoon or fork.

6. Bake for 10 to 12 minutes or until golden brown and still slightly soft on the inside. Transfer the cookies to a wire rack and let cool for 10 minutes, then enjoy!

STORAGE: Store the cookies in an airtight container in the pantry for up to 5 days or in the fridge for up to 7 days, or in a sealable freezer bag in the freezer for up to 3 months. Enjoy frozen or thaw at room temperature or in the microwave.

Tip
Natural peanut butter will give the cookies a more crumbly texture, versus regular peanut butter's softer and chewier texture.

Swaps & Subs
To make the cookies dairy-free, opt for dairy-free chocolate chips. All-purpose or almond flour can be subbed in if you don't have oat flour. If using almond flour, increase the baking time by 1 to 2 minutes.

Afternoon Pick-Me-Up Snack Mix

VEGETARIAN | GLUTEN-FREE

It's hard to even call this one a recipe: all you do is dump four ingredients together and call it a day. It is so simple, yet so satisfying, with satiating plant-based fats from the pecans and almonds, plus the antioxidant power of dark chocolate. This mix makes the perfect snack for hikes or picnics, or even to stash away in your purse or glove box (as long as it's not a hot day). I'm not exaggerating when I say this snack feels like self-care. Whip it up and share it with a friend to spread the love! (Packaging it in a cute little jar also makes for the perfect gift!)

MAKES 4 CUPS

1 cup dark chocolate–covered coffee beans
1 cup pecans
1 cup almonds
1 cup dried cherries

1. In a medium bowl, combine the coffee beans, pecans, almonds, and cherries.

STORAGE: Store the snack mix in an airtight container in the pantry for up to 3 months (if it lasts that long!).

Cheezy Popcorn

VEGETARIAN | GLUTEN-FREE | NUT-FREE

We are big popcorn lovers in our house. Friday nights are movie nights, and they wouldn't be complete without a big bowl of cheezy popcorn. Nutritional yeast has a savory, cheese-like flavor and—nutrition bonus—is packed with vitamin B_{12}, an important vitamin that supports metabolism. I love the combination of butter and coconut oil, but you can opt for one or the other if you prefer. Don't forget the flaky salt to top this crave-worthy snack!

MAKES 10 CUPS

10 cups popped popcorn (about ½ cup unpopped kernels)
2 Tbsp salted butter
2 Tbsp virgin coconut oil
3 to 4 Tbsp nutritional yeast
Flaky salt, to finish

1. Place the popcorn in a large bowl.

2. In a small saucepan, melt the butter and coconut oil over medium heat, about 1 minute, stirring to make sure the mixture doesn't burn. (Or place the butter and coconut oil in a microwave-safe bowl and microwave on high in 20-second increments until completely melted.)

3. Slowly pour half of the butter mixture over the popcorn, tossing lightly to coat evenly. Pour the remaining butter over top.

4. Sprinkle with 3 tablespoons of the nutritional yeast and salt to taste. Toss again to distribute and coat the kernels evenly. Season with more nutritional yeast and salt to taste. Enjoy!

STORAGE: Store the popcorn in a sealable storage bag in the pantry for up to 5 days.

Creamy Homemade Frozen Fudge Bars

VEGETARIAN | GLUTEN-FREE

Creamy, fudgy ice pops always remind me of days running through the sprinkler and cruising down the Slip 'N Slide in my rainbow bathing suit. I still love a store-bought variety, but I also love being able to make my own at home. Cashews give the base a super-creamy texture (which can be hard to accomplish with homemade frozen treats!) and provide additional nutrition and lasting energy with their iron, magnesium, and satiating plant-powered fats. You also get a protein boost from the Greek yogurt, so whether you've got a sprinkler to run through or need a little something to get through that Friday afternoon meeting, these pops have got your back.

MAKES 10 BARS

1 cup raw cashews

3 Tbsp unsweetened cocoa powder

3 cups 5% vanilla Greek yogurt

⅓ cup milk or plant-based milk (see tip)

Pinch of salt

1. Place the cashews in a bowl and cover with boiling water. Cover and soak for 15 minutes to soften, then drain.

2. In a blender (I recommend a high-speed one for the smoothest results), blend the soaked cashews, cocoa, yogurt, milk, and salt on high speed until completely smooth and creamy, about 60 seconds.

3. Pour into ten ice pop molds, dividing evenly, and freeze until solid, at least 4 hours or overnight.

STORAGE: Remove the bars from the ice pop molds and store in a sealable freezer bag in the freezer for up to 2 months (any longer and you risk freezer burn).

Tip

I like to use unsweetened vanilla oat milk for the added sweetness and creaminess, but any milk will do. You can adjust the sweetness to taste by adding maple syrup.

Mangos and Cream Ice Pops

VEGETARIAN | DAIRY-FREE | GLUTEN-FREE | NUT-FREE

We pretty much always have a variation of these ice pops in our freezer at any given time. They are a HUGE hit with the kids and can also be made into a fun adult version with a little splash of coconut rum or tequila. They are so easy to make, they provide immune-supporting and cell-protecting antioxidant vitamin C, and they are beyond delicious. You'll never want to buy store-bought again!

MAKES 10 ICE POPS

3 cups frozen mango

1½ cups water, plus more
   as needed

Juice of 1 lime (about 2 Tbsp)

3 Tbsp honey, divided

1 can (5.4 oz/160 ml) full-fat
   coconut milk

1. In a blender, blend the mango, water, lime juice, and 2 tablespoons of honey until smooth. If too thick, add more water, 1 tablespoon at a time, to thin to a pourable consistency.

2. Open the can of coconut milk and stir the remaining tablespoon of honey directly into the can, making sure it's well combined.

3. Divide the coconut milk mixture evenly between ten ice pop molds. Top with the mango mixture and stir with a chopstick or knife to create a drizzle effect, still keeping the mango and coconut milk components mostly separate. Freeze until solid, at least 4 hours or overnight, and enjoy!

STORAGE: Remove the ice pops from the molds and store in a sealable freezer bag in the freezer for up to 2 months (any longer and you risk freezer burn).

Swaps & Subs

You can swap the mango for pretty much any frozen fruit (we also love strawberry, mixed berry, or watermelon). You can also omit the coconut milk for a straight-up fruity blend!

Elevated Cajun Snack Mix

VEGETARIAN | VEGAN | DAIRY-FREE

I'll take any excuse to add another savory snack mix to the rotation. This one will definitely have you, and everyone else, coming back for more. I put my dietitian spin on classic snack mix favorites like pretzels and cereal squares by adding a variety of nuts and seeds to make it antioxidant-rich and even more satisfying.

MAKES ABOUT 8 CUPS

½ cup extra virgin olive oil

1½ Tbsp Cajun seasoning
  (page 76 or store-bought)

1½ cups mini baguette crisps

1½ cups Chex cereal

1½ cups Shreddies cereal

1 cup pretzel sticks

¾ cup unsalted almonds

¾ cup unsalted cashews

½ cup shelled pumpkin seeds

⅓ cup roasted sunflower seeds

2 Tbsp hemp hearts

1. Preheat the oven to 300°F (150°C). Line a rimmed baking sheet with parchment paper.

2. In a large bowl, whisk together the oil and Cajun seasoning. Add the mini baguette crisps, Chex, Shreddies, pretzels, almonds, cashews, pumpkin seeds, sunflower seeds, and hemp hearts, tossing to coat evenly. (Mixing with your hands works well for this.)

3. Spread the mixture evenly over the prepared baking sheet.

4. Bake for 20 to 25 minutes, stirring halfway through, until golden brown. Enjoy warm or let cool completely before storing.

STORAGE: Store the snack mix in an airtight container in the pantry for up to 1 month (if it lasts that long!) or in a sealable freezer bag in the freezer for up to 3 months.

Time Saver

To make this even quicker, I don't use measuring cups. A handful is about a cup; a half handful, a half cup. You can guesstimate the rest from there. Test a little bit before adding it to the oven, adjust the seasoning accordingly, and voilà!

Salted Peanut Chocolate Freezer Bombs

VEGETARIAN | VEGAN OPTION | DAIRY-FREE OPTION | GLUTEN-FREE

The simplest recipes are sometimes the best, and these freezer bombs fit the bill. They do not last in our house, and I am a big reason why (ha ha!). But for real, we've almost had a few wrestling matches for the last one. It is the best kind of surprise when you bite into that chocolatey coating to find a perfectly salty, nougaty filling. As a bonus, the almond flour base adds protein and fiber to give this snack a little staying power. I'm gonna stop right here, because you just need to see for yourself. Make them now. It will be the best 15 minutes you've spent in a long time.

MAKES 12 TO 16 PIECES

FILLING

3 Tbsp almond flour

2 Tbsp creamy peanut butter

2 Tbsp salted raw or roasted peanuts

2 tsp maple syrup

CHOCOLATE SHELL

¾ cup dark or milk chocolate chips

1 Tbsp + 1 tsp virgin coconut oil

Swaps & Subs

To make these dairy-free and vegan, opt for dairy-free chocolate chips.

1. **Make the filling:** In a small bowl, stir together the flour, peanut butter, peanuts, and maple syrup until well combined.

2. **Make the chocolate shell:** In a small saucepan, melt the chocolate chips and coconut oil over medium heat, stirring frequently to make sure the mixture doesn't burn. (Or place the chocolate chips and coconut oil in a microwave-safe bowl and microwave on high in 20-second increments until completely melted and smooth.)

3. **Assemble:** Divide half of the melted chocolate evenly between an ice cube tray. Roll the filling by heaping teaspoons into oval balls and add one ball to each slot. Pour the remaining chocolate over the balls, dividing evenly. Freeze until the chocolate is completely hard, 30 to 45 minutes.

STORAGE: Remove the freezer bombs from the ice cube trays and store in an airtight container or sealable freezer bag in the freezer for up to 3 months. Enjoy frozen or thaw at room temperature for 5 to 10 minutes.

PB&J Greek Yogurt Snacking Bark

VEGETARIAN | GLUTEN-FREE | NUT-FREE OPTION

Greek yogurt is a staple in our fridge. It is such an easy protein source and is so
versatile, providing the best creamy base for just about anything, sweet or savory.
This fun and delicious snacking bark uses vanilla Greek yogurt for the perfect touch of
sweetness. I've gone with the classic PB&J combo. The peanut butter adds protein and
fat to make this a satisfying blood-sugar-friendly snack, but you can mix things up
and add your favorite fruit, nuts, or seeds, and even a little chocolate if you like!
Pop the bark in the freezer and have fun breaking it apart.

SERVES 4 TO 6

2 cups 5% or higher vanilla
   Greek yogurt
2 Tbsp creamy natural peanut
   butter (see tip)
2 Tbsp Berry Chia Compote
   (page 82), thinned with a
   little water, or store-bought
   jam (I like raspberry)

1. Line a rimmed baking sheet with parchment paper.

2. Pour the yogurt onto the prepared baking sheet, spreading it evenly. Drizzle with peanut butter and place six to eight dollops of jam in different areas. Using a toothpick or chopstick, spread the peanut butter and compote throughout the yogurt mixture, moving in figure eights or swirling patterns.

3. Freeze until the yogurt is completely solid, 1 to 2 hours. To serve, break into pieces and enjoy immediately (it will melt back into a liquid in the fridge or at room temperature).

STORAGE: Store the bark in an airtight container or sealable freezer bag in the freezer for up to 2 months.

Tip
This recipe works best with
natural peanut butter, as the
runnier consistency makes it
easier to drizzle and distribute
throughout the bark.

Swaps & Subs
Make it nut-free by swapping
out the peanut butter for
the seed butter of your
choice, like sunflower seed
butter, tahini, or pumpkin
seed butter.

Crispy Honey Valentina Cauliflower Bites

VEGETARIAN | DAIRY-FREE | NUT-FREE

Cauliflower wings have been on the scene for a while now, but this version mixes things up for the perfect combo of spicy and sweet. Cauliflower is from the cruciferous vegetable family, known for their antioxidant and anti-inflammatory properties. With this recipe, it makes for an addictive snack or appetizer, or a delicious filling for lettuce wraps, burgers, or tacos (as you'll see in the Crispy Honey Valentina Cauliflower Tacos on page 211). Dip them in your favorite blue cheese sauce or make the Famous Kale Caesar with Creamy Greek Yogurt Dressing and Crispy Chickpeas and Capers (page 159) for the perfect pairing!

SERVES 2 TO 4

CRISPY BAKED CAULIFLOWER
Avocado oil spray
2 eggs
1¼ cups panko bread crumbs
⅓ cup all-purpose flour
½ tsp salt
¼ tsp freshly ground
    black pepper
1 head cauliflower, cut into
    bite-size florets (about 6 cups)

HONEY VALENTINA SAUCE
½ cup Valentina hot sauce
¼ cup honey

PREP AHEAD: The cauliflower can be cut ahead of time.

1. **Make the cauliflower:** Preheat the oven to 425°F (220°C). Line two large rimmed baking sheets with parchment paper and spray the paper with avocado oil until covered. This will ensure your cauliflower is crispy.

2. In a large bowl, whisk the eggs until well combined.

3. In a large sealable bag, shake the panko, flour, salt, and pepper until well combined.

4. Add the cauliflower to the eggs and mix until each piece is coated in egg. Using a slotted spoon, shake off any excess egg and transfer the cauliflower to the panko breading bag. Shake the bag until the cauliflower is fully coated with the panko mixture. You may need to press the cauliflower pieces through the bag to ensure the coating sticks.

5. Divide the cauliflower between the prepared baking sheets, spreading it out in a single layer and leaving room between pieces so the cauliflower crisps up and doesn't steam. Spray the heck out of the tops and sides of the cauliflower with avocado oil—this is the key to achieving crispy cauliflower.

6. Bake for 40 to 45 minutes, flipping halfway through, until the coating is golden brown on both sides and the cauliflower is tender but firm when pierced with a fork.

7. **Make the sauce:** Meanwhile, in a small bowl, whisk together the hot sauce and honey.

8. Pour the sauce over the cauliflower and toss to coat. Bake for 5 minutes to heat through.

STORAGE: Store the cooled bites in an airtight container in the fridge for up to 5 days or in a sealable freezer bag in the freezer for up to 2 months. If frozen, thaw in the microwave or overnight in the fridge (they won't be as crispy, but are still delicious). To serve, reheat in a 425°F (220°C) oven or toaster oven for 10 to 15 minutes or until heated through and crisping around the edges.

Mexican Street Corn–Inspired Guacamole

VEGETARIAN | GLUTEN-FREE | NUT-FREE

Homemade guacamole is so easy to make, and when a friend of mine shared her trick of adding a combination of lemon *and* lime, I had a whole new love for it! This version takes inspiration from the famous Mexican street corn (elote) and combines it with this creamy, flavorful fan favorite to make the ultimate topping or delicious standalone dip! The nourishing monounsaturated plant-based fats and fiber from the avocado also support heart health and blood-sugar balance, which keeps you both full and satisfied for longer after eating. You really can't go wrong!

MAKES ABOUT 2 CUPS

2 large avocados

1 clove garlic, grated or finely minced (about ½ tsp)

¼ cup corn kernels

¼ cup crumbled cotija or feta cheese

2 Tbsp finely chopped fresh cilantro

2 Tbsp minced red onion

Juice of ½ lemon (about 2 Tbsp)

Juice of ½ lime (about 1 Tbsp)

Salt and freshly ground black pepper

1. In a medium bowl, mash the avocados to a chunky-smooth consistency. Stir in the garlic, corn, cotija, cilantro, red onion, lemon juice, lime juice, and salt and pepper to taste. Enjoy!

STORAGE: Guacamole is best enjoyed fresh, but if you have leftovers, store it in an airtight container in the fridge for up to 3 days. Squeeze more lemon or lime juice over the top or cover tightly with plastic wrap (so that it's flush against the guacamole) before putting on the lid to keep it from browning.

Swaps & Subs
You can make this dip with only lemon or lime juice if you only have one of the two on hand or want to use up the full fruit.

Creamy Buffalo White Bean Dip

VEGETARIAN | VEGAN | DAIRY-FREE | GLUTEN-FREE | NUT-FREE OPTION

I love using cannellini beans as a base for dips. This one features my favorite condiment, hot sauce, and makes the most delicious, protein-packed snack—like hummus, but even creamier. Use it as a dip for veggies, crackers, or pita, or as a spread for wraps or sandwiches. If you really want to take things to the next level, sprinkle it with cheese and warm it in the oven.

MAKES ABOUT 2 CUPS

¼ cup raw cashews

1 can (19 oz/540 ml) cannellini (white kidney) beans, drained and rinsed (about 2 cups)

3 to 4 Tbsp hot sauce (I like Frank's), plus more for drizzling

2 Tbsp extra virgin olive oil, plus more for drizzling

½ tsp salt, plus more to taste

Juice of ¼ lemon (about 1 Tbsp)

1. Place the cashews in a bowl and cover with boiling water. Cover and soak for 15 minutes to soften, then drain.

2. In a food processor, combine the soaked cashews, beans, 3 tablespoons of hot sauce, oil, salt, and lemon juice. Process until smooth. If the dip is too thick, thin it with water, 1 tablespoon at a time, until the desired consistency is reached. Season with more salt or hot sauce to taste.

3. Transfer to a bowl or airtight container. If serving as a dip, drizzle with oil and hot sauce right before serving.

STORAGE: Store the dip, without the drizzles, in an airtight container in the fridge for up to 5 days or in the freezer for up to 3 months. If frozen, thaw in the microwave or overnight in the fridge, then drizzle with oil and hot sauce.

Swaps & Subs
To make this recipe nut-free, swap the cashews for 2 tablespoons of seed butter, such as tahini or pumpkin seed butter, and skip step 1.

Addictive Edamame Dip

VEGETARIAN | VEGAN | DAIRY-FREE | GLUTEN-FREE | NUT-FREE OPTION

Before the days of kids, whenever I'd go visit my sister in Hawaii, you could find us almost nightly enjoying happy hour on the Waikiki strip while that gorgeous Hawaiian sun set over the water, live reggae humming in the background, a Blue Moon in hand as we chatted our way through a bowl of edamame dip, among other things. I loved it so much I had to create my own at home! Edamame beans are high in fiber and protein, and blend into a beautiful, vibrant dip. My favorite way to eat it is with toasted crostini, but any dipping device will do!

MAKES ABOUT 2 CUPS

2 cups shelled edamame beans

2 Tbsp fresh basil

1 clove garlic, grated or finely minced (about ½ tsp)

⅓ cup extra virgin olive oil, plus more as needed

3 Tbsp warm water, plus more as needed

Juice of ½ lemon (about 2 Tbsp), plus more as needed

½ tsp salt, plus more as needed

Freshly ground black pepper

Diced cucumber (optional)

Thinly shaved radishes (optional)

Toasted pine nuts or chopped walnuts (optional)

Crackers, toasted crostini, or fresh vegetables

1. In a small pot of boiling water, boil the edamame beans for 3 to 4 minutes, until tender-crisp. (Or add the beans to a bowl, cover with water, and microwave on high for 1 to 2 minutes.) Drain the beans.

2. In a food processor, combine the beans, basil, garlic, oil, warm water, lemon juice, and salt. Process until smooth, scraping down the sides as needed, 1 to 2 minutes. If the dip is too thick, thin it with more warm water, 1 tablespoon at a time. Adjust to taste with more salt, pepper, lemon juice, or oil as needed.

3. Transfer to a bowl or airtight container. If desired, top with cucumber, radishes, and nuts right before serving. Serve with crackers, crostini, or vegetables.

STORAGE: Store the dip, without the toppings, in an airtight container in the fridge for up to 5 days or in the freezer for up to 3 months. If frozen, thaw in the microwave or overnight in the fridge, then add the toppings (if using).

Tip
Drizzle with more olive oil or your favorite flavored oil for an extra pop of flavor and a nice finishing touch!

Blender Green Juice the Whole Family Will Love

VEGETARIAN | VEGAN | DAIRY-FREE | GLUTEN-FREE | NUT-FREE

Did you know it's super easy to make your own green juice at home for a fraction of the cost you'd pay at your favorite juice bar? I love making a batch of this stacked green juice for the week to have with breakfast, add to a snack for an extra boost of nutrition and hydration, or even pair with lunch or dinner when I'm too lazy to prep a side salad or veggies. It is so refreshing and even gives a bit of that tropical vibe we all crave, with the pineapple and mint adding a perfect touch of sweetness. I often drink it as is, but if you prefer a smoother, pulp-free juice, just pour through a strainer before popping it in the fridge!

SERVES 4

1 bin (5 oz/142 g) leafy greens, such as a power greens mix, with spinach, kale, and chard (about 8 cups)

4 cups water

2 cups frozen pineapple, plus more to taste

½ large cucumber, cut in half

2 stalks celery, cut into thirds

1 green apple, cut into quarters, core and seeds removed

1 cup fresh mint, plus more to taste

2-inch knob ginger, peeled

Juice of 1 lemon (about ¼ cup)

PREP AHEAD: The cucumber, celery, apple, and ginger can be cut and/or peeled ahead of time.

1. In a high-speed blender, combine the leafy greens, water, pineapple, cucumber, celery, apple, mint, ginger, and lemon juice. (If using a standard blender, cut the ingredients into small, bite-sized pieces.) Blend on high until smooth, 1 to 2 minutes. If the ingredients are getting stuck and not blending, use the tamper to push them down and get them moving. Taste and blend in more mint or pineapple as desired.

2. Enjoy as is or strain to remove the pulp. (I like to keep it in for extra fiber!)

STORAGE: Pour the juice into glass jars, leaving 1 to 2 inches at the top, as the liquid may expand. Store in the fridge for up to 3 days or in the freezer for up to 3 months. If frozen, thaw overnight in the fridge. Before serving, give the juice a good shake to mix any ingredients that may have settled.

Tip

Are you often left with random wilting herbs in the crisper? Stop throwing them out and add them to this juice! Or, if you're not ready to make juice, pop the herbs in the freezer, to pull out when needed!

Time Saver

Using bins of greens saves you a ton of time stemming them.

Nutrition Hack

If you prefer your juice strained, freeze the pulp in ice cube trays and add it to smoothies for extra fiber. (This also prevents food waste!)

Salads

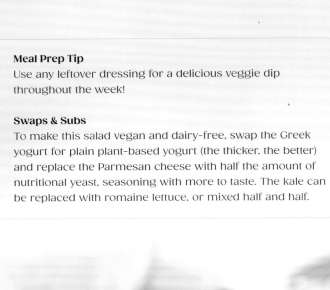

Meal Prep Tip
Use any leftover dressing for a delicious veggie dip throughout the week!

Swaps & Subs
To make this salad vegan and dairy-free, swap the Greek yogurt for plain plant-based yogurt (the thicker, the better) and replace the Parmesan cheese with half the amount of nutritional yeast, seasoning with more to taste. The kale can be replaced with romaine lettuce, or mixed half and half.

Famous Kale Caesar with Creamy Greek Yogurt Dressing and Crispy Chickpeas and Capers

VEGETARIAN | VEGAN OPTION | DAIRY-FREE OPTION | GLUTEN-FREE | NUT-FREE

It ain't called famous for nothin'! This recipe was one of the first on my blog and has been a community favorite ever since, so it only seemed fitting to give it a spot in this book. The Greek yogurt lends the creamiest consistency, while also making it high in protein, and provides just the tang you crave in a Caesar salad dressing. Add in the monounsaturated fats from the olive oil and you've got a dressing that truly satisfies on all fronts! One of the best things about this salad is that—unlike most, where soggy leaves can be an issue—you can totally batch prep this one to enjoy as a quick meal when you need. The dressing soaks into the kale leaves, tenderizing them further over time, while the flavor continues to build. Don't skip the crispy chickpeas and capers. You'll be addicted to this salad topper!

SERVES 6

CRISPY CHICKPEAS AND CAPERS

2 cans (each 19 oz/540 ml) chickpeas, drained and rinsed (about 4 cups)

½ cup drained capers

2 Tbsp avocado oil or other high-heat cooking oil

Salt and freshly ground black pepper

DRESSING

1¼ cups plain Greek yogurt

¾ cup finely grated Parmesan cheese, plus more for garnish

Juice of 1 lemon (about ¼ cup)

3 Tbsp extra virgin olive oil

2 cloves garlic, grated or finely minced (about 1 tsp)

Salt and freshly ground black pepper

SALAD

3 large bunches curly kale, stemmed and cut or torn into bite-size pieces (about 15 cups)

PREP AHEAD: The kale can be cut ahead of time. You can also prepare the dressing up to 4 days ahead and store it in the fridge.

IF YOU'RE FOLLOWING THE MEAL PLAN: Using the kale that was prepped, make all six servings. Serve four now and store the chickpea mixture and the dressed kale in separate airtight containers for lunch tomorrow. If desired, reheat the chickpea mixture (see storage below for reheating instructions).

1. **Make the chickpeas and capers:** Preheat the oven to 425°F (220°C). Line a rimmed baking sheet with parchment paper.

2. Pat the chickpeas and capers as dry as possible to help them crisp up. In a medium bowl, combine the chickpeas, capers, avocado oil, and salt and pepper to taste, stirring to coat evenly.

3. Spread the chickpea mixture in a single layer on the prepared pan. Bake until crispy and golden on the outside, 20 to 25 minutes.

4. **Make the dressing:** Meanwhile, in a salad bowl (this will save you extra dishes), whisk together the yogurt, Parmesan, lemon juice, olive oil, and garlic. Adjust to taste with salt, pepper, and more lemon juice or Parmesan as desired.

5. **Assemble the salad:** Add the kale to the bowl with the dressing and mix together with a fork or clean hands, massaging the dressing into the leaves to ensure they're coated.

6. When ready to serve, top with the chickpea mixture and more Parmesan.

STORAGE: Store the chickpea mixture and the dressed kale in separate airtight containers in the fridge for up to 5 days. Before serving, reheat the chickpea mixture in a 400°F (200°C) oven for 5 to 7 minutes, stirring halfway through, until warmed through and crisped up.

Taco Salad in a Jar

DAIRY-FREE | GLUTEN-FREE | NUT-FREE

I love a good taco salad. There's just something so satisfying about the combination of veggies, perfectly spiced taco meat (ground turkey in this case), and, of course, a good dressing. Black beans are fiber-rich, supporting gut health and making for a more filling salad, while the olive oil provides plant-powered fats that help your body absorb the vitamin K in the leafy greens. In addition to a burst of freshness, lime juice increases absorption of the plant-based iron found in the beans and greens. Pile this up in pretty little jars, or save yourself time by throwing everything into a large bowl to be dished out as needed. Whatever you do, don't forget the chips!

SERVES 4

DRESSING

⅓ cup extra virgin olive oil

Juice of 3 limes (about ⅓ cup)

½ tsp salt

SPICED TURKEY

1 Tbsp avocado oil or other high-heat cooking oil

1 Tbsp chili powder

1 tsp ground cumin

½ tsp salt

1 lb (450 g) ground turkey

TO ASSEMBLE

2 cups cooked quinoa (page 58)

1 can (14 oz/398 ml) black beans, drained and rinsed (about 1½ cups)

1 cup corn kernels (thawed if frozen)

1 cup cherry tomatoes, quartered

½ cup pickled red onion (page 72) or diced raw red onion

4 cups mixed greens (about half a 5 oz/142 g bin)

2 cups nacho chips or tortilla chips, crumbled

PREP AHEAD: The dressing, spiced turkey, quinoa, quartered tomatoes, and pickled red onion can be prepped ahead of time.

IF YOU'RE FOLLOWING THE MEAL PLAN: Before lunchtime on Monday, assemble two servings as described in step 4 (for meal plan method), using half of the prepared turkey and quinoa mixture. Assemble the remaining two servings before lunchtime on Tuesday.

1. **Make the dressing:** In a small bowl, make the dressing by whisking together the olive oil, lime juice, and salt. Adjust to taste with salt and more lime juice as desired.

2. **Make the turkey:** In a large frying pan, heat the avocado oil over medium-high heat. Add the chili powder, cumin, and salt and cook, stirring occasionally, until fragrant, 2 to 3 minutes. Add the turkey and break it into a few large pieces, coating with the seasonings. Cook, without stirring, until the first side is browned, about 4 to 5 minutes. Flip and brown the other side, another 2 to 4 minutes, then break into smaller pieces and cook, stirring, until no pink remains.

3. **Assemble the salads:** Divide the dressing evenly between four jars, then layer in the cooked quinoa, cooked turkey, beans, corn, tomatoes, and pickled red onion, dividing evenly. (Or, if serving right away, combine all these ingredients in a large bowl.)

4. **To serve for meal plan method:** Add 1 cup mixed greens to a bowl and top with a quarter of the prepared salad. Top with ½ cup nacho chips for each serving.

    To serve for jar method: Top each jarred salad with 1 cup of mixed greens and ½ cup nacho chips. Seal the jar closed and enjoy your packed lunch later on in the day!

STORAGE: Prepare the recipe through step 3 and store in the fridge for up to 4 days. To serve, continue with step 4.

Time Saver
While layering is fun, you can store this salad in a large airtight container and dish it up as needed to save time and dishes!

Green Goddess Pasta Salad

VEGETARIAN | NUT-FREE

I haven't always been the biggest fan of pasta salads, but they are a favorite of my husband, Meik—and you know what they say: happy husband, happy life . . . okay, wait, that's not it, but you get the point. Anyway, I am sure glad I got on the pasta salad train, because it would have been a tragedy to miss out on this one. The green goddess dressing is everything you need: a creamy Greek yogurt base, packed with fresh herbs, brightened up with lemon, and turned a vibrant green from a good dose of spinach. Just looking at it makes me happy! As if there weren't already enough reasons to love it, this salad is a nutritional superstar, with an abundance of vitamins and antioxidants (gotta love those green veggies), and has an easy built-in protein source in the edamame beans. This dish makes great leftovers whether cold or heated up.

SERVES 4 TO 6

1½ cups dried orzo pasta

10 stalks asparagus, cut into quarters (about 1 cup)

2 cups shelled edamame beans (thawed if frozen)

1½ cups spinach

1 cup snap peas, cut in half on the diagonal

⅓ cup crumbled Macedonian feta cheese (see swaps & subs)

1 batch Green Goddess Dressing (page 75)

PREP AHEAD: You can prep the asparagus, snap peas, and dressing ahead of time.

1. Bring a pot of salted water to boil and cook the orzo according to package directions.

2. In a large serving bowl, combine the cooked orzo, asparagus, edamame, spinach, peas, and feta. Pour the salad dressing over top and toss to combine. Enjoy!

STORAGE: Store the pasta salad in an airtight container in the fridge for up to 5 days.

Swaps & Subs

Macedonian feta is a softer feta that complements this dish perfectly, but if you can't find it, no worries! Swap in regular feta or goat cheese. You can also play around with the veggies, based on what's in your fridge or in season.

Peach and Burrata Panzanella Salad

VEGETARIAN | NUT-FREE

Bread and salad: two of my favorite things. Enjoying them together? I'm in. Whoever invented panzanella is a straight-up genius. The colors of this salad alone are enough to satisfy my foodie soul, but just wait until you dig in. The way the creamy burrata fills the cracks and crevices between juicy tomatoes and peaches, with fresh mint balancing out the mix of sweet and savory flavors, is pretty dang close to perfection. Best served in good company, with a glass of your favorite cold beverage. This salad works great alongside grilled shrimp or chicken to make it a complete meal. Or top it with a fried or poached egg for a delicious breakfast variation!

SERVES 4 TO 6

CROUTONS

6 cups sourdough bread,
 cut into 1-inch cubes
3 Tbsp extra virgin olive oil
½ tsp flaky salt
Freshly ground black pepper

DRESSING

3 Tbsp extra virgin olive oil
2 Tbsp red wine vinegar
2 tsp honey
1 tsp flaky salt
1 tsp Dijon mustard
1 clove garlic, grated or
 finely minced (about ½ tsp)

SALAD

1 lb (450 g) heirloom tomatoes
2 peaches, thinly sliced
⅓ cup pickled red onion
 (page 72)
¼ cup fresh basil, thinly sliced,
 plus more for garnish if desired
1 Tbsp minced fresh mint
Pinch of flaky salt
9 oz (250 g) burrata cheese,
 broken into 6 to 8 chunks

PREP AHEAD: The pickled red onion can be made and the bread cubes cut ahead of time. Store the bread in an airtight container or storage bag in the pantry for up to 5 days. You can also prepare the dressing up to 5 days ahead and store it in the fridge.

1. Preheat the oven to 375°F (190°C). Line a rimmed baking sheet with parchment paper.

2. **Make the croutons:** Add the bread, oil, salt, and a generous sprinkle of pepper to the prepared baking sheet. Using clean hands, toss to coat the bread evenly, then spread out in a single layer. Bake for 10 to 12 minutes, flipping halfway through, until the croutons are crisp and golden on the outside.

3. **Make the dressing:** In a small bowl, whisk together the oil, vinegar, honey, salt, mustard, and garlic.

4. **Assemble the salad:** On a large serving platter, toss together the croutons, tomatoes, peaches, pickled red onion, basil, mint, dressing, and salt, coating evenly. Distribute the burrata over top and garnish with more basil, if desired. Serve immediately.

STORAGE: This salad is best served fresh, but if it makes more than you can serve at one time, leave out the croutons when tossing the salad together. Transfer the portion of salad you're not serving immediately to an airtight container and store in the fridge for up to 5 days. Add the croutons to each portion as you serve it, and top with fresh basil, if desired.

Swaps & Subs

If you can't find burrata cheese (or for a more budget-friendly option), try buffalo mozzarella. If heirloom tomatoes aren't available, swap in a combination of vine-ripened tomatoes and tricolored cherry tomatoes.

Time Saver

To make this a super-quick meal, swap the pickled red onion for fresh, or omit altogether.

Charcuterie Salad

GLUTEN-FREE

Back in the day, my girlfriends and I would get together every Thursday.
One of us would host and the others would bring a bottle of wine. We'd eat,
we'd chat, we'd eat some more. Charcuterie was often involved and, call me basic,
but it's got to be one of my favorite things in life. One night I was cleaning up the
charcuterie leftovers and threw everything into one container. Out of pure laziness,
I threw these remnants onto my salad the next day, and the result was nothing
short of amazing. Now you can enjoy this fancy favorite as a meal on the go,
with the most delicious touch of freshness from the greens!

SERVES 4

DRESSING

¼ cup extra virgin olive oil

3 Tbsp red wine vinegar

Salt and freshly ground
    black pepper

SALAD

10 cups arugula (about one
    and a half 5 oz/142 g bins)

4 feta-stuffed jalapeño peppers
    (these are typically red),
    sliced crosswise into rounds

1 pint cherry tomatoes, halved

1 can (14 oz/398 ml) chickpeas,
    drained and rinsed (about
    1½ cups)

7 oz (200 g) thinly sliced
    prosciutto

3.5 oz (100 g) baby bocconcini,
    halved

⅓ cup fresh basil leaves,
    roughly torn

¼ cup sun-dried kalamata olives,
    pitted (optional)

¼ cup Marcona almonds

¼ small red onion, thinly sliced
    (about ¼ cup)

Balsamic glaze, for garnish

1. **Make the dressing:** In a small bowl, whisk together the oil, vinegar,
   and salt and pepper to taste.

2. **Assemble the salad:** Arrange the arugula on a large platter. Evenly
   distribute the stuffed peppers, tomatoes, chickpeas, prosciutto,
   bocconcini, basil, olives, almonds, and red onion on top.

3. Right before eating, drizzle the salad with the dressing and toss until
   evenly coated. Season with more salt and pepper and finish with a drizzle
   of balsamic glaze. Enjoy!

Tip
I love serving salads on a large platter to show
off the beautiful ingredients and make it easier
to dish up so everyone gets a bit of everything!

Swaps & Subs
While I love Marcona almonds in this dish
(they're the ones that are typically lightly fried,
then salted), they can be replaced with regular
roasted almonds.

Easiest Arugula Salad

VEGETARIAN | NUT-FREE

Don't let the simplicity of this salad fool you—the flavor is next-level. I could seriously eat it every night. It stands alone with grilled chicken or a piece of fish, but most days I eat it as a flavor-packed side salad, ready in 5 minutes, or even as the perfect topping for pizza, pasta, or burgers. The zip of the garlic and creaminess of the Parm are perfectly balanced out by the brightness of the lemon. Okay, be right back—going to make this ASAP!

SERVES 2 TO 4

DRESSING

1 clove garlic, grated or finely minced (about ½ tsp)

¼ cup finely grated Parmesan cheese, plus more for garnish if desired

1½ Tbsp extra virgin olive oil

Juice of ½ lemon (about 2 Tbsp)

Pinch of flaky sea salt (I like Maldon salt)

SALAD

1 bin (5 oz/142 g) arugula (about 6 to 8 cups)

2 Tbsp panko bread crumbs (see tip)

Freshly ground black pepper

PREP AHEAD: The dressing can be made up to 1 week ahead and stored in the fridge.

IF YOU'RE FOLLOWING THE MEAL PLAN: If you'd like to serve this salad alongside the turkey burgers, whip it together while the burgers are cooking.

1. **Make the dressing:** In a large serving bowl, whisk together the garlic, Parmesan, oil, lemon juice, and salt until well combined.

2. **Assemble the salad:** Add the arugula to the dressing and toss with tongs to coat evenly. Finish with the panko and more Parmesan, if desired. Season with salt and pepper to taste.

STORAGE: This salad does not store well once dressed.

Tip

If you have a little extra time, toast the panko for extra flavor. In a small frying pan, heat 1 tablespoon of salted butter and one clove of minced garlic over medium-low heat. Add the panko and cook, stirring, for 2 to 3 minutes or until golden brown.

Strawberry Summer Salad

NUT-FREE

What started as a kitchen sink salad from barbecue leftovers and the last of my farmers' market haul is now a salad I crave on the regular! It's got everything you need for a satisfying, balanced meal, or you can omit the couscous and chicken for an easy side salad. Strawberries are high in vitamin C, which supports the immune system and improves iron absorption, found in the deep-green leaves of spinach. Although the salad reminds me of summer on a plate, it can truly be made year-round.

SERVES 4

8 cups spinach
(about one 5 oz/142 g bin)

2 cups cooked whole wheat couscous (page 58)

2 cups sliced strawberries

1½ cups sugar snap peas, sliced diagonally in half

⅔ cup crumbled feta or goat cheese

¼ cup roasted salted sunflower seeds

1 large avocado, cut into cubes

⅛ small red onion, very thinly sliced (about 2 Tbsp)

½ cup Basic Balsamic Vinaigrette (page 75 or store-bought)

4 cooked Cajun-seasoned chicken thighs (page 68)

PREP AHEAD: The couscous and chicken can be cooked, the snap peas and onion cut, and the vinaigrette (if using homemade) made ahead of time.

1. In a large serving bowl, combine the spinach, couscous, strawberries, peas, feta, sunflower seeds, avocado, and red onion. Toss with vinaigrette and top with Cajun chicken.

STORAGE: This salad does not store well once dressed. If you think you will have leftovers, separate out a portion of the salad (including chicken) before dressing it, transfer the salad to an airtight container, and store in the fridge for up to 4 days.

Meal Prep Tip
While you're at it, double up on cooking the Cajun-seasoned chicken thighs for leftovers. They are delicious on Rainbow Power Bowls (page 179) or Summer Pasta (page 241), or in 10-Minute Chicken, Fig, and Brie Sourdough Sandwiches (page 212) or Chicken, Corn, and Feta Quesadillas (page 232).

Kale, Apple, and Crispy Cajun White Bean Salad

VEGETARIAN | GLUTEN-FREE | NUT-FREE

This recipe comes together in record time, using many of my favorite "fast foods," like rainbow slaw and canned cannellini beans (a household favorite for a quick protein, even for my once skeptical husband). You want the Cajuny crust on the beans to get nice and crispy, so be sure not to stir while cooking! And don't be afraid to add more oil, which plant-based dishes often need—we're over that fear of fat from the 90s, right?! Fats are essential for the absorption of vitamins A, D, E, and K, and provide a feeling of increasing satiety after a meal. Olive oil, in particular, is heart-healthy, with the potential to decrease LDL cholesterol levels. Okay, enough nutrition nerding out—go enjoy this salad!

SERVES 4

2 Tbsp extra virgin olive oil

2 cloves garlic, grated or finely minced (about 1 tsp)

1 can (19 oz/540 ml) cannellini (white kidney) beans, drained, rinsed, and patted dry (about 2 cups)

4 tsp Cajun seasoning (page 76 or store-bought)

⅓ to ½ cup Basic Balsamic Vinaigrette (page 75 or store-bought)

Juice of 1 lemon (about ¼ cup)

1 bunch lacinato kale, stemmed and torn (about 5 cups)

1 apple (I like Gala), cut into bite-size pieces

2 cups rainbow slaw mix

½ cup crumbled feta cheese

¼ cup unsweetened dried cranberries

¼ cup roasted salted shelled pumpkin seeds (pepitas)

Pinch of flaky salt (optional)

PREP AHEAD: The garlic and kale can be cut and the Cajun seasoning and vinaigrette (if using homemade) made ahead of time.

1. In a large frying pan, heat the oil over medium-high heat until shimmering, about 2 minutes. Add the garlic and cook until fragrant, about 1 minute. Add the beans and season with the Cajun seasoning. Cook, without stirring, allowing the beans to brown, for 4 to 5 minutes. Flip as many beans over as possible, add more oil if needed, and cook, without stirring, until browned on both sides, another 4 to 5 minutes.

2. Meanwhile, in a small bowl, whisk together the vinaigrette and lemon juice.

3. On a large serving platter, combine the kale, apple, slaw, feta, cranberries, and pumpkin seeds. Drizzle with dressing and toss to combine. Top with beans and finish with a sprinkle of flaky salt, if desired.

STORAGE: This salad gets better with time. Store the fully dressed salad, separate from the beans, in an airtight container in the fridge for up to 5 days, letting the kale and apple soak up the dressing. Reheat the beans in a frying pan with a splash of oil over medium heat until heated through and crispy again, about 4 to 6 minutes or in the microwave on high in 30-second increments until heated through. Alternatively, bake in the oven or toaster oven at 400°F (200°C) until heated through and crispy again, 5 to 10 minutes.

Greek Chickpea Salad

VEGETARIAN | NUT-FREE

Batch-prep salads are a thing of beauty. Every time I make one, I find myself opening the fridge with a little more love for myself. They are so easy to throw together, and they ensure that no matter what you have going on, you've always got a lunch to look forward to that will keep you going through the day! This one takes the classic Greek salad and adds chickpeas for an easy plant-based protein source, couscous for a fiber-rich carbohydrate, and a ton of vibrant, vitamin-rich vegetables, making a satisfying, balanced meal almost instantly!

SERVES 4

DRESSING

½ cup extra virgin olive oil

⅓ cup red wine vinegar

Juice of 1 lemon (about ¼ cup)

2 tsp Dijon mustard

2 tsp dried oregano

1 tsp salt

Freshly ground black pepper

SALAD

2 cups cooked whole wheat couscous, cooled (page 58)

1 can (19 oz/540 ml) chickpeas, drained and rinsed (about 2 cups)

1 cup cherry tomatoes, quartered

4 mini cucumbers, diced (about 2 cups)

1 bell pepper, cut into 1-inch squares (about 1 cup)

½ cup pitted sun-dried or regular kalamata olives

⅛ small red onion, thinly sliced (about 2 Tbsp)

1 cup crumbled feta cheese

1 head romaine lettuce, chopped

½ cup loosely packed fresh basil, roughly chopped

Salt and freshly ground black pepper

IF YOU'RE FOLLOWING THE MEAL PLAN: Before lunchtime on Monday, divide half of the prepared salad between two bowls (or two medium containers). Add one-quarter of the lettuce to each bowl, one-quarter of the basil, and salt and pepper to taste. Just before eating, toss to coat evenly with the dressing. On Thursday, repeat with the remaining salad, lettuce, and basil.

1. **Make the dressing:** In a small bowl, whisk together the oil, vinegar, lemon juice, mustard, oregano, salt, and pepper until well combined.

2. Divide the dressing evenly between four large jars. Add layers of couscous, chickpeas, tomatoes, cucumbers, bell pepper, olives, onion, and feta, then the romaine and the basil. Make sure to finish with the romaine and basil so they don't get soggy.

3. To serve, season with salt and pepper to taste, and toss the ingredients together. (If the jar is too full to toss ingredients together, pour into a bowl and toss to combine.)

STORAGE: Store the assembled salad in the individual jars for up to 5 days.

Meal Prep Tip

While you're at it, cook double the couscous and freeze some for later use. Try swapping it for rice or quinoa in one of your favorite dishes—it soaks up flavor perfectly!

Time Saver

While layering is fun, you can store this salad in a large airtight container to dish up as needed for a quick meal! Wait to add the lettuce and basil until right before serving, so they don't get soggy in storage.

Build-Your-Own Big-Batch Salad

VEGETARIAN OPTION | GLUTEN-FREE OPTION | NUT-FREE OPTION

Even though salads feel like something you should be able to throw together quickly, when it comes down to it, I often don't feel like making the effort of washing, chopping, and mixing from scratch every time. Having a big-batch salad in the fridge makes it easy to get those extra veggies on your plate for filling fiber and cell-nourishing antioxidants, vitamins, and minerals. This choose-your-own-adventure salad template, specifically showcasing ingredients that will hold up through the week, offers endless options for the perfect salad to pair with meals like burgers, pizza, or pasta!

SERVES 8 TO 10 AS A SIDE, OR 4 TO 5 AS A MEAL

SALAD TEMPLATE

10 cups hearty greens
   (like kale, arugula, or romaine)

3 cups shredded cabbage or
   slaw mix

3 cups diced or sliced vegetables
   (like bell peppers, zucchini,
   mushrooms, or cucumber)

1¼ cups crumbled feta cheese

½ cup nuts or seeds (like
   sunflower seeds, shelled
   pumpkin seeds, slivered
   almonds, or chopped walnuts)

**MAKE IT A MEAL
(OPTIONAL)**

2 cups cooked grains (quinoa,
   couscous, or barley)

2 cups leftover cooked protein
   (eggs, chicken breast or thighs,
   salmon, chickpeas, or beans)

DRESSING

½ to 1 cup Basic Balsamic
   Vinaigrette (page 75 or
   store-bought)

Salt and freshly ground
   black pepper

1. In a large salad bowl or airtight container, combine the greens, cabbage, diced vegetables, feta, and nuts. If desired, add the grains and protein.

2. Serve up the desired amount, drizzle with vinaigrette, and toss until evenly coated. Season with salt and pepper to taste.

STORAGE: Store the undressed salad in an airtight container in the fridge for up to 5 days.

Tip
I usually omit the grains and protein if I want a side salad, and include them if I'm looking for a full meal.

Rainbow Power Bowls

VEGETARIAN OPTION | GLUTEN-FREE | NUT-FREE

These gorgeous little bowls were a collaboration with my good friend, Barbora, who owns the most beautiful salad shops here in Vancouver, called Field & Social. When she asked me to create a bowl for their menu, I was both honored and immediately inspired by the array of vibrant ingredients they had for me to work with. We knew we wanted color, texture, and all the nourishing goodness that has you leaving a meal feeling satisfied, body, mind, and soul. Here, kale and cabbage provide a hefty dose of antioxidants, with vitamin C–rich sweet potatoes for a slow-digesting carbohydrate and chicken to round out the meal with a delicious protein. This dish is no longer on their menu, and I know some of you have been after it ever since (with special requests for the dressing), so I was beyond excited when I got the okay to share the details so you can make it at home! There's nothing better than when food and community come together. So sit back, stop multitasking, take a breath, and enjoy each perfect little bite (you know, when you get the ideal combo of a bit of everything on your fork) as a respite in your day. You might just hear your body say "Thank you."

SERVES 4

DRESSING

¼ cup extra virgin olive oil

Juice of 1 lemon (about ¼ cup)

1 Tbsp tahini

1 Tbsp white wine vinegar

1 clove garlic, grated or finely minced (about ½ tsp)

¼ tsp ground turmeric

¼ tsp salt

Pinch of freshly ground black pepper

POWER BOWLS

2 cups cooked quinoa (page 58)

2 cups roasted sweet potatoes (page 62)

1 bin (5 oz/142 g) baby kale (about 6 to 9 cups)

1½ cups thinly shredded purple cabbage

½ cup pickled red onion (page 72)

¼ cup salted roasted sunflower seeds

2 avocados, halved

4 grilled chicken thighs (page 68), sliced (if you like a little kick, season with Cajun seasoning!)

2 Tbsp roasted sesame seeds

Lemon wedges, to finish

PREP AHEAD: You can cook the chicken, sweet potato, and quinoa, and prep the cabbage, pickled red onion, and dressing ahead of time.

IF YOU'RE FOLLOWING THE MEAL PLAN: On Tuesday, use half of the prepped salad mixture and top with half of the avocado, kale, cooked chicken, sunflower seeds, and sesame seeds. Toss to combine and enjoy. Serve the last two portions with the additional fresh ingredients on Thursday.

1. **Make the dressing:** In a small bowl, whisk together the oil, lemon juice, tahini, vinegar, garlic, turmeric, salt, and pepper.

2. **Assemble the bowls:** In a large bowl, combine the quinoa, sweet potatoes, kale, cabbage, pickled red onion, and sunflower seeds. Toss to combine.

3. Divide the salad evenly between four bowls and top each with half an avocado and a chicken thigh. Sprinkle sesame seeds over the avocado. Drizzle with the dressing and finish with a squeeze of lemon. Enjoy!

STORAGE: After step 2, store the quinoa mixture in one airtight container or four individual ones in the fridge for up to 4 days. To serve, assemble as in step 3.

Meal Prep Tip

While you're at it, make extra roasted sweet potatoes for A Vegan Chili the Meat Lovers Will Beg For (page 270) or a mix of sweet potatoes and cauliflower for the Thai Peanut Red Curry (page 206).

Swaps & Subs

Replace the chicken with Perfectly Prepped Jammy Eggs (page 71) for a vegetarian option.

Flavor-Packed Farro Salad with Toasted Walnuts and Blue Cheese

VEGETARIAN

I first fell in love with grain salads during my cooking lab in university. Yep, us food nerds got to cook and enjoy delicious food as one of our classes (but organic chemistry more than balanced things out). Grain salads are the perfect batch-prep meal. They soak up the flavors of the dressing without getting soggy and truly taste better with time. Some of the nutrition highlights of this one include brain-healthy omega-3 fats, gut-nourishing prebiotics, and a flood of antioxidant and anti-inflammatory properties. Bursting with the pomegranate arils' jewel tones, the richness of toasted walnuts and creamy blue cheese, and a slightly sour crunch from the green apple, this salad's somewhat loud flavors have a way of complementing each other and leaving you with the perfect balanced energy to move through the afternoon.

SERVES 6 TO 8

SALAD

4 cups cooked farro
1 bunch curly kale, finely chopped (about 5 cups)
1 small radicchio, finely chopped (about 3 cups)
1 can (19 oz/540 ml) chickpeas, drained and rinsed (about 2 cups)
1 green apple, diced
Arils of 1 pomegranate (about 1 cup)
1 cup roughly chopped toasted walnut halves
1 cup crumbled blue cheese
1 cup fresh flat-leaf parsley, roughly chopped

DRESSING

1 shallot, minced (about 2 Tbsp)
½ cup extra virgin olive oil
Juice of 1 lemon (about ¼ cup)
2 Tbsp apple cider vinegar
1 Tbsp honey
1 Tbsp Dijon mustard
1 tsp salt
1 tsp freshly ground black pepper

PREP AHEAD: The farro can be cooked and the kale and dressing prepped ahead of time.

1. **Assemble the salad:** In a large serving bowl or airtight container, combine the farro, kale, radicchio, chickpeas, apple, pomegranate arils, walnuts, blue cheese, and parsley.

2. **Make the dressing:** In a small bowl, whisk together the shallot, oil, lemon juice, vinegar, honey, mustard, salt, and pepper.

3. Pour the dressing over the salad and toss until evenly coated.

STORAGE: Store the dressed salad in an airtight container in the fridge for up to 5 days.

Swaps & Subs

If you're not a fan of blue cheese, you can swap in goat cheese or feta. You can also use wheat berries or barley if you can't find farro.

Noodles and Rice Bowls

Coconut Thai Green Curry Noodle Soup in a Jar

VEGETARIAN OPTION | VEGAN OPTION | DAIRY-FREE | GLUTEN-FREE | NUT-FREE

This might just become your new favorite batch-prep lunch. With a total prep time of 10 minutes, setting yourself up for the week never felt so easy. Tofu is one of the best sources of plant-based iron and is also rich in fiber, potassium, and magnesium. That said, if you've got leftover protein kicking around, feel free to swap it for the tofu. This easy-peasy lunch is sure to make your co-workers jealous!

SERVES 4

SAUCE

1 can (14 oz/400 ml) full-fat coconut milk

¼ cup Thai green curry paste

2 Tbsp vegetable bouillon powder or paste

1 Tbsp fish sauce

2 cloves garlic, grated or finely minced (about 1 tsp)

NOODLES

1 lb (450 g) medium-firm tofu, cut into 1-inch cubes

7 oz (200 g) rice vermicelli noodles

4 cups spinach, roughly torn (about half a 5 oz/142 g bin)

3.5 oz (100 g) snap peas, ends trimmed (about 1 cup)

6 cups boiling water

> **Swaps & Subs**
> To make it vegetarian or vegan, swap the fish sauce for soy sauce and a splash of lime juice!

PREP AHEAD: Follow steps 1 to 3 to prep these jars ahead of time.

IF YOU'RE FOLLOWING THE MEAL PLAN: Before serving on Tuesday, follow step 4 to add the boiling water to your prepped jars, stir, let sit, and enjoy! Do the same for your remaining two jars on Friday.

1. **Make the sauce:** In a medium bowl, whisk together the coconut milk, curry paste, bouillon, fish sauce, and garlic until well combined.

2. Divide the sauce evenly between four large jars or airtight containers, covering the bottom evenly.

3. **Assemble the noodles:** Evenly distribute the tofu, noodles, spinach, and snap peas between the jars, ensuring the tofu is on the bottom so it can marinate in the sauce.

4. To serve, top each jar with 1½ cups boiling water. Stir in the curry sauce until fully incorporated. Let sit for 5 to 7 minutes or until the noodles are cooked and the peas are tender-crisp. Enjoy!

STORAGE: Prepare the recipe through step 3 and store in the fridge for up to 5 days. To serve, continue with step 4.

20-Minute Miso Ramen with Jammy Eggs

VEGETARIAN | DAIRY-FREE | NUT-FREE

One of my earliest memories is sitting at the kitchen table with my dad, eating ramen noodles. He said to me, "Linds—don't ever forget this. Just me and you, eating noodles." When I close my eyes, I can hear him saying those words. It was in my first childhood home, so I couldn't have been older than four or five, and while I'm not sure if it's a true memory or just something we've continued to talk about so much over the years that it has stuck with me, it doesn't matter. To me, ramen will forever be a physical reminder of how food connects us, and in a strange way it will always be this reminder of how much my dad loves me. Deep, for a bowl of ramen, hey? But I hope that as you sit down to eat this dish, you savor the smells and flavors and think a loving thought. Your body will thank you for this meal, which is brimming with nutrient-rich vegetables and the most delicious jammy eggs for protein.

SERVES 4

2 Tbsp white (shiro) miso paste

1 Tbsp soy sauce

1 Tbsp toasted sesame oil

3.5 oz (100 g) shiitake mushrooms, thinly sliced (about 6 to 7 mushrooms/ 1¼ cups)

8 baby bok choy, ends trimmed and leaves separated (about 4 cups)

1 Tbsp extra virgin olive oil

2 cloves garlic, grated or finely minced (about 1 tsp)

6 cups chicken or vegetable stock

2 cups water

9 oz (250 g) baked ramen noodles (also called instant noodles)

1 cup frozen corn, pea, and carrot mix

8 Perfectly Prepped Jammy Eggs (page 71), halved lengthwise

2 green onions, green parts only, thinly sliced (about 2 Tbsp)

Chili Crisp Oil (page 78 or store-bought), for garnish (optional)

Toasted sesame seeds, for garnish (optional)

PREP AHEAD: The mushrooms, bok choy, and garlic can be prepped, the chili crisp oil (if using homemade) made, and the jammy eggs cooked ahead of time (although the jammy eggs are best when made right before eating).

IF YOU'RE FOLLOWING THE MEAL PLAN: Make the jammy eggs. Continue preparing all four servings and enjoy now!

1. In a small bowl, whisk together the miso paste and soy sauce. Set aside.

2. In a large pot, heat the sesame oil over medium heat. Add the mushrooms and bok choy and sauté until tender, 3 to 4 minutes. Transfer the mushroom mixture to a bowl and set aside.

3. To the same pot, add the olive oil and garlic and sauté until fragrant, 30 to 60 seconds.

4. Stir in the miso mixture, stock, and water and bring to a boil. Add the noodles and vegetable mix, return to a boil, and cook until the noodles are cooked through, 3 to 4 minutes.

5. Ladle the soup into four bowls and evenly divide the mushroom mixture, eggs, and green onions between them. If desired, garnish with chili oil and sesame seeds. Enjoy!

STORAGE: Store the broth and noodles in separate airtight containers (or together and add more broth as needed when reheating, as the noodles will soak up the broth) in the fridge for up to 5 days. To serve, reheat on the stove or in the microwave until heated through.

Swaps & Subs

You can substitute any mushrooms you prefer!

Charlie's Lo Mein

DAIRY-FREE | NUT-FREE

I have such fond memories of my yeh-yeh (grandpa), Charlie, making his famous lo mein. My ma-ma (grandma) did most of the cooking, but he had this recipe down to a T. To this day, it is comfort in a bowl for me! We would go to the butcher in Chinatown, pick out a piece of char siu pork (a flavorful Chinese barbecue pork), and off to cooking he'd get. Shredded cabbage adds the perfect crunch and complement to the noodles, while also adding antioxidants and some extra filling fiber! I hope this meal feels like a hug in a bowl to you, just like when Charlie made it for me!

SERVES 6

CHAR SIU PORK

2 lb (900 g) pork tenderloin, cut into strips

6 Tbsp char siu sauce

½ tsp salt

NOODLES AND ASSEMBLY

12 oz (350 g) lo mein noodles

3 Tbsp avocado oil or other high-heat cooking oil, divided

5 cloves garlic, grated or finely minced (about 2½ tsp)

1½-inch knob ginger, minced (about 1½ Tbsp)

10 cups thinly shredded green cabbage (see time saver)

3 Tbsp soy sauce

1½ Tbsp oyster sauce

White vinegar, for serving (optional)

Swaps & Subs

If you can't find lo mein noodles, you can replace them with ramen noodles, egg noodles, or even linguini or spaghetti.

Time Saver

Swap the shredded cabbage for ready-to-go store-bought slaw mix. If you can find ready-made char siu pork (depending on where you live, it's often found in Chinese groceries), don't hesitate to pick it up!

PREP AHEAD: The pork can be cut and marinated as in step 1, and the garlic, ginger, and cabbage can be prepped ahead of time.

IF YOU'RE FOLLOWING THE MEAL PLAN: With the prepped cabbage, garlic, ginger, and marinated pork, make all six servings. Serve four now and store the other two in airtight containers for lunch tomorrow.

1. **Make the pork:** In a medium bowl, combine the pork, char siu sauce, and salt. Set aside, or cover and refrigerate for up to 2 days for intensified flavors.

2. **Make the noodles:** Bring a large pot of water to a boil and cook the noodles according to package directions. Drain and set aside.

3. Meanwhile, in a large frying pan, heat 1 tablespoon of oil over medium heat. Add the pork and cook until lightly browned on the bottom, 2 to 3 minutes. Flip and brown the other side, another 2 to 3 minutes. Transfer the pork and any juices to a bowl and set aside.

4. In the same pan, heat the remaining 2 tablespoons of oil over medium heat. Add the garlic and ginger and cook, stirring, until fragrant, 30 to 60 seconds. Add the cabbage and sauté until tender-crisp, 3 to 4 minutes.

5. Return the pork and any juices to the pan and stir in the noodles, soy sauce, and oyster sauce, tossing to coat. (Note: If the noodles have clumped up, run them under hot water to separate them before adding them to the pan.)

6. Serve immediately, drizzled with vinegar (if using)—a Chinese favorite way to serve this! Enjoy!

STORAGE: Store the cooled lo mein in an airtight container in the fridge for up to 4 days or in a sealable freezer bag in the freezer for up to 3 months. To serve, reheat on the stove or in the microwave (thawing first, if frozen).

Better-than-Takeout
Tender Beef and Broccoli Udon

DAIRY-FREE | NUT-FREE

I owe my love of beef and broccoli to my dad, the stir-fry master. He's got it nailed. He also taught me the power of black bean paste to add major flavor to this and any other stir-fry. Quick-cooking beef and ready-to-go udon noodles make this a weeknight dinner you'll look forward to on all fronts! Oh, and we can't forget the queen of cruciferous vegetables, broccoli, for a major nutrition boost!

SERVES 6

1½ lb (680 g) flank or skirt steak

MARINADE

6 cloves garlic, minced or grated
(about 1 Tbsp)

3-inch knob ginger, minced
(about 3 Tbsp)

1½ Tbsp soy sauce

1 Tbsp unseasoned rice vinegar

Salt and freshly ground
black pepper

**BEEF AND BROCCOLI
SAUCE**

¾ cup chicken stock

1½ Tbsp oyster sauce

1½ Tbsp soy sauce

1 Tbsp black bean paste

STIR-FRY

3 Tbsp toasted sesame oil,
divided, plus more as needed

1 small white onion, thinly sliced
(about 1 cup)

2 crowns broccoli, cut into bite-
size florets (about 6 to 7 cups)

1¾ lb (800 g) udon noodles

Green onion, thinly sliced,
for garnish

Sesame seeds, for garnish

PREP AHEAD: The steak can be cut and marinated as in steps 1 and 2, and the broccoli and onion cut ahead of time.

IF YOU'RE FOLLOWING THE MEAL PLAN: With the prepped marinated steak, sliced onions, chopped broccoli, and garlic on hand, make all six servings, starting from step 3. Serve four now and store the other two for lunch tomorrow.

1. Thinly slice the steak against the grain, cutting the slices in half if needed to make strips about 2 inches long and ¼ inch thick.

2. **Make the marinade:** In a small bowl, make the marinade by whisking together the garlic, ginger, soy sauce, vinegar, and salt and pepper to taste. Add the beef and toss to coat. Marinate for at least 5 minutes or, for the most tender and flavorful meat, cover and refrigerate for up to 3 days.

3. **Make the sauce:** In another small bowl, make the sauce by whisking together the stock, oyster sauce, soy sauce, and black bean paste. Set aside.

4. **Make the stir-fry:** In a wok or large frying pan, heat 2 tablespoons of the oil over medium-high heat. Lift the beef out of the marinade, letting any excess drip off, and add to the pan in a single layer. (This may need to be done in batches, depending on the size of your pan; add more oil as needed.) Discard any remaining marinade. Sear the beef, without stirring, until nicely browned, 1 to 2 minutes. Flip and sear the other side, 1 to 2 minutes more. Transfer the beef to a plate and set aside.

5. In the same pan, heat the remaining tablespoon of oil. Add the onion and cook until translucent, 1 to 2 minutes. Add the broccoli, cover, and steam until the broccoli starts to become a vibrant green, 1 to 2 minutes (do not overcook, as it will continue to cook with the noodles). Add the noodles and sauce and cook for another 5 to 7 minutes, tossing to coat and separate the noodles. Return the beef and any accumulated juices to the pan and cook until heated through.

6. Serve sprinkled with green onion and sesame seeds and enjoy!

STORAGE: After step 5, let the stir-fry cool, then store in an airtight container in the fridge for up to 4 days or in a sealable freezer bag in the freezer for up to 3 months. Reheat on the stove or in the microwave (thawing first, if frozen), then sprinkle with green onion and sesame seeds.

Time Saver
To speed up this recipe,
buy pre-chopped broccoli.

Swaps & Subs
You can substitute black bean
sauce if paste is not available,
but you may need to add more,
as it's not as concentrated.

Peanutty Soba Noodle Bowls

VEGAN | DAIRY-FREE

This gorgeous bowl has been on repeat in our meal rotation for years. It's actually the first plant-based meal my husband started requesting regularly. The peanut butter sauce is to die for! A bit dramatic? Maybe, but it doesn't feel like an exaggeration. It is creamy and a bit spicy, and the balanced depth of the toasted sesame seeds and sesame oil with the tangy rice vinegar hits just right. I love how the abundant veggies add so much to the overall enjoyment of the dish. Antioxidant-rich cabbage gives the perfect crunch (big texture girl over here), the tender kale and mushrooms offer a dose of vitamins K and D, and the edamame lends an almost-instant source of plant-based protein. It all comes together for a flavor explosion in your mouth!

SERVES 6

PEANUTTY SOBA NOODLE SAUCE

2 cloves garlic, grated or finely minced (about 1 tsp)

⅔ cup hot water

⅓ cup creamy peanut butter

¼ cup soy sauce

¼ cup hoisin sauce

2 Tbsp unseasoned rice vinegar

1 Tbsp toasted sesame oil

1 to 2 tsp sriracha (depending on the heat level you like)

BOWLS

12 oz (350 g) soba noodles

1½ cups shelled edamame beans

1 Tbsp toasted sesame oil

10.5 oz (300 g) mixed mushrooms (I like shiitake and cremini), thinly sliced (about 20 mushrooms/4 cups)

1 bunch lacinato kale, stemmed and thinly sliced (about 4 cups)

3 cups thinly shredded purple cabbage

2 green onions, thinly sliced (about 2 Tbsp)

Toasted sesame seeds, for garnish

PREP AHEAD: The kale, mushrooms, and cabbage can be prepped ahead of time. You can also prepare the sauce up to 5 days ahead and store it in the fridge.

IF YOU'RE FOLLOWING THE MEAL PLAN: With the prepped mushrooms, kale, and cabbage on hand, make all six servings. Serve four now and store the other two for lunch tomorrow.

1. **Make the sauce:** In a small bowl, make the sauce by whisking together the garlic, hot water, peanut butter, soy sauce, hoisin, vinegar, oil, and sriracha until smooth. Set aside.

2. **Make the noodle bowls:** Bring a large pot of salted water to a boil and cook the soba noodles for 6 to 7 minutes or according to package directions. Add the edamame for the last 2 to 3 minutes of cooking time. Drain and set aside.

3. In a large frying pan, heat the oil over medium heat. Add the mushrooms and cook, stirring occasionally, until tender, 3 to 4 minutes. Add the kale and cook, stirring, until vibrant green, another 2 to 3 minutes. Add the noodles, cabbage, and sauce. Cook for another 3 to 4 minutes, stirring and tossing to coat, until heated through and the sauce has thickened to coat the noodles.

4. Top with green onions and sesame seeds.

STORAGE: Let cool and store in an airtight container in the fridge for up to 5 days. To serve, reheat on the stove or in the microwave, or enjoy cold!

Meal Prep Tip

This large-batch recipe makes incredible leftovers, delicious either hot or cold.

Time Saver

Swap the cabbage and kale for store-bought bagged kale slaw and/or buy pre-sliced mushrooms.

Mila's Sticky Orange Chicken

VEGETARIAN OPTION | DAIRY-FREE | NUT-FREE

I've got to give credit to my niece Mila for this one. This is the first dish she ever requested, and I was instantly inspired to make my own version! The chicken is so crispy and delicious, and creates the most amazing flavor as it gets coated with the sticky, just-sweet-enough orange sauce. Your immune system will thank you for this one, as it's brimming with vitamin C from the colorful peppers and orange juice. I love this dish with a little spice, so I always add the sriracha or red pepper flakes, but feel free to leave them out to suit the spice preferences of your household.

SERVES 6

ORANGE SAUCE

Juice of 5 large navel oranges (about 1½ cups) (see time saver)

⅓ cup soy sauce

¼ cup honey

¼ cup water

3 cloves garlic, grated or finely minced (about 1½ tsp)

1½ Tbsp cornstarch

½ tsp salt

ORANGE CHICKEN

1½ lb (680 g) boneless skinless chicken thighs, cut into bite-size pieces (about 6 to 8 thighs)

½ cup cornstarch

½ tsp salt

½ tsp freshly ground black pepper

4 Tbsp avocado oil or other high-heat cooking oil, divided, plus more as needed

1 large white onion, thinly sliced (about 3 cups)

3 bell peppers (red or orange), cut into 1-inch squares (about 3 cups)

5 cups cooked rice (I like white), reheated if prepped ahead (page 58)

4 green onions, green parts only, cut diagonally into 1-inch pieces (about ¼ cup), for garnish

Toasted sesame seeds, for garnish (optional)

Sriracha or red pepper flakes, for garnish (optional)

PREP AHEAD: The rice can be cooked and the chicken, garlic, onion, and bell peppers prepped ahead of time. You can also prepare the sauce up to 5 days ahead and store it in the fridge.

IF YOU'RE FOLLOWING THE MEAL PLAN: Make the sauce, if you haven't already. With the prepped chicken, onion, pepper, and garlic, continue preparing all six servings. Reheat four servings of rice and serve four servings of the orange chicken now, garnishing with desired toppings. Store the other two for lunch tomorrow and serve with reheated rice and desired toppings. (Note: Take the turkey burgers for tomorrow's dinner out of the freezer now and thaw overnight in the fridge.)

1. **Make the sauce:** In a small bowl, make the sauce by whisking together the orange juice, soy sauce, honey, water, garlic, cornstarch, and salt. Set aside.

2. **Make the chicken:** Place the chicken in a medium bowl, sprinkle with the cornstarch, salt, and pepper, and stir to coat the chicken evenly.

3. In a large frying pan, heat 3 tablespoons of oil over medium-high heat until shimmering, about 2 minutes. Add the chicken in a single layer. (This may need to be done in batches depending on the size of the pan; add more oil as needed.) Cook, without stirring, until the bottom of the chicken is nicely browned and crisp, 5 to 6 minutes. Flip and cook the other side, without stirring, until browned and the juices run clear when the chicken is pierced, another 3 to 4 minutes. Transfer the chicken to a plate, leaving the juices in the pan.

4. In the same pan, heat the remaining tablespoon of oil. Add the onion and sauté until translucent, 2 to 3 minutes. Add the peppers and sauté until tender-crisp, another 3 minutes. Add the orange sauce and bring to a boil.

5. Reduce the heat to medium-low, return the chicken and any accumulated juices to the pan, and bring to a simmer, tossing to coat the chicken in sauce and heat through.

6. Serve the chicken mixture over hot rice, garnishing with green onions and, if desired, sesame seeds and sriracha.

STORAGE: Prepare the chicken mixture through step 5, let cool, and store in an airtight container in the fridge for up to 4 days or in an airtight container or sealable freezer bag in the freezer for up to 3 months. To serve, reheat on the stove or in the microwave (thawing first, if frozen), then continue with step 6.

Swaps & Subs

This dish is also delicious with tofu! For the crispiest result, buy pressed tofu, which already has much of the moisture removed. Alternatively, press extra-firm tofu yourself by wrapping the block of tofu with a cloth or paper towel and placing something heavy, like a stack of books, on top to squeeze out the moisture.

Time Saver

Save a step by using store-bought 100% orange juice instead of squeezing the oranges.

Crispy Black Pepper and Maple Tofu Stir-Fry

VEGAN | DAIRY-FREE | GLUTEN-FREE OPTION

We ate a lot of tofu in our house growing up, but I get it, it's not for everyone . . .
until you've tried it this way. The beauty and the curse of tofu is that it's rather bland—
which makes it extremely versatile. It picks up the flavor of whatever you cook it with,
so having a flavorful sauce or marinade is key, and this recipe delivers big time!
Now go on, try it. Yep, you tofu skeptics too, even if just to prove me wrong.

SERVES 4

MAPLE SOY SAUCE

4-inch knob ginger, minced
    (about ¼ cup)

6 cloves garlic, grated or finely
    minced (about 1 Tbsp)

1 Tbsp cornstarch

¼ tsp salt

¼ tsp freshly ground
    black pepper

Pinch of red pepper flakes

⅓ cup soy sauce or gluten-free
    tamari

¼ cup water

3 Tbsp maple syrup

1½ Tbsp unseasoned rice vinegar

TOFU AND VEGETABLES

12 oz (350 g) pressed tofu

¼ cup cornstarch

½ tsp salt

½ tsp freshly ground
    black pepper

3 Tbsp + 1 tsp avocado oil or other
    high-heat cooking oil, divided

4 cups snap peas or snow peas,
    ends trimmed

1 cup diced purple cabbage

TO SERVE

3 cups cooked rice, reheated
    if prepped ahead (page 58)

3 green onions, thinly sliced on
    the diagonal, for garnish

¼ cup roasted cashews, roughly
    chopped, for garnish

Red pepper flakes, for garnish
    (optional)

PREP AHEAD: If you did not purchase "pressed tofu" the tofu can be pressed, and the snap peas and cabbage can be cut ahead of time. You can also cook the rice and prepare the sauce up to 5 days ahead and store it in the fridge.

1. **Make the sauce:** In a medium bowl, make the sauce by whisking together the ginger, garlic, cornstarch, salt, pepper, red pepper flakes, soy sauce, water, maple syrup, and vinegar. Set aside.

2. **Make the tofu and vegetables:** Cut the tofu in half crosswise, then into ¾-inch cubes. Add the tofu, cornstarch, salt, and pepper to a large airtight container, seal the lid, and shake to coat the tofu completely and evenly.

3. In a large frying pan, heat 2 tablespoons of oil over medium-high heat. Add the tofu in a single layer and cook, without stirring, until the bottom is browned, 4 to 5 minutes. Drizzle with 1 tablespoon of oil, flip the tofu, and cook the other side, without stirring, until it crisps and turns golden brown, another 3 to 4 minutes. Transfer the tofu to a plate and set aside.

4. In the same pan, heat the remaining teaspoon of oil over medium-high heat. Add the snap peas and cabbage and sauté until the peas are tender-crisp and their color becomes more vibrant, 2 to 3 minutes. Add the sauce, bring to a boil, and cook until thickened, 2 to 3 minutes. Return the tofu to the pan and toss to coat.

5. **Assemble the stir-fry:** Serve the tofu mixture over hot rice, garnished with green onions, cashews, and, if desired, red pepper flakes.

STORAGE: Prepare the stir-fry through step 4, let cool, and store in an airtight container in the fridge for up to 5 days or in a sealable freezer bag in the freezer for up to 3 months. To serve, reheat on the stove or in the microwave (thawing first, if frozen), then continue with step 5.

Korean-Inspired Beef and Rice Bowls with Pickled Cukes

DAIRY-FREE | NUT-FREE

You might have noticed I am a sucker for bold flavors, especially when they come together quickly. These bowls are inspired by that perfect combo of sweet and salty that Korean dishes are famous for, balanced out with the tang of homemade pickled cucumbers (which are so much easier to make than you'd think, by the way!). Packed with colorful, antioxidant-rich veggies for good measure, these are pretty near bowl perfection, if I do say so myself! Plus, they make amazing leftovers!

SERVES 6

KOREAN-INSPIRED BEEF SAUCE

¼ cup packed brown sugar

½ tsp salt

⅓ cup soy sauce

2 Tbsp unseasoned rice vinegar

BEEF

2 Tbsp toasted sesame oil, plus more as needed

4-inch knob ginger, minced (about ¼ cup)

6 cloves garlic, grated or finely minced (about 1 Tbsp)

1½ lb (680 g) extra-lean ground beef

Salt and freshly ground black pepper

BOWLS

4½ cups cooked rice (I like jasmine), reheated if prepped ahead (page 58)

3 cups thinly shredded purple cabbage, for garnish

2 large carrots, grated (about 2 cups), for garnish

1½ cups pickled cucumbers (page 72), for garnish

3 green onions, thinly sliced (about 3 Tbsp), for garnish

Toasted sesame seeds, for garnish (optional)

PREP AHEAD: The rice can be cooked, the pickled cucumbers made, and the garlic, ginger, cabbage, and carrots cut ahead of time. You can also prepare the sauce up to 5 days ahead and store it in the fridge.

IF YOU'RE FOLLOWING THE MEAL PLAN: Make the sauce, if you haven't already. Continuing on to step 2, prepare all six servings using the prepped garlic, ginger, cabbage, carrots, and pickled cucumbers. Reheat four portions of rice and serve four now. Store the other two for lunch tomorrow.

1. **Make the sauce:** In a small bowl, whisk together the sugar, salt, soy sauce, and vinegar. Set aside.

2. **Make the beef:** In a large frying pan, heat the oil over medium-high heat. Add the ginger and garlic and cook until fragrant, about 1 minute. Add the beef in a single layer (see tip), cooking in batches and adding more oil if needed. Season generously with salt and pepper and break the beef into a few large pieces. Without stirring, brown the beef on one side, about 4 to 5 minutes. Flip, season with more salt and pepper, and brown the other side, another 2 to 4 minutes, then break into smaller pieces and cook, stirring, until no pink remains.

3. Add the sauce and reduce the heat to medium-low. Cook for 3 to 5 minutes, stirring only once or twice, allowing the sauce to thicken and caramelize the meat.

4. **Assemble the bowls:** Divide the hot rice and the beef mixture between bowls and top with cabbage, carrots, pickled cucumbers, green onions, and sesame seeds (if using). Enjoy!

STORAGE: Prepare the beef mixture through step 3, let cool, and store in an airtight container in the fridge for up to 4 days or in the freezer for up to 3 months. To serve, reheat on the stove or in the microwave (thawing first, if frozen) and continue with step 4.

> **Time Saver**
> You can buy rainbow slaw mix (blend of carrots and cabbage) to use in place of the shredded cabbage and carrots. You will need 5 cups.

Tip
Cooking the beef in a single layer allows
it to brown evenly and prevents it from
being steamed.

Sweet and Spicy
Soy-Glazed Salmon Bowls

DAIRY-FREE | GLUTEN-FREE OPTION | NUT-FREE

Is it just me or does everything taste better in bowl form? Especially when it's packed with vibrant colors and big flavor—it can't help but draw in your senses and inspire mindful eating! The sweet, salty, and spicy marinade makes the perfect glossy coating for tender salmon, and by adding a splash of rice vinegar, it doubles as a tangy dressing (you may want to make extra for other salads throughout the week). Salmon is one of my favorite anti-inflammatory foods, and I love how fast it cooks, making this a quick and easy dinner pick any night of the week!

SERVES 4

SWEET AND SPICY SOY MARINADE AND DRESSING

6 Tbsp honey

⅓ cup soy sauce or gluten-free tamari

2 to 3 tsp sriracha (depending on the heat level you like)

1 clove garlic, grated or finely minced (about ½ tsp)

1½ Tbsp unseasoned rice vinegar

1½ tsp sesame oil

Salt and freshly ground black pepper

BOWLS

1 lb (450 g) skinless salmon, cut into chunks

Salt and freshly ground black pepper

1 tsp toasted sesame oil

4 cups arugula

3 cups cooked brown rice, reheated if prepped ahead (page 58)

1 small English cucumber, diced (about 1 to 1½ cups)

1 large avocado, cubed

½ cup pickled red onion (page 72)

Green onion, for garnish

Black sesame seeds, for garnish

PREP AHEAD: The pickled red onion can be made and the rice cooked ahead of time. You can also prepare the marinade and dressing up to 5 days ahead and store it in the fridge. The salmon can be cut into chunks and marinated as in step 3.

1. **Make the marinade and dressing:** In a medium bowl, make the marinade by whisking together the honey, soy sauce, and sriracha.

2. Pour two-thirds of the marinade into a separate medium bowl and add the garlic, vinegar, and oil to make the dressing. Season with salt and pepper to taste. Set aside.

3. **Make the salmon bowls:** Add the salmon to the marinade, season generously with salt and pepper, and toss to coat. Marinate for at least 10 minutes, or cover and refrigerate for up to 1 day.

4. In a large frying pan, heat the oil over medium-high heat. Lift the salmon out of the marinade, letting any excess drip off, and add to the pan in a single layer. Sear on one side until golden brown, 2 to 3 minutes (if using wild salmon, go with the shorter cooking time, as it has less fat and can dry out more easily). Flip the salmon and pour in any remaining marinade. Sear the other side until golden brown and the salmon is opaque and flakes easily with a fork, another 2 to 3 minutes.

5. Divide the arugula between four bowls and top with hot rice, cucumber, avocado, pickled red onion, and salmon. Drizzle with the reserved dressing. Garnish with green onion and sesame seeds. Enjoy!

STORAGE: Store the cooked salmon in an airtight container in the fridge for up to 3 days. To serve, reheat on the stove or in the microwave, then assemble the bowls as in step 5.

Meal Prep Tip

Plan ahead for Ready-in-a-Pinch Sweet and Spicy Soy-Glazed Sushi Tacos (page 220) by cooking extra rice, doubling the marinade and storing half. I recommend cooking the salmon the night of, since it can dry out when reheated.

Waikiki Tuna Poke Bowls

DAIRY-FREE | GLUTEN-FREE OPTION | NUT-FREE

Hawaii has a very special place in my heart. Not only does my sister live there, but it is home to poke, something I could (and do when I'm there) eat morning, noon, and night. While poke may seem intimidating to make at home, it is actually super easy! The array of colors in this beautiful dish speaks to its nutritional vibrancy, including antioxidants like vitamin C and carotenoids. It's like a vacation in a bowl!

SERVES 6

TUNA POKE SAUCE

4 green onions, sliced (about ¼ cup)

⅔ cup soy sauce or gluten-free tamari

¼ cup toasted sesame oil

2 tsp red pepper flakes

TUNA POKE BOWLS

1½ lb (680 g) sushi-grade tuna, cut into 1-inch cubes

5 cups cooked rice (I like short-grain brown or sushi rice), reheated if desired (page 58)

4 mini cucumbers, thinly sliced (about 2 cups)

2 mangos, diced (or 2 cups frozen mango cubes, thawed)

1½ cups shelled edamame beans (thawed if frozen)

1½ cups pickled cabbage (page 72)

2 small avocados, peeled, pitted, and sliced

TO SERVE (OPTIONAL)

Sriracha Aioli (page 77 or store-bought)

1 Tbsp toasted sesame seeds

Pickled ginger

Wasabi

PREP AHEAD: The cucumbers can be cut, the rice cooked, and the pickled cabbage and aioli (if using homemade) made ahead of time. You can also prepare the sauce up to 5 days ahead and store it in the fridge. The tuna can be cubed, tossed with the sauce, and stored in an airtight container in the fridge up to 1 day ahead.

IF YOU'RE FOLLOWING THE MEAL PLAN: On Monday, make the poke sauce and sriracha aioli (if using homemade), if you haven't already. Assemble four servings as described in steps 2 to 4. Divide the remaining tuna poke bowl ingredients (except the rice) between two airtight containers and refrigerate for lunch tomorrow. Before serving, reheat the remaining rice, divide it between two bowls, and top with the tuna poke bowl mixture and the optional garnishes.

1. **Make the sauce:** In a small bowl, whisk together the green onions, soy sauce, oil, and red pepper flakes until well combined.

2. **Make the tuna:** In a medium bowl, toss together the tuna and one-third of the sauce until evenly coated (see tip).

3. Divide the hot rice between six bowls. Top with the tuna and arrange the cucumbers, mangos, edamame, cabbage, and avocados on top. Drizzle with the remaining sauce.

4. Serve with aioli, sesame seeds, pickled ginger, and wasabi (if using). Enjoy!

STORAGE: Without the rice, the tuna poke bowl ingredients can be stored in an airtight container in the fridge for up to 3 days. To serve, reheat the rice, divide it between bowls, and top with the tuna poke mixture, toppings, and optional garnishes.

Swaps & Subs

If you can't find sushi-grade tuna, simply sear the outside of a tuna steak (it can still be pink inside) and thinly slice it to top the bowl. You can also replace the tuna with salmon, again buying sushi-grade if you want to eat it raw (but cooked is delicious too!).

Tips
Sushi-grade tuna is not always clearly labeled, but many places do carry it! Ask your local fishmonger or grocery store seafood department staff.

This dish can be pulled together quickly on the night of eating, but for maximum flavor, marinate the tuna in the fridge for 20 minutes or in the fridge up to 1 day.

Jangs' Famous Fried Rice

DAIRY-FREE | NUT-FREE

It's funny the things you take for granted. Growing up in a half-Chinese household, we ate a lot of rice, fried rice being one of those dishes. (My maiden name is Jang, so you see how this recipe came to be!) When I asked Meik if fried rice was too boring to include in the book, he looked at me wide-eyed in disbelief—apparently fried rice is one of his favorites, which I was only just learning fourteen years in. So thank you, cookbook, for earning me some wife brownie points and reminding me how much I also love fried rice. This dish comes together quickly, especially since it's best with leftover rice and works with pretty much any protein. Whatever you do, do *not* leave out the Chinese sausage. You'll see why!

SERVES 6

4 Tbsp toasted sesame oil, divided

3 Chinese sausages, diced

6 cloves garlic, grated or finely minced (about 1 Tbsp)

2 shallots, minced (about 3 Tbsp)

5 cups cooked white rice (I like jasmine; leftover works best) (page 58)

4 cooked chicken thighs (page 68), diced (about 2 cups)

2½ cups frozen corn, pea, and carrot mix

2½ Tbsp soy sauce

5 eggs, beaten

3 cups spinach, chopped

Green onion, thinly sliced on the diagonal, for garnish

Sriracha or Chili Crisp Oil (page 78 or store-bought), for garnish (optional)

PREP AHEAD: The rice and chicken can be cooked, the garlic, shallots, and spinach cut, and the chili crisp oil (if using homemade) made ahead of time.

IF YOU'RE FOLLOWING THE MEAL PLAN: With the prepped rice, chicken, spinach, shallots, and garlic, make all six servings. Serve four now and store the other two for lunch tomorrow.

1. In a wok or cast-iron pan (see tip), heat 3 tablespoons of sesame oil over medium-high heat. Add the sausages, garlic, and shallots and cook, stirring occasionally, until fragrant, 1 to 2 minutes.

2. Add the rice and cook, without stirring, for 3 to 4 minutes until rice starts to crisp up. Using a wooden spoon or spatula, stir the rice, scraping up any that's stuck to the bottom of the pan. Cook, again without stirring, until more of the rice becomes crispy and golden, 2 to 4 minutes. Stir in the chicken, vegetable mix, and soy sauce.

3. Reduce the heat to low and push the rice to the sides of the pan, making a well in the middle. Add the remaining tablespoon of sesame oil, then the eggs. Scramble until just cooked. Add the spinach and stir everything together to combine.

4. Serve topped with green onion and sriracha, if desired. Enjoy!

STORAGE: Store the cooled fried rice, without the toppings, in an airtight container in the fridge for up to 4 days or in a sealable freezer bag in the freezer for up to 3 months. To serve, reheat on the stove or in the microwave (thawing first, if frozen), then add the toppings.

Tip

If you don't have a wok or cast-iron pan, a regular large frying pan will do. Make sure to follow the instructions and not stir too frequently, so the rice can crisp up!

Nutrition Hack

For an extra dose of antioxidant- and fiber-rich vegetables, add 1 to 2 cups of riced cauliflower!

Swaps & Subs (+ Time Saver)

The chicken can be swapped for pretty much any other leftover protein. Shrimp, tofu, and pork are all delicious in this dish and I love using cooked rotisserie chicken to speed things up. The corn, pea, and carrot mix can be replaced with any leftover vegetables you want to use up; I love mushrooms, bok choy, and asparagus, to change things up.

Thai Peanut Red Curry

VEGAN | DAIRY-FREE | GLUTEN-FREE OPTION

If you want flavor, this is your dish! The vibrant flavor of Thai red curry paste is perfectly complemented by the creamy coconut milk, while peanut butter adds a richness that is just right, and the salty roasted peanuts and fresh cilantro cause a flavor explosion in your mouth. I will warn you, it does have a bit of a kick; if spicy is not your jam, feel free to start with half the amount of curry paste. If you're feeling it, dunk in some pitas or fluffy naan bread to soak up the sauce.

SERVES 6

1 sweet potato, cubed

1 cauliflower, cut into bite-size florets

3 Tbsp avocado oil or other high-heat cooking oil, divided

Salt and freshly ground black pepper

1 can (28 oz/796 ml) chickpeas, drained, rinsed, and patted dry (about 4 cups)

1 Tbsp virgin coconut oil

1 small onion, diced (about 1 cup)

2-inch knob ginger, minced (about 2 Tbsp)

4 cloves garlic, grated or finely minced (about 2 tsp)

2 Tbsp Thai red curry paste (sometimes just called red curry paste)

1 can (14 oz/400 ml) full-fat coconut milk

1½ cups water

3 Tbsp creamy peanut butter

2 Tbsp soy sauce or gluten-free tamari

5 cups cooked rice (I like basmati or jasmine), reheated if prepped ahead (page 58)

⅓ cup chopped salted roasted peanuts, for garnish

Minced fresh cilantro, for garnish

Warm pitas or naan (optional)

PREP AHEAD: The rice can be cooked and the sweet potatoes, cauliflower, onion, garlic, and ginger prepped ahead of time.

1. Preheat the oven to 425°F (220°C). Line two rimmed baking sheets with parchment paper.

2. In a large bowl, toss the sweet potato and cauliflower with 2 tablespoons of avocado oil. Season generously with salt and pepper. Spread in a single layer over one and a half of the prepared baking sheets.

3. In the same bowl, toss the chickpeas with the remaining tablespoon of avocado oil. Season generously with salt and pepper. Spread evenly over the empty half of the second baking sheet.

4. Roast the cauliflower, sweet potato, and chickpeas for 45 minutes, stirring halfway through. Transfer the cauliflower and sweet potato to a bowl.

5. Set the oven to broil and cook the chickpeas until crispy, 3 to 4 minutes, watching to make sure they don't burn.

6. Meanwhile, heat a large frying pan over medium-high heat. Add the coconut oil, onion, ginger, and garlic and sauté until the onion is translucent, 2 to 3 minutes. Reduce the heat to medium, add the curry paste, and cook for another 3 to 4 minutes until fragrant.

7. Whisk in the coconut milk, water, peanut butter, and soy sauce. Increase the heat and bring to a boil, then reduce the heat and simmer for 10 minutes.

8. Stir in the cauliflower and sweet potato and simmer until heated through, about 5 minutes.

9. Serve the curry over hot rice, topped with the crispy chickpeas, peanuts, and cilantro. Serve with warm pitas, if desired.

STORAGE: Prepare the curry through step 8, let cool, and store in an airtight container in the fridge for up to 5 days or in a sealable freezer bag in the freezer for up to 3 months. To serve, reheat on the stove or in the microwave (thawing first, if frozen), then continue with step 9.

Nutrition Hack

Try replacing 1 to 2 cups of rice with an equal amount of riced cauliflower, for an extra dose of fiber and antioxidants!

Handhelds

Tip
I love making a crunchy version by breading the cauliflower, like in the Crispy Honey Valentina Cauliflower Bites recipe. If you have the time (or leftover bites—these go great in the same week's meal plan), follow the breading and baking method on page 147.

Crispy Honey Valentina Cauliflower Tacos

VEGETARIAN | GLUTEN-FREE OPTION | NUT-FREE

Cauliflower tacos first became a staple in my 3-2-1 Method meal plans. (Anyone remember those?) No word of a lie, at least once a week I'd get a note from someone saying, "My husband/kid/<fill in the blank> was sure they wouldn't like these, but they came back asking for more!" Cauliflower is such a versatile vegetable, with potent nutrition benefits to boot. Don't let its lack of color deceive you; it's one of the richest dietary sources of vitamin C, which has strong antioxidant properties. Now these Crispy Honey Valentina Cauliflower Tacos take things to a whole other level. Inspired by similarly flavored lettuce wraps at one of my favorite patios on our gorgeous Vancouver seawall, I knew I had to recreate them at home, and they did not disappoint!

SERVES 4

1 head cauliflower, cut into bite-size florets (about 6 cups)

1 can (19 oz/540 ml) chickpeas, drained, rinsed, and patted dry (about 2 cups)

2 Tbsp avocado oil or other high-heat cooking oil

Salt and freshly ground black pepper

HONEY VALENTINA SAUCE

½ cup Valentina hot sauce

¼ cup honey

TACOS

Eight 6-inch tortillas

¼ cup thinly sliced shredded green cabbage

Lime Crema (page 84)

Fresh cilantro, roughly chopped, for garnish

Salted roasted shelled pumpkin seeds, for garnish

PREP AHEAD: The cauliflower and cabbage can be cut and the crema made ahead of time. You can also prepare the sauce up to 1 week ahead and store it in the fridge.

1. Preheat the oven to 425°F (220°C). Line two large rimmed baking sheets with parchment paper and spray the paper with avocado oil until covered. This will ensure your cauliflower is crispy.

2. Divide the cauliflower and chickpeas between the two prepared baking sheets. Drizzle the cauliflower and chickpeas with oil and season generously with salt and pepper. Stir to make sure everything is evenly coated, then spread out in a single layer, leaving room between cauliflower pieces so it crisps up and doesn't steam.

3. Bake for 40 to 45 minutes, flipping halfway through, until the cauliflower and chickpeas are a nice golden brown and chickpeas are crispy.

4. **Make the sauce:** Meanwhile, in a medium bowl, whisk together the hot sauce and honey.

5. Combine the cauliflower and chickpeas on one baking sheet. Pour half of the sauce over top and toss to coat. Bake for 5 minutes to heat through.

6. **Assemble the tacos:** Divide the tortillas between four plates and top with the cabbage, cauliflower mixture, the remaining sauce, lime crema, cilantro, and pumpkin seeds and enjoy!

STORAGE: Prepare the cauliflower mixture through step 5, let cool, and store in an airtight container in the fridge for up to 5 days. To serve, reheat in a 400°F (200°C) oven or toaster oven for 10 to 12 minutes, until heated through and beginning to crisp back up. (Alternatively, reheat on the stove or in the microwave.) Continue with step 6.

Swaps & Subs

To make these tacos gluten-free, opt for gluten-free tortillas.

10-Minute Chicken, Fig, and Brie Sourdough Sandwiches

NUT-FREE

If I could marry a sandwich, this would be it. I first fell in love with this combo while working my very first serving job at Earls, and over the years have adapted it to this perfection of a homemade version. Ooey-gooey Brie, sticky fig jam, and the most perfectly cooked chicken, stuffed between slices of my favorite bread: sourdough. Oh, and we can't forget the spinach for good measure, packed with iron and antioxidants. The best part is that these come together in no time, with barely any dishes. Serve them with a side salad, kick your feet up, and enjoy!

MAKES 4 SANDWICHES

4 cooked chicken breasts (page 67)

5 to 7 oz (150 to 200 g) Brie cheese, sliced

8 slices sourdough bread

6 Tbsp fig jam

2 cups spinach

Salt and freshly ground black pepper

¼ to ½ cup Garlic Aioli (page 77 or store-bought)

PREP AHEAD: The chicken can be cooked and the aioli (if using homemade) made ahead of time.

IF YOU'RE FOLLOWING THE MEAL PLAN: With the prepped chicken on hand, make all four sandwiches and, if desired, serve with the optional bagged salad.

1. Preheat the oven to 400°F (200°C). Line a rimmed baking sheet with parchment paper.

2. Add the chicken to the prepared pan and top each breast with the Brie. Bake until the cheese is melted and chicken is heated through, 4 to 6 minutes.

3. Meanwhile, place the bread on the top rack of the oven to toast slightly, 3 to 4 minutes.

4. Spread fig jam on four slices of toast and top each with spinach, chicken and Brie, and a sprinkle of salt and pepper. Spread aioli on the other four slices, close the sandwiches, and enjoy!

STORAGE: Store the sandwiches in an airtight container in the fridge for up to 4 days. Enjoy cold or reheat open-faced in the toaster oven or oven until warmed through.

Meal Prep Tip
While you're at it, cook up some extra chicken to make the Chicken, Corn, and Feta Quesadillas (page 232) a super-quick meal. Using leftovers from this meal is actually how I created those quesadillas! Serve with a store-bought salad kit for a quick side, or the Easiest Arugula Salad (page 168) or Build-Your-Own Big-Batch Salad (page 176).

Time Saver
To make this a super-quick meal, use leftover cooked chicken breasts or use shredded meat from a store-bought rotisserie chicken!

Seared Salmon Burgers with the Easiest Tartar Sauce Ever

GLUTEN-FREE OPTION | NUT-FREE

I love how quickly salmon burgers come together while still feeling a little more special than regular burgers (not that there's anything wrong with those!). This recipe is a favorite with our whole family—chef included. Salmon is known for being rich in heart- and brain-supporting omega-3 fatty acids, and not only is the homemade tartar sauce easy and delicious, but its Greek yogurt base adds an extra dose of nutrients, including protein and calcium! If you're serving these burgers with fries, dip them in more of the aioli!

MAKES 4 BURGERS

BURGERS

Four 4 oz (125 g) skinless salmon fillets (about 1 inch thick)

Salt and freshly ground black pepper

1 Tbsp avocado oil or other high-heat cooking oil

4 small burger buns (regular or gluten-free), toasted

2 cups arugula

1 tomato, sliced

½ cup pickled red onion (page 215)

"TARTAR" SAUCE

¼ cup Garlic Aioli (page 77 or store-bought)

1 large pickle, diced

PREP AHEAD: The pickled red onion and "tartar" sauce can be made ahead of time.

1. **Make the burgers:** Pat the salmon dry and generously season both sides with salt and pepper.

2. In a large frying pan, heat the oil over medium-high heat. Add the salmon and sear on one side until golden brown, 3 to 4 minutes. Flip and sear the other side until the salmon is opaque and flakes easily with a fork, another 2 to 3 minutes (the cooking time depends on the thickness of your fillets).

3. **Make the sauce:** In a small bowl, combine the aioli and pickles.

4. **Assemble:** Spread tartar sauce over one or both sides of each bun. Layer arugula, tomato, salmon, and pickled red onion on the bottom half of each bun and cover with the top half.

STORAGE: Store the cooked salmon in an airtight container in the fridge for up to 3 days. To reheat, transfer it to a parchment-lined baking sheet, add 1 tablespoon of oil or butter (to prevent it from drying out), cover loosely with foil, and bake in a 300°F (150°C) oven until warmed through, 7 to 10 minutes. (Alternatively, heat in the microwave until warmed through.) Assemble the burgers as in step 4.

Time Saver

Use store-bought tartar sauce to save a step! To make a super-quick meal, pickle the onions ahead of time.

15-Minute Cajun Fish Tacos with Quick Pickled Cabbage

GLUTEN-FREE OPTION | NUT-FREE

I can't even believe this is true, but I haven't always been a fan of fish tacos. I can only think to blame it on my previously delicate relationship with cilantro. Anyway, I am happy to say this tale is history and fish tacos are now one of my favorite meals. Fish is a great way to quickly add protein to a meal, and tacos are the perfect vehicle for the beautiful color and texture of fruits and veggies—in this case, antioxidant-rich purple cabbage and mango! They come together quickly, are packed with flavor, and all the fresh toppings make them the meal of your dreams.

SERVES 4

1 lb (450 g) skinless white fish (I like cod, halibut, or tilapia)

Salt and freshly ground black pepper

1 Tbsp Cajun seasoning (page 76 or store-bought)

2 Tbsp avocado oil or other high-heat cooking oil

2 cloves garlic, grated or finely minced (about 1 tsp)

Twelve 6-inch tortillas (I prefer flour tortillas for these)

TOPPINGS

1 mango, cubed (or 1 cup frozen mango cubes, thawed)

1 large avocado, sliced

¼ cup loosely packed fresh cilantro, chopped (optional)

½ cup Lime Crema (page 84)

1 lime, cut into wedges

Dash of hot sauce (optional)

Pickled red onion and/or pickled cabbage (page 72), for garnish (optional)

PREP AHEAD: The crema, pickled cabbage, pickled red onion, and Cajun seasoning (if using homemade) can be made ahead of time.

IF YOU'RE FOLLOWING THE MEAL PLAN: Make the crema, pickled cabbage, and pickled red onion (if using), if you haven't already. If using homemade Cajun seasoning, make it now, if you haven't already. Make all four servings of tacos for Monday dinner.

1. Pat the fish dry. Sprinkle both sides with salt and pepper, then coat with Cajun seasoning.

2. In a large cast-iron pan or frying pan, heat the oil over medium-high heat. Add the garlic and cook, stirring, until fragrant, 30 seconds. Add the fish and cook one side until browned, 3 to 4 minutes. Flip the fish, cover, and cook until the fish is opaque and flakes easily with a fork, about 2 to 3 minutes.

3. Divide the tortillas between four plates and top with the fish, mango, avocado, cilantro, and crema. Finish with a squeeze of lime and, if desired, hot sauce, pickled red onion, and pickled cabbage. Enjoy!

STORAGE: Store the cooked fish in an airtight container in the fridge for up to 3 days. To serve, reheat on the stove or in the microwave, then assemble the tacos as in step 3.

Tip
Serve leftovers on a bed of rice or lettuce for the most delicious fish taco bowl!

Swaps & Subs
To make these tacos gluten-free, opt for gluten-free tortillas.

Time Saver
To make this a super-quick meal, pickle the onions and/or cabbage ahead of time.

Sheet Pan Margarita Shrimp Fajitas

DAIRY-FREE OPTION | GLUTEN-FREE OPTION | NUT-FREE

Another sheet pan favorite. I love how these meals minimize dishes and free up your time while the oven does the cooking! With over ten servings of vegetables, this is a nutrition-packed meal the whole family will devour. (It even got five stars from friends who said, "No one in our family likes fajitas.") Plus, everyone loves a good top-your-own-style dish. Enjoy as an easy weeknight meal or for entertaining guests without spending all your time in the kitchen. These babies are also delicious barbecued in a grilling basket!

SERVES 6

FILLING

5 bell peppers (yellow, orange, or red), thinly sliced (about 5 cups)

1 white onion, thinly sliced (about 2 cups)

1 Tbsp avocado oil or other high-heat cooking oil

1½ lb (680 g) frozen raw peeled shrimp, thawed, rinsed, and patted dry

MARINADE

6 cloves garlic, grated or finely minced (about 1 Tbsp)

1 jalapeño, seeds removed and minced

1½ Tbsp packed brown sugar

1 Tbsp chili powder

1 Tbsp ground cumin

1½ tsp salt

Freshly ground black pepper

3 Tbsp extra virgin olive oil

TO ASSEMBLE

Twelve 6-inch tortillas (regular or gluten-free)

Sour cream or plain yogurt (optional)

Salsa (optional)

Guacamole (optional)

Chopped fresh cilantro (optional)

Shredded cheese, such as marble or Tex-Mex mix (optional)

Hot sauce (optional)

Lime wedges (optional)

PREP AHEAD: The peppers, onion, and garlic can be prepped ahead of time. You can also prepare the marinade up to 5 days ahead and store it in the fridge.

IF YOU'RE FOLLOWING THE MEAL PLAN: Make the marinade, if you haven't already. With your already-prepped peppers, onion, and garlic, make all six servings through step 5. For Thursday dinner, continue with step 6 for four servings. Divide the remaining shrimp mixture between two airtight containers, let cool, and refrigerate. Store the remaining tortillas and desired toppings separately so the fajitas don't get soggy. For Friday lunch, reheat the filling and assemble the fajitas.

1. Preheat the oven to 425°F (220°C), with one rack set in the top third of the oven and the other in the middle. Line two rimmed baking sheets with parchment paper.

2. **Make the filling:** Divide the peppers and onions between the baking sheets and drizzle with the oil. Toss to coat, then spread out in a single layer. Roast for 15 minutes with one baking sheet on the top rack and the other on the middle rack.

3. **Make the marinade:** In a medium bowl, whisk together garlic, jalapeño, sugar, chili powder, cumin, salt, pepper, and oil.

4. Add the shrimp to the marinade, tossing to coat evenly, and let marinate while the peppers and onions cook.

5. At the 15-minute mark, remove the peppers and onions from the oven. Divide the shrimp and any excess marinade between the baking sheets, tossing everything together to coat in the marinade. Return the baking sheets to the oven and turn the oven to broil. Broil for 3 minutes, then switch the trays between racks. Broil for another 3 minutes, until the vegetables are lightly charred and the shrimp are pink, firm, and opaque.

6. **Assemble:** Serve on warm tortillas. (I do this in the microwave: lay out on a plate—it's okay if they overlap slightly—in 20-second increments.) Top with sour cream, salsa, guacamole, cilantro, cheese, hot sauce, and a squeeze of lime, as desired.

STORAGE: Store the cooled shrimp and pepper mixture in an airtight container in the fridge for up to 3 days. To serve, reheat on the stove or in the microwave, then assemble the fajitas as in step 6.

Ready-in-a-Pinch Sweet and Spicy Soy-Glazed Sushi Tacos

DAIRY-FREE | GLUTEN-FREE OPTION | NUT-FREE

This recipe made it into the book right before the buzzer, and I am SO happy it did! Trial after trial, I just couldn't get the recipe for the Sweet and Spicy Soy-Glazed Salmon Bowls (page 201) quite right. As a result, I ended up eating variations of it almost every night for a whole week. While I love that recipe, after multiple nights of eating the same thing, I needed to switch things up. I was craving sushi but didn't want the food in the fridge to go to waste—so this gorgeous, fun little combo was born! It was an epiphany moment, and I just knew it had to go in the book. I love the texture and nutrients the seaweed wrappers add, including antioxidant vitamins A and C and anti-inflammatory omega-3 fats (which you'll also get from the salmon)!

SERVES 4

SALMON

2 Tbsp honey

1½ Tbsp soy sauce or gluten-free tamari

1 tsp sriracha

1 lb (450 g) skinless salmon, cut into chunks

Salt and freshly ground black pepper

1 tsp toasted sesame oil

SUSHI TACOS

8 sheets seaweed (nori), cut into quarters

Wasabi paste

2 avocados, sliced

3 cups cooked rice, reheated if prepped ahead (page 58)

Toasted sesame seeds, for garnish

Green onion, thinly sliced, for garnish

PREP AHEAD: The rice can be cooked ahead of time and the salmon marinated as in step 1.

1. **Make the salmon:** In a medium bowl, whisk together the honey, soy sauce, and sriracha. Add the salmon, season generously with salt and pepper, and toss to coat. Marinate for at least 10 minutes, or cover and refrigerate for up to 1 day.

2. In a large frying pan, heat the oil over medium-high heat. Lift the salmon out of the marinade, letting any excess drip off, and add to the pan in a single layer. Sear on one side until golden brown, 2 to 3 minutes (if using wild salmon, go with the shorter cooking time, as it has less fat and can dry out more easily). Flip the salmon and pour in any remaining marinade. Sear the other side until golden brown and the salmon is opaque and flakes easily with a fork, another 2 to 3 minutes.

3. **Assemble the sushi tacos:** Divide the seaweed pieces between four plates and top with wasabi paste, avocados, hot rice, and salmon. Garnish with sesame seeds and green onion. Enjoy!

STORAGE: Store each sushi taco ingredient (except the seaweed) separately in an airtight container in the fridge for up to 3 days. When ready to assemble and eat the sushi tacos, reheat salmon then top with remaining ingredients.

Meal Prep Tip

I prefer white rice for this dish, but any rice will do! If you're making it with leftovers from the Sweet and Spicy Soy-Glazed Salmon Bowls or another recipe using brown rice, just use what you've already prepped!

Thai-Inspired Lettuce Wraps

VEGAN OPTION | DAIRY-FREE

I love lettuce wraps—another dish commonly found on our dinner table when I was growing up—for a quick throw-together dinner. These ones are packed with vegetables and have the rice mixed right in to soak up the flavors of the sauce and make a balanced, filling meal. For a more beautiful presentation, opt for butter lettuce cups, but nothing compares to the traditional crunch of iceberg lettuce, which also holds up better to the jam-packed filling!

SERVES 4

FILLING

2 Tbsp toasted sesame oil

2-inch knob ginger, minced (about 2 Tbsp)

3 cloves garlic, grated or finely minced (about 1½ tsp)

1 lb (450 g) ground turkey

Salt and freshly ground black pepper

10.5 oz (300 g) cremini mushrooms, diced (about 20 mushrooms/4 cups)

3 cups cooked rice (I like brown) (page 58)

¼ small purple cabbage, diced (about 2 cups)

2 Tbsp soy sauce

1 Tbsp hoisin sauce

2 tsp fish sauce

WRAPS

1 head butter lettuce or iceberg lettuce, leaves removed

2 mini cucumbers, diced (about 1 cup), for garnish

¼ cup chopped roasted salted peanuts, for garnish

Thinly sliced Thai red chilis or sriracha, for garnish

Chopped fresh cilantro, for garnish

Lime wedges, for garnish

PREP AHEAD: The rice can be cooked and the mushrooms, cabbage, garlic, and ginger can be prepped ahead of time.

1. **Make the filling:** In a large frying pan, heat the oil over medium-high heat. Add the ginger and garlic and cook, stirring, until fragrant, about 2 minutes. Add the turkey and season generously with salt and pepper, breaking the turkey into a few large pieces. Cook, without stirring, until the turkey is browned on one side, 4 to 5 minutes. Flip and brown the other side, another 2 to 4 minutes, then break into smaller pieces and cook, stirring, until no pink remains.

2. Add the mushrooms and cook, stirring only once or twice to allow them to brown, for 5 minutes. Add the rice, cabbage, soy sauce, hoisin, and fish sauce, stirring to combine and coat all the ingredients evenly. Cook for 2 to 3 minutes, until the cabbage is tender-crisp.

3. **Assemble the wraps:** Divide the lettuce leaves between four plates, top with filling, and garnish with cucumbers, peanuts, chilis, cilantro, and a squeeze of lime. Enjoy!

STORAGE: Store the cooled filling in an airtight container in the fridge for up to 4 days or in a sealable freezer bag in the freezer for up to 3 months. To serve, reheat on the stove or in the microwave (thawing first, if frozen), then assemble the wraps as in step 3.

Tip

For a less messy lunch revamp, chop up lettuce and pile it with the filling and toppings for a deconstructed lettuce wrap bowl!

Swaps & Subs

Make this recipe plant-based by swapping the ground turkey for veggie ground round or crumbled tofu. Replace the fish sauce with soy sauce and a splash of either lime juice or unseasoned rice vinegar.

Pear and Blue Cheese Pizza

DAIRY-FREE OPTION | GLUTEN-FREE OPTION | NUT-FREE

I am a sucker for a good "bite"—you know, when you get that perfect combo of a little bit of everything? My passion for "bites" inspired this pizza, and it delivers with every mouthwatering morsel. Fresh pear is the perfect complement to the salty blue cheese and prosciutto, all delivered on a warm, doughy crust. Once you taste this you'll be craving more, so I made the recipe for two pizzas. Enjoy the leftovers (and time saved for your next meal)!

SERVES 4 TO 6

Two 12-inch pizza crusts
½ cup pizza sauce
1 large pear, thinly sliced
⅔ cup blue cheese
5 oz (150 g) thinly sliced prosciutto
1½ cups shredded mozzarella cheese
3 cups arugula
Roughly chopped basil, for garnish
Extra virgin olive oil, for garnish
Balsamic glaze, for garnish
Flaky salt, for garnish

1. Preheat the oven to 425°F (220°C), with one rack set in the top third of the oven and the other in the middle. Line two large rimmed baking sheets with parchment paper. (If using pizza stones, do not line with parchment paper.)

2. Place one pizza crust on each prepared baking sheet. Spread pizza sauce evenly over both crusts and top with pear, blue cheese, prosciutto, and mozzarella.

3. With one baking sheet on the top rack and the other on the middle rack, bake until the edges are golden and the crust is cooked through, about 18 to 20 minutes or per package instructions. Halfway through the baking time, switch the positions of the baking sheets in the oven, moving the lower to the upper and vice versa.

4. Let cool for 5 minutes, then top with the arugula, basil, and a drizzle of olive oil and balsamic glaze. Finish with a pinch of flaky salt, cut into slices, and enjoy!

STORAGE: Store the cooled pizza in an airtight container in the fridge for up to 5 days or in a sealable freezer bag in the freezer for up to 3 months. To serve, reheat on a baking sheet in a 375°F (190°C) oven until warmed through, 7 to 10 minutes for refrigerated or 15 to 18 minutes for frozen. (Or reheat in the microwave.)

Serving Tip
The Build-Your-Own Big-Batch Salad (page 176), Easiest Arugula Salad (page 168), or any big salad work great as a side for this pizza!

Swaps & Subs
To make these pizzas gluten-free, opt for gluten-free crusts. To make these pizzas dairy-free, opt for dairy-free cheese.

Nutrition Hack
Serve with a ready-to-go salad kit for an instant extra dose of greens!

Sun-Dried Tomato and Pesto Shrimp Pizza

DAIRY-FREE OPTION | GLUTEN-FREE OPTION

We didn't go out for dinner a ton when I was growing up, but when we did, the spot to go in Kamloops was Earls. It was either the hot wings (yes, even as a child I was hot sauce–obsessed; my son, Wylder, comes by his love of hot sauce honestly) or this perfection of a pizza. Perfectly cooked shrimp, pesto, and sun-dried tomatoes are a flavor match made in heaven! I loved it so much, I had to come up with my own version, and this one is often on the menu when we have homemade pizza night. I hope you love it as much as we do!

SERVES 4 TO 6

12 oz (350 g) raw peeled shrimp, thawed, rinsed, and patted dry

2 Tbsp extra virgin olive oil

Juice of ½ lemon (about 2 Tbsp)

1 clove garlic, grated or finely minced (about ½ tsp)

Salt and freshly ground black pepper

Two 12-inch pizza crusts

⅓ cup store-bought pesto

½ cup drained oil-packed sun-dried tomatoes, chopped

2 cups shredded mozzarella cheese

⅔ cup crumbled feta cheese

¼ cup fresh basil, roughly chopped, for garnish

1. Preheat the oven to 425°F (220°C), with one rack set in the top third of the oven and the other in the middle. Line two large rimmed baking sheets with parchment paper. (If using pizza stones, do not line with parchment paper.)

2. In a small bowl, combine the shrimp, oil, lemon juice, garlic, salt, and pepper, tossing to coat. Set aside to marinate.

3. Place one pizza crust on each prepared baking sheet. Spread pesto evenly over both crusts and top with sun-dried tomatoes, mozzarella, and feta.

4. With one baking sheet on the top rack and the other on the middle rack, bake for 13 minutes. Add the shrimp, drizzle any remaining marinade over the pizza, and switch the placement on the baking sheets in the oven, with the lower moving to the upper position and vice versa. Bake until the shrimp are firm, pink, and opaque and the crust is cooked through, about 5 to 7 minutes or per package instructions.

5. Let cool for 5 minutes, then top with the basil, cut into slices, and enjoy!

STORAGE: Store the cooled pizza in an airtight container in the fridge for up to 3 days or in a sealable freezer bag in the freezer for up to 3 months. To serve, reheat on a baking sheet in a 375°F (190°C) oven until warmed through, 7 to 10 minutes for refrigerated or 15 to 18 minutes for frozen. (Or reheat in the microwave.) Add more fresh basil to garnish, if desired.

Tip

If you have time, feel free to make your own favorite pizza dough, or, my favorite hack, buy premade dough from a bakery, pizza shop, or the freezer aisle at the grocery store! Just like with homemade dough, and all you need to do is roll it out!

Swaps & Subs

To make these pizzas gluten-free, opt for gluten-free crusts. To make these pizzas dairy-free, opt for dairy-free cheese.

Juicy Spinach and Feta Turkey Burgers

Biting into a juicy burger—there's nothing like it. Although turkey is a lean meat, it can still be juicy when made right, and it provides a good source of iron and B vitamins. Mixing the salty tang of feta, the freshness of spinach, and the perfect flavor boost of red onion right into the patties ensures you get maximum flavor in every bite and also helps to keep them juicy. The recipe yields eight patties, making it perfect for a backyard barbecue with friends or an easy meal prep recipe that will bring a little party vibe to your week. You know how you like your burgers, so top away as you like. I've included some of my favorites as suggestions. Dig in!

MAKES 8 BURGERS

PATTIES

2 lb (900 g) ground turkey

2 eggs

2 cloves garlic, grated or finely minced (about 1 tsp)

1 small red onion, diced (about 1 cup)

4 cups spinach, finely chopped

⅔ cup crumbled feta cheese

½ tsp salt

½ tsp pepper

1 to 2 Tbsp olive oil

BURGERS

Burger buns (I like brioche)

Tzatziki (page 82 or store-bought)

Mini cucumber, thinly sliced

Lettuce (optional)

Sliced tomato (optional)

Sliced cheese (I like aged white Cheddar) (optional)

Pickled red onion (page 72) (optional)

Sliced avocado (optional)

Meal Prep Tip

Serve with Easiest Arugula Salad (page 168), a store-bought salad kit, or fries.

IF YOU'RE FOLLOWING THE MEAL PLAN: In Week 2, cook the four refrigerated patties for Sunday dinner, starting from Step 3, and optionally, make and serve with the arugula salad. In Week 4, pull the frozen patties out of the freezer on Wednesday night and thaw them overnight in the fridge to cook for Thursday dinner. Optionally, make and serve with the arugula salad.

1. **Make the patties:** In a medium bowl, combine the turkey, eggs, garlic, red onion, spinach, feta, salt, and pepper.

2. Shape the turkey mixture into eight evenly sized patties, pressing the middles down with your thumb to make a small dip in the center (the center expands when cooking).

3. In a large frying pan, heat 1 tablespoon of oil over medium-high heat. (If cooking all eight at once, you may need to cook in batches, depending on the size of your pan.) Cook for 6 minutes on the first side. Flip the patties over, cover, and cook for another 6 minutes or until no pink remains inside. Let sit for 2 to 3 minutes while you toast the buns.

4. **Assemble the burgers:** Lightly toast the buns, then top each with a burger patty, tzatziki, cucumber, and any other desired toppings.

STORAGE: Store raw patties in an airtight container in the fridge for up to 4 days, separating each layer with parchment paper so the patties don't stick together. Or wrap each patty in plastic wrap and store in a sealable storage bag in the freezer for up to 3 months. Thaw frozen patties overnight in the fridge before cooking.

Store cooked patties in an airtight container in the fridge for up to 4 days or in a sealable freezer bag in the freezer for up to 3 months. To serve, reheat the patties on the stove or in the microwave (thawing first, if preferred), then assemble the burgers.

Sesame Seared Wasabi Tuna Wraps

DAIRY-FREE | GLUTEN-FREE OPTION | NUT-FREE

Hawaii is my happy place, and home to my sister and her sweet fam. While I wish I could just pop over to her house for Sunday dinner or call her up for a walk, if there's anywhere in the world I'd want to have to go to visit her, Hawaii is pretty much the dream. These wraps are inspired by an offering at one of our favorite beachfront restaurants in Lanikai, the beach near her house. When I bite into one, I can hear the waves crashing and taste the crisp local beer on my lips. They are fresh, flavorful, and packed with antioxidant-rich vegetables, and they come together with ease in 15 minutes flat. When you can't just jump on a plane, this recipe is the next best thing.

SERVES 4

1 lb (450 g) tuna steaks

1 tsp soy sauce or gluten-free tamari

Salt and freshly ground black pepper

3 Tbsp toasted sesame seeds

1 Tbsp toasted sesame oil

2 cups rainbow slaw mix

½ cup Wasabi Aioli (page 77 or store-bought)

Four 10-inch tortillas

1 large avocado, sliced

¼ English cucumber, thinly sliced (about ¼ cup)

2 cups mixed greens

PREP AHEAD: The aioli (if using homemade) can be made and the cucumber sliced ahead of time.

1. Place the tuna in a medium bowl, add the soy sauce, and season generously with salt and pepper. Marinate for 5 to 10 minutes.

2. Sprinkle all sides of the tuna steaks with sesame seeds until fully covered.

3. In a large frying pan, heat the oil over medium-high heat until shimmering, about 2 minutes. Add the tuna and sear for 1 to 2 minutes per side or until golden brown on both sides. Remove from the heat and let sit for 5 minutes, then cut into ¼-inch-thick slices.

4. Meanwhile, in a medium bowl, toss the slaw mix and aioli until the slaw is fully coated.

5. Lay the tortillas flat and evenly distribute the avocado, cucumber, greens, wasabi slaw mix, and tuna slices in the center of each wrap, leaving 2 inches on each end. Fold the short ends in, then roll one long end over the filling until no more tortilla remains. Cut the wraps in half.

STORAGE: Store the wraps in an airtight container in the fridge for up to 3 days. Enjoy cold!

Swaps & Subs

To make these wraps gluten-free, opt for gluten-free tamari and gluten-free tortillas.

Chicken, Corn, and Feta Quesadillas

GLUTEN-FREE OPTION | NUT-FREE

This recipe was a happy accident (I have a lot of those in the kitchen) of leftovers that needed to be eaten up but could use a little jazz. Quesadillas of all kinds are staples in our home because they are so versatile—by throwing in any veg and protein with a little cheese, you're guaranteed a balanced meal with an array of nutrients and a crowd-pleaser all in one. These quesadillas were created with leftover chicken from the 10-Minute Chicken, Fig, and Brie Sourdough Sandwiches on page 212, some wilting asparagus, and an ingredient we always have in the freezer: corn. If you've got leftover barbecued corn, even better, but this quick trick to broil your veggies gives nearly the same effect in record time!

SERVES 6

1 bunch asparagus, cut into 1-inch pieces (about 2 cups)

1½ cups corn kernels (thawed if frozen)

1 Tbsp avocado oil or other high-heat cooking oil, plus more for brushing or spraying

Salt and freshly ground black pepper

Six 10-inch flour tortillas

2½ cups shredded cheese (I like Monterey Jack)

1 cup crumbled feta cheese

2½ cups cooked chicken breasts (page 67), diced (about 2 to 3 breasts, see time saver)

Flaky salt

Chili powder

Salsa, for serving (optional)

Sour cream, for serving (optional)

Guacamole, for serving (optional)

PREP AHEAD: The chicken can be cooked, the cheese shredded, and the asparagus cut ahead of time.

IF YOU'RE FOLLOWING THE MEAL PLAN: With the prepped chicken and asparagus on hand, make all six servings through step 4. Serve four now, following step 5, with an optional bagged salad. Store the other two for lunch tomorrow.

1. Preheat the broiler. Line two rimmed baking sheets with parchment paper.

2. On one of the prepared baking sheets, toss the asparagus and corn with the oil and salt and pepper to taste. Broil until lightly charred, 3 to 5 minutes. Remove from the oven and set the oven to 425°F (220°C). Transfer the vegetables to a plate.

3. Arrange the tortillas on the two prepared baking sheets (they should all fit once folded in half after filling). On one half of each tortilla, evenly distribute half of the shredded cheese, followed by the feta, the chicken, and the veggies. Sprinkle with the remaining shredded cheese and fold the quesadillas in half to close. Brush or spray the tops lightly with oil and sprinkle with flaky salt and a light dusting of chili powder.

4. Bake until the cheese is melted and the tops of the quesadillas are crisp and golden brown, 10 to 15 minutes. Let cool for 5 minutes, then cut each quesadilla into quarters.

5. Serve with salsa, sour cream, and guacamole. Enjoy!

STORAGE: Store the cooled quesadillas in an airtight container in the fridge for up to 4 days or in a sealable freezer bag in the freezer for up to 3 months. To serve, thaw in the microwave or overnight in the fridge. Reheat in a 325°F (160°C) oven or toaster oven until warmed through, 7 to 12 minutes. Alternatively, reheat in a panini press or a frying pan on medium heat.

Swaps & Subs

To make these quesadillas gluten-free, opt for gluten-free tortillas.

Time Saver

Use cooked rotisserie chicken for a quick protein option. You can also skip the step of broiling the corn and asparagus, although I recommend it for extra flavor if you have the time!

Pastas, Bakes, and Family Meals

Swaps & Subs

If you don't have red wine, or prefer not to use it, you can substitute 1 tablespoon of balsamic vinegar. The taste will be slightly different, but the vinegar will still give the sauce that delicious burst of acidity. To make this recipe vegan, use nutritional yeast instead of Parmesan.

Best-Ever Veggie Bolognese

VEGETARIAN | VEGAN OPTION | DAIRY-FREE OPTION | NUT-FREE

What makes this the best-ever veggie Bolognese? Not to toot my own horn, but every time I make it, there are requests for seconds. The meat eaters never notice it's vegetarian, and even the more selective kiddos gobble it up. When delicious, satisfying pasta is also packed to the brim with veggies (nearly twenty servings go into this recipe!), I'd call that a major win. I love how much you get out of this recipe, making it the perfect batch-prep meal for busy weeks.

SERVES 8 TO 10
(MAKES 8 CUPS SAUCE)

1 lb (450 g) pasta (I like pappardelle, spaghetti, or rotini)

3 Tbsp extra virgin olive oil, divided

1 small white onion, diced (about 1 cup)

3 cloves garlic, grated or finely minced (about 1½ tsp)

1½ lb (680 g) veggie ground round

Salt and freshly ground black pepper

10.5 oz (300 g) cremini mushrooms, diced (about 20 mushrooms/4 cups)

3 large carrots, grated (about 3 cups)

3 stalks celery, grated (about ⅔ to 1 cup)

½ cup red wine

1 can (28 oz/796 ml) crushed tomatoes

¼ cup nutritional yeast

1 Tbsp tomato paste

2 tsp dried oregano

Grated Parmesan cheese or nutritional yeast, for garnish (optional)

Flat-leaf parsley, for garnish (optional)

IF YOU'RE FOLLOWING THE MEAL PLAN: On Sunday evening, cook the pasta and reheat the sauce over the stove. Toss together, plate, and garnish four servings. Let the remaining pasta and sauce cool, mix together in an airtight container, and refrigerate. Reheat for dinner on Wednesday.

1. Bring a large pot of salted water to boil and cook the pasta according to package directions. If eating right away, before draining, set aside ½ cup of the pasta water. Drain the pasta and set aside.

2. Meanwhile, in a large frying pan, heat 2 tablespoons of the oil over medium heat. Add the onion and garlic and cook until the onion is translucent, 3 to 4 minutes. Add the veggie ground round, breaking it apart, and season generously with salt and pepper. Without stirring, brown the veggie ground round on one side, 5 to 7 minutes. Flip and brown the other side, another 4 to 5 minutes.

3. Increase the heat to medium-high and add the remaining tablespoon of oil and the mushrooms, carrots, and celery. Cook until the vegetables are soft, another 4 to 5 minutes. Stir in the wine to deglaze the pan and cook until most of the wine has evaporated, about 1 minute.

4. Reduce the heat to medium-low and add the tomatoes, nutritional yeast, tomato paste, and oregano. (If you have extra tomato paste, fill an ice cube tray with it, freeze, and use as needed.) Season with salt and pepper to taste. Reduce the heat to low and simmer for another 5 to 10 minutes (longer if you have time, as the flavor will continue to build).

5. If you've made fresh pasta, add the pasta water to the sauce and stir to combine, cooking for another 2 to 3 minutes, until the sauce has thickened again.

6. Divide the pasta between serving plates or bowls, top with sauce, and finish with Parmesan and parsley (if using), and a drizzle of olive oil.

STORAGE: The sauce can be stored on its own or mixed with the pasta in an airtight container in the fridge for up to 5 days or in a sealable freezer bag in the freezer for up to 3 months. To serve, reheat sauce on its own over medium-low heat until it simmers, then pour over freshly cooked pasta and add the garnishes. (If frozen, first thaw it in the microwave or overnight in the fridge.) Or reheat sauce and pasta together on the stove or in the microwave.

Time Saver

You can buy pre-shredded carrots instead of grating them yourself.

Roasted Tomato and Seared Scallop Capellini

DAIRY-FREE | NUT-FREE

When you want to treat yourself to a nice dinner, this is it. There's something about seared scallops that just make a dish feel special, and man, are they delicious! The juicy, blistered tomatoes build sweetness when roasted, plus I love this hands-off method of preparing them. Make this easy-to-prep, antioxidant-rich dish for your next date night or dinner with friends—the rest of that bottle of wine needs to get finished up somehow!

SERVES 4

3 pints cherry tomatoes

5 cloves garlic, minced (about 2½ tsp)

3 Tbsp avocado oil or other high-heat cooking oil

Salt and freshly ground black pepper

½ cup white wine

1 Tbsp tomato paste

12 oz (350 g) capellini or spaghettini pasta

1 Tbsp extra virgin olive oil

14 oz (400 g) large scallops (about 12 to 16), patted dry

Fresh basil, for garnish

Meal Prep Tip

Pasta makes a delicious brunch leftover. Add a handful of arugula, fry up an egg with a runny yolk to pop on top, and voilà!

PREP AHEAD: The sauce can be made ahead as in steps 1 to 3 and stored in the fridge for up to 5 days.

1. Preheat the oven to 450°F (230°C).

2. In a cast-iron frying pan or oven-safe dish, combine the tomatoes, garlic, avocado oil, and salt and pepper to taste. Bake until the tomatoes start to blister, about 20 minutes.

3. Transfer the pan to the stove, over medium heat. Add the wine and tomato paste and bring to a simmer. Simmer, stirring occasionally, until most of the liquid has cooked off and a thick sauce has formed, about 5 minutes.

4. Meanwhile, bring a pot of salted water to a boil and cook the pasta according to package directions.

5. In another frying pan, heat the olive oil over medium-high heat for 30 seconds.

6. Sprinkle the scallops generously with salt and pepper on both sides. Add to the hot oil and sear on one side for about 1 minute. Cover and cook for 2 minutes. Flip the scallops and sear, uncovered, until firm and opaque, about 2 minutes.

7. When the pasta is cooked, add it to the tomato sauce and toss to coat.

8. Plate the pasta, top with the scallops, and garnish with basil.

STORAGE: Store the pasta and scallops in an airtight container in the fridge for up to 3 days. To serve, reheat on the stove or in the microwave.

Summer Pasta

VEGETARIAN | GLUTEN-FREE OPTION | NUT-FREE

This recipe kind of came together by accident. We were up in the Okanagan, at the lakeside cabin of one of our best friends, soaking in the abundance of summer tomatoes, some leftover grilled corn, and a garden exploding with basil. (Besides adding gorgeous color and a fresh flavor, herbs count towards your daily dose of greens too!) I got assigned to help with a birthday dinner, and working with what we had, this simple yet flavor-packed dish was born. It has since become a favorite among friends and family. As a nice little bonus, it makes for super-tasty leftovers, even cold—ideally paired with a glass of sauv blanc on a dock somewhere.

SERVES 4

4 to 6 in-season tomatoes (I like heirloom or Roma), chopped (about 4 cups)

3 cloves garlic, grated or finely minced (about 1½ tsp)

¼ cup extra virgin olive oil

Salt and freshly ground black pepper

9 oz (250 g) spaghettini pasta

1½ cups corn kernels (frozen or leftover from grilled corn)

1 cup crumbled feta cheese

Fresh basil, for garnish

Grated Parmesan cheese, for garnish

Swaps & Subs

To make it gluten-free, opt for a gluten-free pasta.

PREP AHEAD: The tomatoes and garlic can be cut and the corn grilled (if using grilled) and cut off the husks ahead of time.

1. In a medium bowl, combine the tomatoes, garlic, oil, and salt and pepper to taste. Set aside or refrigerate for 30 minutes or up to overnight for intensified flavors.

2. Meanwhile, bring a pot of salted water to a boil and cook the pasta according to package directions. Drain, reserving ½ cup of the pasta water, and set aside.

3. In a large frying pan, heat the tomato mixture and corn over medium heat. Season with more salt and pepper to taste. Cook down for 6 to 8 minutes until most of the liquid has cooked off. Add the pasta and reserved pasta water and cook until the sauce thickens and clings to the noodles, another 3 to 5 minutes. Remove from the heat and stir in the feta.

4. Divide between four bowls and garnish with basil and Parmesan. Enjoy!

STORAGE: Store the pasta in an airtight container in the fridge for up to 5 days. To serve, reheat on the stove or in the microwave, adding more fresh basil and Parmesan if desired.

Helen's One-Pan Sun-Dried Tomato and Basil Balsamic Chicken Orzo

DAIRY-FREE OPTION | NUT-FREE

You know how smells bring back memories? This dish does that for me. I remember stepping into my granny's house, after (what seemed like) the longest drive ever from Kamloops down to the coast, to the smell of roasting chicken, sometimes with rosemary and crisp potatoes and sometimes this tangy and vibrant balsamic chicken. I've tweaked the recipe a bit to make it a fast and easy one-pot wonder. Flavor-packed sun-dried tomatoes add to the tangy balsamic vinegar, and it's all balanced out with fresh basil and iron-rich spinach, added at the very end to cozily wilt into the perfect little orzo bites. Truly like a warm hug from Granny.

SERVES 4

1 lb (450 g) boneless skinless chicken thighs

Salt and freshly ground black pepper

1 Tbsp extra virgin olive oil, plus more for drizzling

2 cloves garlic, grated or finely minced (about 1 tsp)

1 shallot, minced (about 2 Tbsp)

1⅓ cups orzo pasta

2 Tbsp balsamic vinegar

4 cups chicken stock

4 cups spinach, roughly chopped

¾ cup oil-packed sun-dried tomatoes, drained and chopped

½ cup basil, julienned, divided

Fresh lemon wedges, for garnish

Grated Parmesan cheese, for garnish

Flaky salt, for garnish (optional)

Red pepper flakes to serve, for garnish (optional)

PREP AHEAD: The shallots and garlic can be cut and the chicken cooked ahead of time.

1. Season both sides of the chicken generously with salt and pepper.

2. In a large frying pan, heat the oil over medium-high heat. Add the chicken when the oil is hot; it should sizzle when the chicken hits the pan. Sear, allowing the edges to brown, for 4 to 5 minutes on each side, until the juices run clear when the chicken is pierced. Transfer the chicken to a plate, keeping the oil and chicken juices in the pan, and set aside.

3. Add the garlic and shallot to the pan and sauté until fragrant and shallot is translucent, about 1 minute. Add the orzo and toast until slightly browned, 2 to 3 minutes, stirring frequently.

4. Stir in the vinegar and scrape up any brown bits from the bottom of the pan. Add the stock, and bring to a boil. Boil, stirring occasionally, until most of the liquid is absorbed, 12 to 14 minutes.

5. Add the spinach, sun-dried tomatoes, and ¼ cup of the basil, tossing to coat. Place the chicken on top of the mixture and drizzle with any accumulated juices. Cover the pan, reduce the heat to medium-low, and cook until the chicken is heated through, 2 to 3 minutes (if chicken was prepped ahead, heat for an additional 3 to 4 minutes or until heated through).

6. Serve with a squeeze of lemon and a drizzle of oil, garnished with Parmesan and the remaining basil. If desired, sprinkle with flaky salt and red pepper flakes.

STORAGE: Store the orzo in an airtight container in the fridge for up to 4 days or in the freezer for up to 3 months. To serve, reheat on the stove or in the microwave.

Swaps & Subs

To make it dairy-free, omit the Parmesan garnish or swap it for a plant-based cheese or a sprinkle of nutritional yeast.

Nutrition Hack

To amp up the veggies in this dish, diced mushrooms or peppers are delicious additions!

Creamy Roasted Vegetable Sheet Pan Gnocchi

VEGETARIAN OPTION | NUT-FREE

This recipe is jam-packed with flavor and comes together easily with everything tossed right onto the same pan to bake away and create the perfect sauce for perfectly plump and slightly crispy gnocchi. The arugula adds a nice touch of freshness (plus antioxidants via vitamins A and C, along with folate and vitamin K) and instantly elevates the dish to taste like it's being served at your favorite restaurant. I love making it when guests come over, because it's super easy to prep ahead so that all you have to do is pop it in the oven when it's time to eat. (Bonus: the cleanup is pretty much nonexistent!)

SERVES 6

1 lb (450 g) gnocchi

2 pints cherry tomatoes

2 bell peppers (I like red, orange, or yellow), cut into 1-inch squares (about 2 cups)

2 cloves garlic, grated or finely minced (about 1 tsp)

1 small red onion, cut into squares (about 1 cup)

¼ cup extra virgin olive oil

½ tsp salt

¼ tsp red pepper flakes, plus more for garnish if desired

1 lb (450 g) mild Italian sausage, removed from casing and broken apart (see time saver)

1 cup crumbled feta cheese

4 cups baby arugula (about half a 5 oz/142 g bin)

Chopped fresh basil, for garnish

Time Saver

Use ground Italian sausage, if available.

Swaps & Subs

I like making this recipe with ground chicken sausage when I can find it! For a vegetarian meal, you can use vegetarian sausage in place of the Italian sausage.

PREP AHEAD: The peppers, onions, and garlic can be prepped ahead of time.

IF YOU'RE FOLLOWING THE MEAL PLAN: With the prepped peppers, onion, and garlic on hand, make all six servings. Serve four now and store the other two for lunch tomorrow.

1. Preheat the oven to 425°F (220°C), with racks set in the top third and the middle. Line two rimmed baking sheets with parchment paper.

2. In a medium bowl, combine the gnocchi, tomatoes, peppers, garlic, onion, oil, salt, and red pepper flakes. Add the sausage and feta and toss to combine.

3. Spread the gnocchi mixture out in a single layer on the two prepared pans. Place one pan on each rack and roast for 20 minutes, stirring halfway through and swapping the pans' position in the oven, until the vegetables are tender-crisp, the sausage is no longer pink, and the gnocchi are plump and slightly golden.

4. Set the oven to broil and cook until the tomatoes and peppers on the top rack char slightly, about 2 minutes. Switch the pans and broil for another 2 minutes.

5. Serve topped with arugula, basil, and more red pepper flakes, if desired.

STORAGE: Store the cooled gnocchi mixture, without the toppings, in an airtight container in the fridge for up to 4 days or in a sealable freezer bag for up to 3 months. To serve, reheat on the stove or in the microwave (thawing first, if frozen), then add the toppings.

Better-than-Boxed
Homemade Mac 'n' Cheese

VEGETARIAN | GLUTEN-FREE OPTION | NUT-FREE

I feel like this dish doesn't need an intro, because who doesn't like mac 'n' cheese? (If you say you don't, I'm not sure I believe you.) This recipe has become a staple in our house over the years and comes together just as quickly as the boxed stuff! For real. Whip up the creamy sauce while the noodles boil, and eat as is or bake for the perfect bubbly, melty crust. The dietitian and momma in me loves some green, so I added broccoli. Keyword: *added*—this isn't about replacing the noodles or cutting back in any way. I truly love how the broccoli adds color, flavor, and, of course, fiber and those good ole antioxidants we all love! So dig in and enjoy the looks of pure pleasure as you serve this gorge little dish!

SERVES 4 TO 6

8 oz (225 g) shell pasta (about 2½ cups)

3 Tbsp salted butter

3 Tbsp unbleached all-purpose flour

2 cups milk

½ tsp salt

3 cups shredded old Cheddar cheese, divided

1 small crown broccoli, cut into ½-inch florets (about 2 cups)

¼ cup panko bread crumbs

Flaky sea salt (I love Maldon salt)

Swaps & Subs

To make it gluten-free, use gluten-free flour in the roux and opt for a gluten-free pasta and panko bread crumbs.

Time Saver

Use pre-shredded cheese and/or, to make this meal even quicker, enjoy it after adding the pasta to the sauce, skipping the baking step. In this case, omit the broccoli, since it will be raw, or sub in 2 cups of peas or riced cauliflower, cooking until heated through.

1. Preheat the oven to 400°F (200°C). Line an 8-inch square baking dish with parchment paper.

2. Bring a large pot of salted water to a boil and cook the pasta according to package directions. Drain and set aside.

3. Meanwhile, in a large pot, melt the butter over medium-low heat. Add the flour and whisk to form a smooth paste. Cook, continuing to whisk frequently in a figure-eight motion so the roux doesn't burn, until lightly browned, 4 to 6 minutes.

4. Increase the heat to medium-high and slowly add the milk, ½ cup at a time. Add the salt and bring to a simmer. Reduce the heat to medium-low and continue to simmer, whisking frequently, until the sauce thickens, 4 to 5 minutes.

5. Remove from the heat and stir in 2 cups of the Cheddar, whisking until the cheese is fully melted. Add the pasta and broccoli, stirring to coat evenly.

6. Spoon the pasta mixture into the prepared baking dish and sprinkle with the remaining Cheddar, panko, and flaky salt.

7. Bake, uncovered, for 10 minutes. Set the oven to broil and cook until the cheese is bubbling at the edges of the dish, 2 to 3 minutes. Enjoy!

STORAGE: Let the baked mac 'n' cheese cool, then store in an airtight container in the fridge for up to 5 days or in the freezer for up to 3 months. To serve, reheat refrigerated or thawed mac 'n' cheese in an oven-safe dish by covering with foil and baking at 350°F (180°C) until warmed through, 20 to 30 minutes. You can reheat individual servings in the microwave. Reheat from frozen at 350°F (180°C) until warmed through, 30 to 60 minutes (depending on the serving size).

Swaps & Subs
Make it dairy-free or vegan! Swap
the butter for plant-based butter
(or leave it out altogether) and
substitute nutritional yeast for
the Parmesan cheese.

Creamy Oven-Baked Mushroom Risotto

VEGETARIAN | VEGAN OPTION | DAIRY-FREE OPTION | GLUTEN-FREE | NUT-FREE

Risotto is one of my all-time favorite dishes. What's not to love? Creamy rice, cheesy flavor . . . What I *don't* love about it is standing over the stove for hours. This oven-baked version has all the flavor, without the babysitting, so you can enjoy it on even the busiest of weeknights! I add seared scallops for an extra-special meal, and grilled shrimp or a poached or fried egg for a quick protein option. I hope you love this much easier risotto as much as I do! As an added bonus, nutrition-packed mushrooms provide vitamin D, antioxidants, and a range of B vitamins, which help support energy metabolism in the body.

SERVES 6

1½ lb (680 g) mixed mushrooms, such as shiitake and cremini, thinly sliced (about 9 cups)

3 cloves garlic, grated or finely minced (about 1½ tsp)

15 sprigs fresh thyme, leaves removed and roughly chopped

Salt and freshly ground black pepper

5 Tbsp extra virgin olive oil, divided

2 shallots, peeled and minced (about ¼ cup)

1½ cups arborio rice

¾ cup dry white wine

4½ cups vegetable stock, plus more as needed

2 cups grated Parmesan cheese, plus more for garnish if desired

3 Tbsp unsalted butter

Meal Prep Tip

This risotto is designed as a large-batch recipe to provide built-in leftovers for the Crispy Arancini Cakes with Fried Eggs (page 250).

Time Saver

Buy pre-sliced mushrooms.

PREP AHEAD: The mushrooms, shallots, and garlic can be prepped ahead of time.

1. Preheat the oven to 400°F (200°C). Line a rimmed baking sheet with parchment paper.

2. On the prepared pan, toss the mushrooms with the garlic, thyme, salt and pepper to taste, and 3 tablespoons of oil until evenly coated. Roast for 20 minutes, stirring halfway through. Remove the mushrooms from the oven and set aside. Turn the oven down to 350°F (180°C).

3. Meanwhile, in an ovenproof Dutch oven, heat the remaining 2 tablespoons of oil over medium heat until shimmering, about 2 minutes. Add the shallots and cook, stirring occasionally, until fragrant, 2 to 3 minutes. Add the rice and cook until translucent, 3 to 4 minutes, stirring frequently so it doesn't burn.

4. Stir in the wine and cook, scraping up any brown bits from the bottom of the pan, until most of the wine has evaporated. Add the stock, cover, and bring to a simmer.

5. Once the rice mixture is simmering, transfer it to the oven, still covered, and bake until the liquid is mostly absorbed, 18 to 20 minutes.

6. Return the rice to the stove, over medium-high heat. If the risotto is too dry, or you desire a creamier consistency, add more broth, ½ cup at a time, stirring until most of the liquid is absorbed and the desired consistency is achieved. Stir in the roasted mushrooms.

7. Remove the risotto from the heat and stir in the Parmesan and butter. Season with salt and pepper to taste. Serve with more Parmesan, if desired.

STORAGE: Store the cooled risotto in an airtight container in the fridge for up to 5 days or in the freezer for up to 3 months. If frozen, thaw in the microwave or overnight in the fridge. To serve, bring ¼ cup of stock or water per 1 cup of risotto to a boil. Add the risotto and stir until it's warmed through, 5 to 10 minutes. Alternatively, reheat in the microwave (you do not need the extra stock or water for this method).

Crispy Arancini Cakes with Fried Eggs

VEGETARIAN | NUT-FREE

What I love about this arancini recipe is that it is so quick and easy but makes you feel like you're at a nice Italian restaurant! This version is majorly sped up by using leftovers from the Creamy Oven-Baked Mushroom Risotto (page 249) and combining the mozzarella right into the rice mixture so you don't have to manually stuff each ball. The fried egg on top provides protein and, as a bonus, antioxidant vitamin E. Paired with a tangy marinara sauce that complements the crisp golden-brown crust, these arancini are heaven in your mouth!

SERVES 4 (MAKES 8 CAKES)

Avocado oil spray

2 cups leftover risotto (page 249)

1 cup shredded mozzarella cheese

10 eggs, divided

1 cup panko bread crumbs

¼ cup unbleached all-purpose flour

Salt and freshly ground black pepper

1⅓ cups store-bought marinara sauce

1 to 2 Tbsp extra virgin olive oil

Serving Tip

I love serving arancini with the Easiest Arugula Salad (page 168)!

1. Preheat the oven to 425°F (220°C), with a rack set in the top third. Line a rimmed baking sheet with parchment paper and spray the paper with avocado oil until well covered. This is the key to making the cakes crispy.

2. In a medium bowl, stir together the risotto, mozzarella, and one egg until combined.

3. Set up a breading station by whisking one egg in a small bowl. In a second bowl, combine the panko, flour, ½ teaspoon salt, and ¼ teaspoon pepper.

4. Scoop a heaping ¼ cup of risotto mixture and roll it into a ball. Dip the ball in the egg, ensuring the outside is completely covered, then roll it in panko mix until completely coated. Place on the prepared baking sheet and press down to flatten it into a ½-inch-thick cake. Repeat to make eight arancini cakes. Spray the tops and sides well with avocado oil.

5. Bake on the top rack for 20 to 25 minutes, flipping halfway through, until both sides are golden brown. If needed, spray with more avocado oil when you flip them.

6. Meanwhile, in a small saucepan, heat the marinara sauce over medium heat until heated through. (Or microwave it in 20-second increments until heated through.)

7. In a large frying pan, heat 1 tablespoon of olive oil over medium heat. Crack the remaining 8 eggs into the pan (this may need to be done in batches, depending on the size of your pan). Cook the eggs, without moving them, for 2 to 3 minutes or until the whites start to turn opaque and bubble. Using a nonstick spatula, flip the eggs. Season with salt and pepper and cook until the whites are fully set but the yolk remains runny, about 1 more minute.

8. Divide the arancini cakes between four plates, top each with a fried egg, and serve the marinara alongside!

STORAGE: Store any leftover arancini in an airtight container in the fridge for up to 5 days. To serve, reheat in the microwave or, for crispier arancini, in a 350°F (180°C) oven or toaster oven until heated through, 10 to 12 minutes. Meanwhile, fry the eggs to top the arancini.

Creamy Roasted Tomato and White Bean Soup

VEGETARIAN | VEGAN OPTION | DAIRY-FREE OPTION | GLUTEN-FREE OPTION | NUT-FREE

Everyone needs a good tomato soup—one of the OG comfort food meals—in their repertoire. Tomatoes are special in that cooking them actually increases their nutritional benefits, making antioxidant lycopene more bioavailable (easier for our body to absorb and use). Going with the theme of ease, I turned this classic into a complete meal by blending in a can of beans. Not only do they add an easy source of fiber-rich protein, but they thicken the soup, giving it the perfect creamy consistency. That said, I won't be mad if you serve a grilled cheese on the side or cut it up to make grilled cheese croutons!

SERVES 4 TO 6

2 cans (each 28 oz/796 ml) whole tomatoes, pierced and drained, liquid reserved

1 onion, peeled and cut into eighths

4 cloves garlic, smashed

2 Tbsp fresh thyme leaves, plus more for garnish

2 Tbsp extra virgin olive oil, plus more for drizzling if desired

½ tsp salt

¼ tsp freshly ground black pepper, plus more for garnish

1 can (19 oz/540 ml) cannellini (white kidney) beans, drained and rinsed (about 2 cups)

1 cup milk (I recommend 2% or higher)

½ cup lightly drained oil-packed sun-dried tomatoes

Warm bread (sourdough or focaccia recommended!) or croutons, for serving

1. Preheat the oven to 425°F (220°C), with a rack placed in the top third. Line a large rimmed baking sheet with parchment paper.

2. Arrange the tomatoes, onion, garlic, and thyme on the prepared baking sheet. Drizzle with oil and season with salt and pepper. Stir to coat the ingredients evenly, then spread in a single layer.

3. Roast on the top rack for 20 minutes. Set the oven to broil and cook for another 5 minutes, until the tomatoes and onions are slightly charred.

4. Transfer the roasted tomato mixture to a blender and add the reserved tomato juice, beans, milk, and sun-dried tomatoes. Blend until smooth, then season with more salt to taste.

5. Pour the soup into a large pot and heat through over medium-high heat, 3 to 5 minutes.

6. Divide the soup into bowls and top with more pepper, thyme (if desired), and a drizzle of oil, if desired. Serve with warm bread or croutons.

STORAGE: Store the soup in an airtight container in the fridge for up to 5 days or in a sealable freezer bag in the freezer for up to 3 months. If frozen, thaw in the microwave or overnight in the fridge. Reheat on the stove over medium heat until warmed through, about 5 to 7 minutes, or in the microwave.

Swaps & Subs

To make the soup vegan and dairy-free, opt for a plant-based milk. To make it gluten-free, serve with gluten-free bread or croutons.

Save-the-Day Freezer Enchiladas

NUT-FREE

Every time you finish eating enchiladas, you just want more—right? That's why I decided to make this one heck of a big-batch meal, with sixteen enchiladas for the taking. It barely takes any additional time to scale up the amount of filling, versus making it from scratch each time. This super-satisfying dish is also packed with nourishing goodness, from the antioxidant-rich beans to the vitamin-packed zucchini to iron from the chicken, all rolled up into a delicious, balanced meal. I recommend popping one batch into the freezer to have ready when you need them most. There is nothing like pulling out a homemade freezer meal and appreciating the efforts of your past self!

**MAKES 2 BATCHES
OF 8 ENCHILADAS
(4 SERVINGS EACH)**

ENCHILADAS

3 Tbsp extra virgin olive oil

1 small white onion, diced
(about 1 cup)

3 cloves garlic, grated or finely
minced (about 1½ tsp)

1 tsp ground cumin

½ tsp chili powder

½ tsp salt

2 small zucchini, diced
(about 3 cups)

1 rotisserie chicken, shredded
(about 6 cups)

1 can (19 oz/540 ml) black
beans, drained and rinsed
(about 2 cups)

2 cups red enchilada sauce, divided

Sixteen 6-inch tortillas

3 cups shredded Tex-Mex cheese

TOPPINGS

1 avocado, diced

Sour cream or plain Greek yogurt,
(optional)

Salsa (optional)

Chopped fresh cilantro (optional)

Thinly sliced green onion
(optional)

Thinly sliced jalapeños (optional)

Hot sauce (optional)

1. Preheat the oven to 400°F (200°C).

2. In a large frying pan, heat the oil over medium-high heat. Add the onion, garlic, cumin, chili powder, and salt. Sauté until the onion is translucent, 2 to 3 minutes. Add the zucchini and cook, stirring occasionally, until beginning to brown, 8 to 10 minutes. Stir in the chicken, beans, and ½ cup of the enchilada sauce until well combined.

3. Lay out all of the tortillas in an assembly line on a flat surface. Evenly distribute half of the cheese among the tortillas, then top with the chicken mixture, dividing evenly.

4. Spread ¼ cup of enchilada sauce over the bottom of each of two 9 × 13-inch baking dishes. Roll up the tortillas, leaving the ends open, and place eight in each baking dish, seam side down. Top each batch with ½ cup of enchilada sauce, then sprinkle the remaining cheese over top, dividing evenly. Cover one dish tightly with plastic wrap and then foil, and freeze.

5. Place the other dish in the oven and bake, uncovered, until the cheese melts and begins to bubble, 15 to 20 minutes. Remove from the oven and let cool for 5 to 10 minutes.

6. Serve the enchiladas with the desired toppings.

STORAGE: Label the freezer batch with these instructions: 1) Preheat the oven to 425°F (220°C). 2) Remove the plastic wrap from under the foil, then recover with foil and bake from frozen until warmed through, 50 to 60 minutes. 3) Remove the foil, set the oven to broil, and broil until the cheese is golden brown, about 3 minutes.

Store any leftover cooled enchiladas, without toppings, in an airtight container in the fridge for up to 4 days or in a sealable freezer bag in the freezer for up to 3 months. Reheat in the microwave or in a 350°F (180°C) oven or toaster oven until heated through, about 15 to 20 minutes if thawed, or 30 to 60 minutes from frozen (depending on the amount and how tightly packed they are).

Tip

To brighten up any frozen meal, whether homemade or store-bought, add something fresh, like diced avocado and fresh cilantro.

Sheet Pan Chimichurri Salmon with Crispy Roasted Potatoes and Green Beans

DAIRY-FREE | GLUTEN-FREE | NUT-FREE

Sheet pan meals are a thing of beauty: minimal prep, minimal cleanup, and usually great leftovers. Salmon is one of my favorite proteins, packed with flavor and the anti-inflammatory benefits of omega-3s. Enjoy this dish for an easy weeknight meal or to impress guests while *actually* getting to visit rather than fussing over the stove. The chimichurri will have everyone raving! I often say that recipes are just a template, and while I love green beans in this dish, they can easily be replaced with almost any vegetable you have on hand. Broccoli, cauliflower, broccolini, bell peppers, or zucchini are just a few you could try. So here's your reminder to have fun in the kitchen and never make unnecessary grocery trips. *Bon appétit!*

SERVES 6

2¼ lb (1 kg) Little Gems or other baby potatoes, halved

4 Tbsp extra virgin olive oil, divided

Salt and freshly ground black pepper

1¼ lb (550 g) green beans, trimmed (about 6 cups)

1 large lemon, thinly sliced into 10 to 12 rounds

1½ lb (680 g) skinless salmon, cut into 6 fillets

1 cup Chimichurri (page 81 or store-bought)

Lemon wedges, for serving

Tip

I recommend doubling up the chimichurri recipe and popping half in the freezer so that it's ready to go the next time you want to make this meal!

Time Saver

Swap the chimichurri for your favorite store-bought pesto. I love sun-dried tomato pesto on this!

PREP AHEAD: The salmon can be cut, the green beans trimmed, and the chimichurri made ahead of time.

IF YOU'RE FOLLOWING THE MEAL PLAN: With the prepped salmon, green beans, and chimichurri on hand, make all six servings. Serve four now and store the other two for lunch tomorrow.

1. Preheat the oven to 400°F (200°C). Line two rimmed baking sheets with parchment paper.

2. In a large bowl, toss the potatoes with 2 tablespoons of olive oil and season generously with salt and pepper. Arrange the potatoes in a single layer across both of the prepared pans and bake for 25 minutes.

3. Remove the pans from the oven and evenly divide the green beans, lemon slices, and 1 tablespoon of oil between the pans. Stir to coat the beans in oil and mix them with the potatoes. Create three divots on each pan for the salmon. Lay a salmon fillet in each divot and brush with the remaining tablespoon of oil. Season the fillets generously with salt and pepper.

4. Bake until the potatoes are golden brown and the salmon is opaque and flakes easily with a fork, 12 to 15 minutes. (For wild salmon, check at 9 to 10 minutes for doneness.)

5. Divide the salmon and vegetables between serving plates and top each fillet with chimichurri and more lemon wedges, salt, or pepper, as desired.

STORAGE: Store the cooled fish and vegetables in an airtight container in the fridge for up to 3 days. To serve, reheat on the stove or in the microwave, and top with chimichurri.

Skillet Turkey Nacho Bake

DAIRY-FREE OPTION | GLUTEN-FREE | NUT-FREE

I've said it before and I'll say it again: food should be fun, and it should feel good! So I'll take any chance I get to amp up both the nutrition and fun of a dish. This recipe is packed with antioxidant-rich veggies, fiber-rich whole grains, and plant-powered legumes—and you get to dip chips in it. It also makes amazing leftovers and is a freezer-friendly meal, so feel free to double it up or, if you're cooking for a smaller crowd, throw half in the freezer. Your future self will thank you.

SERVES 6 TO 8

1 Tbsp avocado oil or other high-heat cooking oil

1 lb (450 g) ground turkey

1 Tbsp chili powder

1 Tbsp ground cumin

1 tsp salt

1 can (28 oz/796 ml) diced tomatoes, half of the juice drained

1 can (14 oz/398 ml) mixed beans, drained and rinsed (about 1½ cups)

2 cups cooked brown rice (page 58)

1½ cups corn kernels

1 cup riced cauliflower

3 cups shredded Tex-Mex cheese, divided

Thinly sliced green onion, for garnish

Sliced avocado, for serving (optional)

Diced jalapeños, for serving (optional)

Salsa, for serving (optional)

Tortilla chips, for serving

PREP AHEAD: The rice can be cooked ahead of time. The turkey mixture can be cooked as in step 2 up to 3 days ahead and stored in an airtight container in the fridge.

1. Preheat the oven to 400°F (200°C).

2. In a large cast-iron or ovenproof pan, heat the oil over medium-high heat. Add the turkey and season with the chili powder, cumin, and salt, breaking the turkey into a few large pieces. Cook, without stirring, until the first side is browned, 4 to 5 minutes. Flip and brown the other side, another 2 to 4 minutes, then break into smaller pieces and cook, stirring, until no pink remains. Turn off the heat.

3. Stir in the tomatoes with their remaining juice, beans, rice, corn, cauliflower, and half of the cheese. Sprinkle the remaining cheese on top.

4. Bake until the cheese is bubbling around the edges of the pan, 25 to 30 minutes.

5. Serve the turkey mixture garnished with green onion and, if desired, avocado, jalapeños, and salsa. Serve with tortilla chips for dipping and enjoy!

STORAGE: Prepare the turkey mixture through step 4, let cool, and store in an airtight container in the fridge for up to 4 days or in the freezer for up to 3 months. If refrigerated, reheat on the stove or in the microwave. If frozen, reheat in a 350°F (180°C) oven until warmed through, 15 to 20 minutes, or in the microwave. Once the turkey mixture is reheated, continue with step 5.

Swaps & Subs

To make this recipe dairy-free, opt for a plant-based cheese.

Chinese Ginger Garlic Fish en Papillote

DAIRY-FREE | NUT-FREE

The flavors of this easy and delicious fish dish are inspired by a staple we enjoyed at special dinners when I was growing up. If you've never been to one, Chinese banquet dinners are something special. Often held to celebrate a marriage, a new baby, or a big birthday, they are a time to gather and celebrate over good food—and a lot of it! My Chinese side of the family is big! I've always loved seeing grandparents, aunts, uncles, and cousins—lots of cousins—at these family gatherings. There's an energy about them that's hard to match. This dish takes those celebratory flavors, but in a packet you can pop into the oven and pull out fifteen or so minutes later, steamed to perfection. Garlic and ginger not only add big flavor, but contribute powerful anti-inflammatory compounds, making them two of my favorite ingredients. Serve the fish over rice and make it a celebration, just because!

SERVES 4

GINGER GARLIC SAUCE

4-inch knob ginger, minced (about ¼ cup)

4 green onions, thinly sliced (about ¼ cup)

4 cloves garlic, grated or finely minced (about 2 tsp)

¼ cup warm water

¼ cup avocado oil or other high-heat cooking oil

2 Tbsp soy sauce

Pinch of granulated sugar

½ tsp salt

FISH PACKETS

3 cups chopped bok choy

1 lb (450 g) white fish (I like cod, black cod, or sea bass)

Salt and freshly ground black pepper

3 cups cooked white rice, reheated if prepped ahead (page 58)

1 bunch fresh cilantro, roughly chopped, for garnish

PREP AHEAD: The rice can be cooked and the bok choy can be prepped ahead of time. You can also prepare the sauce up to 5 days ahead and store it in the fridge.

1. Preheat the oven to 400°F (200°C). Cut a large piece of parchment paper that measures one and a half times the width of a large rimmed baking sheet. Cover the baking sheet so that equal amounts are hanging over each side.

2. **Make the sauce:** In a small bowl, whisk together the ginger, green onions, garlic, water, oil, soy sauce, sugar, and salt.

3. **Make the fish packets:** Spread the bok choy lengthwise on one half of the creased parchment paper. Top with the fish and half of the sauce, reserving the other half to drizzle over the cooked fish. Season with salt and pepper. Fold the top half of the paper over the fish, like closing a book. Starting at one end, start folding and crimping the edges of the paper, working your way around to create a tight seal around the fish. It should end up looking like a half-moon. Don't wrap the fish too tightly: heat and air need to be able to circulate well to properly steam it.

4. Bake until the fish is opaque and flakes easily with a fork, 14 to 16 minutes. (If your fillets are on the thicker side, they may need to cook for an additional 3 to 5 minutes.) Open the packet carefully to avoid escaping steam.

5. Serve the fish and bok choy over hot rice, sprinkled with cilantro and drizzled with the remaining sauce. Enjoy!

STORAGE: Prepare the fish through step 4, then transfer the contents of the packet to an airtight container, let cool, and store in the fridge for up to 3 days. To serve, reheat on the stove or in the microwave, then continue with step 5.

Creamy Parmesan Polenta with Tomato Cajun Shrimp

GLUTEN-FREE | NUT-FREE

Polenta has been a fairly recent addition to my kitchen, and I have no idea what took me so long. It has a delicious, creamy texture and provides somewhat of a blank canvas to pick up the flavors of whatever you cook it in or serve it with. In this recipe, it makes a perfect bed for flavorful Cajun shrimp that have been tossed with fresh tomatoes at the last minute to create the most delicious sauce. The whole meal comes together in just 20 minutes or so (thanks to quick-cooking and selenium-rich cornmeal), making it a go-to for busy nights!

SERVES 4

POLENTA

2 Tbsp salted butter

2 cups milk

2 cups chicken or vegetable stock

1 cup ground yellow cornmeal

½ cup grated Parmesan cheese, plus more for garnish if desired

Salt and freshly ground black pepper

SHRIMP

1 Tbsp salted butter

1 lb (450 g) raw peeled shrimp, thawed, rinsed, and patted dry

1 Tbsp Cajun seasoning (page 76 or store-bought)

1 pint mixed color cherry tomatoes, quartered

¼ cup chopped fresh parsley (optional)

Lemon wedges, for serving

IF YOU'RE FOLLOWING THE MEAL PLAN: Make all four servings now and enjoy!

1. **Make the polenta:** In a medium pot, melt 2 tablespoons of butter over medium heat. Add the milk, stock, and cornmeal, stirring so all the cornmeal is coated. Bring to a low boil, stirring until the polenta is thick and creamy, 3 to 5 minutes. Stir in the Parmesan and season with salt and pepper to taste. Turn off the heat, cover the pot, and let sit for 5 minutes.

2. **Make the shrimp:** In a large frying pan, heat 1 tablespoon of butter over medium-high heat. Add the shrimp and Cajun seasoning, toss to coat, then cook, without stirring, for 1 to 2 minutes. Flip the shrimp and cook, again without stirring, for another 1 to 2 minutes, until the shrimp are firm, pink, and opaque. Add the tomatoes and toss to combine and heat slightly. Remove from the heat.

3. Spoon the polenta into bowls and top with the shrimp and tomatoes. If desired, garnish with parsley and more Parmesan. Finish with a squeeze of lemon.

STORAGE: Store the polenta and shrimp, without the garnishes, in an airtight container in the fridge for up to 3 days. To serve, reheat on the stove or in the microwave, then garnish as desired.

Coconut Red Curry Mussels

GLUTEN-FREE | NUT-FREE

One of the things I love most about mussels is that they feel like a fun restaurant meal but are so easy to make at home. The creamy coconut red curry sauce is jam-packed with flavor, and the whole dish comes together in 20 minutes. On top of being delicious, mussels are a great source of protein, iron, and zinc. Could there be anything better? These are best enjoyed in good company—open a bottle of crisp white wine, invite some friends over, and slurp up the delicious sauce to your heart's content!

SERVES 4

¼ cup salted butter

2-inch knob ginger, minced (about 2 Tbsp)

4 large cloves garlic, grated or finely minced (about 2 tsp)

8 Roma (plum) tomatoes, diced

2 cans (each 14 oz/400 ml) full-fat coconut milk

¼ cup Thai red curry paste (sometimes just called red curry paste)

¼ cup chopped fresh cilantro, divided

2 Tbsp fish sauce

Juice of 1 lime (about 2 Tbsp)

3 lb (1.4 kg) mussels, debearded and scrubbed

Toasted sourdough bread or focaccia, for serving (optional, see tip)

PREP AHEAD: The ginger, garlic, and tomatoes can be cut ahead of time.

1. In a large pot, melt the butter over medium heat. Add the ginger and garlic and cook until fragrant, about 1 minute. Add the tomatoes and sauté for 4 to 5 minutes, until they begin to soften.

2. Stir in the coconut milk, curry paste, 2 tablespoons of the cilantro, fish sauce, and lime juice, ensuring the curry paste breaks up and fully mixes in. Bring to a low boil.

3. Add the mussels, cover the pot, and cook at a low boil until the mussels open, about 5 minutes. Remove from the heat, stir, and discard any mussels that did not open.

4. Serve immediately, sprinkled with the remaining cilantro, with bread to sop up the sauce. Enjoy!

STORAGE: Store the mussels and sauce in an airtight container in the fridge for up to 2 days. To serve, reheat on the stove over medium-low heat until warmed through, 5 to 7 minutes.

Tip

To keep it gluten-free, use a gluten-free bread or omit the bread altogether.

Ma-Ma's 100 Wontons

DAIRY-FREE | NUT-FREE

When I was growing up, my ma-ma (grandma) would come visit us in Kamloops every summer, and one thing sure to be on her agenda was stocking our freezer with enough wontons to last us through the winter. I remember sitting at the kitchen table, feet not yet touching the ground, and watching as she meticulously folded them one by one into perfect, tiny little packages of love and flavor. I know this experience contributed to my love of food and being in the kitchen, and I am so grateful to have learned from the best and to be able to pass this family recipe on to you. It is also a reminder that perspective is everything: folding 100 wontons could easily feel like a daunting task, but if you let it, fold by fold, it can be a mindfulness exercise, therapeutic as you become immersed in the repetitive action, knowing that your actions of today will serve as nourishment and ready-to-go meals when you need them most.

MAKES 100

2 lb (900 g) extra-lean or lean ground pork

2-inch knob ginger, minced (about 2 Tbsp)

4 cloves garlic, grated or finely minced (about 2 tsp)

2 green onions, thinly sliced (about 2 Tbsp)

1 can (8 oz/227 g) water chestnuts, diced

1 tsp red pepper flakes

1 tsp freshly ground black pepper

2 eggs

2 Tbsp soy sauce

2 tsp toasted sesame oil

100 square wonton wrappers

1. In a medium bowl, combine the pork, ginger, garlic, green onions, water chestnuts, red pepper flakes, pepper, eggs, soy sauce, and oil. Use a fork to mix well.

2. To set up your wonton-making station, line a baking sheet with parchment paper. Clean a large area on your counter and lay out as many wrappers as will fit. Fill a small bowl with water—this will be used to moisten the edges of the wrappers and seal the wontons.

3. Spoon ½ to 1 teaspoon of the filling onto a wonton wrapper (see tip). Dip your fingers or a pastry brush in water and moisten the edges of the wrapper, being careful not to wet them too much. Fold the top corner of the wrapper over the filling to meet the bottom corner, making a triangle. Press the edges firmly to seal. Bring the left and right corners together above the filling. Overlap the tips of these corners, moisten with water, and press together (see the step-by-step photos opposite). Place the wonton on the prepared baking sheet. Repeat until all the filling has been used up.

4. Cook immediately (see page 269 for Ma-Ma's Wonton Soup) or freeze until ready to use.

STORAGE: To freeze, make sure the wontons are sitting upright on the baking sheet and not touching each other. Place the baking sheet in the freezer until the wontons are firm, 1 to 2 hours, then transfer them to a large sealable freezer bag and store in the freezer for up to 3 months. To serve, cook from frozen, following the recipe for Ma-Ma's Wonton Soup (page 269).

Swaps & Subs

While ground pork is my preferred filling, it can be swapped for ground turkey or chicken, or even mixed half and half!

Tip

Wonton wrappers come in different sizes. Test one wrapper with 1 teaspoon of filling and see if it will seal properly. If it does, continue adding 1 tsp to all the wrappers. If it doesn't, reduce to ½ teaspoon or as much as will fit while allowing wontons to seal.

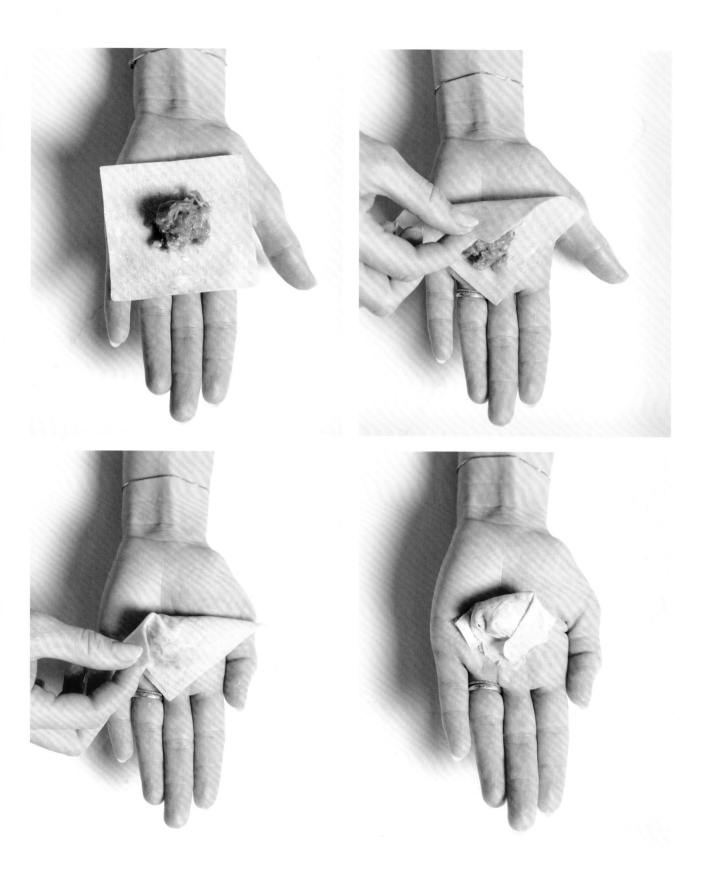

Ma-Ma's Wonton Soup

DAIRY-FREE | NUT-FREE

It's the best feeling pulling my Ma-Ma's Wontons out of the freezer—ready to be cooked in a warming soup. This is one of our best family kitchen hacks, allowing us to enjoy the gift of time with loved ones while the pot of broth on the stove does the heavy lifting for you. Before you know it, you've got a comforting meal on the table with very little effort from you!

SERVES 4

6 cups chicken stock

2 tsp sesame oil

25 to 30 frozen wontons (page 266)

10½ oz (300 g) mushrooms (I like shiitake or enoki), sliced (about 4 cups)

2 cups snow peas, trimmed

2 green onions, thinly sliced (about 2 Tbsp), for garnish

Sriracha or Chili Crisp Oil (page 78 or store-bought), for serving (optional)

PREP AHEAD: The snow peas and mushrooms can be prepped and the wontons made and frozen ahead of time.

1. In a large pot, bring the stock and oil to a boil. Add the wontons and mushrooms and boil for 5 minutes. Add the snow peas and cook for 1 to 2 minutes or until the peas are cooked but still slightly firm and the wontons have cooked through.

2. Ladle the soup into bowls and top with green onions and sriracha or chili oil, if desired. Enjoy!

STORAGE: After step 1, remove the wontons from the broth using a slotted spoon and let cool. Store the wontons and broth in separate airtight containers in the fridge for up to 4 days. To serve, reheat the broth and wontons together on the stove or in the microwave, then continue with step 2.

A Vegan Chili the Meat Lovers Will Beg For

VEGAN | DAIRY-FREE | GLUTEN-FREE | NUT-FREE

There is something so comforting about a bowl of chili. It's also one of my favorite batch-prep meals, with the flavor only getting better over time. Dump everything into a big pot or a slow cooker and let it do its thing! You can rest easy knowing that beans have your back: they're one of the most cost-effective and nutrient-dense protein sources, packed with soluble fiber (known for its blood-sugar-balancing properties and cholesterol-lowering potential), B vitamins for energy metabolism, and minerals such as iron, zinc, and magnesium. I love the slightly sweet addition of roasted sweet potato, but feel free to skip this step if you want to speed things up!

SERVES 8

1 sweet potato, cut into ½-inch cubes (about 2 cups)

1 Tbsp avocado oil or other high-heat cooking oil

Salt and freshly ground black pepper

2 Tbsp extra virgin olive oil

1 red onion, diced (about 1 cup)

1½ lb (680 g) veggie ground round

2 cans (each 28 oz/796 ml) diced tomatoes, with juice

1 can (19 oz/540 ml) kidney beans, drained and rinsed (about 2 cups)

1 can (19 oz/540 ml) mixed beans, drained and rinsed (about 2 cups)

1 can (10 oz/285 g) sliced mushrooms, drained

1 can (5.5 oz/156 ml) tomato paste

1½ Tbsp chili powder

5 dashes of hot sauce

Sour cream, for garnish (optional; omit to keep it vegan)

Shredded cheese, for garnish (optional; use plant-based cheese to keep it vegan)

Cilantro leaves, for garnish

Sliced avocado, for garnish (optional)

Green onion, for garnish (optional)

1. Preheat the oven to 425°F (220°C). Line a large rimmed baking sheet with parchment paper.

2. Place the sweet potato on the prepared baking sheet and drizzle with the avocado oil. Season generously with salt and pepper and toss to coat, then spread out in a single layer. Roast for 40 to 45 minutes, stirring halfway through, until fork-tender.

3. Meanwhile, in a large frying pan, heat the olive oil over medium-high heat. Add the onion and cook until translucent, 3 to 4 minutes. Add the ground round, break into large pieces, and cook, without stirring, for another 5 minutes, allowing it to brown. Flip and break into smaller pieces and cook for another 3 to 4 minutes until the other side is browned (it doesn't have to be fully cooked through, as it will finish cooking in the slow cooker).

4. Transfer the onion and ground round to a slow cooker (or see the tip for stovetop cooking instructions). Stir in the roasted sweet potato, tomatoes with juice, kidney beans, mixed beans, mushrooms, tomato paste, chili powder, and hot sauce. Cover and cook on low for 8 to 12 hours or on high for 4 hours.

5. Ladle the chili into bowls and, if desired, top with sour cream, cheese, cilantro, avocado, and green onion. Enjoy!

STORAGE: Store the cooled chili in an airtight container in the fridge for up to 5 days or in an airtight container or sealable freezer bag in the freezer for up to 3 months. To serve, reheat on the stove or in the microwave (thawing first, if frozen), and top as desired.

Tip
I like to make chilis in a slow cooker for the best flavor, but if you don't have one, simply use a large pot and let it simmer on the stovetop for at least 30 minutes or up to 2 hours.

Swaps & Subs
Swap the veggie ground round for ground beef or turkey if you prefer a meatier version. In step 3, cook the meat until both sides are browned before adding it to the slow cooker.

Meal Prep Styles Recipe List

Ingredient Prep

10-Minute Chicken, Fig, and Brie Sourdough Sandwiches (page 212)

15-Minute Cajun Fish Tacos with Quick Pickled Cabbage (page 216)

20-Minute Miso Ramen with Jammy Eggs (page 186)

Better-than-Takeout Tender Beef and Broccoli Udon (page 190)

Charlie's Lo Mein (page 189)

Chicken, Corn, and Feta Quesadillas (page 232)

Chinese Ginger Garlic Fish en Papillote (page 261)

Coconut Red Curry Mussels (page 265)

Creamy Roasted Vegetable Sheet Pan Gnocchi (page 245)

Crispy Black Pepper and Maple Tofu Stir-Fry (page 197)

Crispy Honey Valentina Cauliflower Bites (page 147)

Crispy Honey Valentina Cauliflower Tacos (page 211)

Easiest Arugula Salad (page 168)

Famous Kale Caesar with Creamy Greek Yogurt Dressing and Crispy Chickpeas and Capers (page 159)

Helen's One-Pan Sun-Dried Tomato and Basil Balsamic Chicken Orzo (page 242)

Jangs' Famous Fried Rice (page 205)

Kale, Apple, and Crispy Cajun White Bean Salad (page 172)

Korean-Inspired Beef and Rice Bowls with Pickled Cukes (page 198)

Ma-Ma's Wonton Soup (page 269)

Mila's Sticky Orange Chicken (page 194)

One-Pan Green Goddess Hash (page 114)

Peach and Burrata Panzanella Salad (page 164)

Peanutty Soba Noodle Bowls (page 193)

Ready-in-a-Pinch Sweet and Spicy Soy-Glazed Sushi Tacos (page 220)

Roasted Tomato and Seared Scallop Capellini (page 238)

Seared Salmon Burgers with the Easiest Tartar Sauce Ever (page 215)

Sesame Seared Wasabi Tuna Wraps (page 231)

Sheet Pan Chimichurri Salmon with Crispy Roasted Potatoes and Green Beans (page 257)

Sheet Pan Margarita Shrimp Fajitas (page 219)

Sheet Pan Pancakes with Blueberry Chia Compote (page 117)

Skillet Turkey Nacho Bake (page 258)

Strawberry Summer Salad (page 171)

Summer Pasta (page 241)

Sweet and Spicy Soy-Glazed Salmon Bowls (page 201)

Thai-Inspired Lettuce Wraps (page 223)

Thai Peanut Red Curry (page 206)

Waikiki Tuna Poke Bowls (page 202)

Batch Prep

Super-Quick

Freezer-Friendly

Acknowledgments

To my readers and community, with this book in your hands—this book is for you! You've asked for more meal prep and meal planning and I'm so grateful to have been able to bring this to life! Without you, none of this would be possible. Thank you for supporting me and allowing me to be a small part of your life and your kitchens. Whether you're part of my blog and newsletter communities or we've connected on social media, every single message or kind word you've shared, every like or comment on a recipe, and every time you choose to spend your precious time to try one of my recipes, it truly means the world!

To the incredible team who made this book a reality, it truly takes a village and I could not have dreamt up a better one.

THE INCREDIBLE APPETITE AT PENGUIN RANDOM HOUSE CANADA TEAM: To my amazing editors Rachel Brown and Whitney Millar, thank you for making this dream of mine a reality, for seeing something in me I didn't yet see in myself, and for guiding me every step of the way. Thank you for sharing your insane talent and pouring your hearts into the process to make this book the best version it could possibly be, while always honoring my vision and encouraging me to "do what feels right to you!" I am forever grateful. To Lindsay Paterson, editorial director; Robert McCullough, publisher; Matt Flute, designer, Sue Sumeraj, copyeditor; Lana Okerlund, proofreader— you are a dream team!

SAMMI FABBRO: My right-hand woman and wearer of all hats. There are truly no words. This book would not be here without you. From your ability to organize and visualize how to get from point A to point B in a way my brain simply cannot (and create a process and spreadsheet for it), to your other-worldly multitasking abilities in the kitchen and unwavering commitment through countless recipe-testing days, photoshoots, cooking, cooking, and more cooking, and so much more. Everyone needs a Sammi and I am beyond grateful, not only for your professional support, but for your friendship. "Thank you" simply is not enough!

MOM AND DAD: Writing this book while pregnant with Indie and during the first year of her life was not without its challenges. Your support throughout this process should not come as a surprise, as it parallels the support and unconditional love you have always shown me. From late-night phone calls to share exciting news or reassure me when overwhelm and doubt got the best of me, to dropping everything to come help with Indie on recipe-testing and shoot days before I had childcare, and running countless errands, doing it all with patience, love, and kindness. Thank you for always encouraging me to go after my dreams, to follow my passions, and to trust that nothing is ever a failure if it's done with heart and integrity.

TO MY HUBBY MEIK: How did I get so lucky to do life with you? To the guy who loves an organized space, thank you for putting up with the absolute chaos that was our kitchen for the better part of a year (although I know you didn't mind the recipe testing). Thank you for picking up the slack around the house, taking on extra daycare drops and pick-ups, countless emergency grocery store runs for the missing ingredient, and everything in between. Most of all, thank you for always believing in me and my dreams, even when I've doubted myself. You are always there to listen patiently as I ramble on about my ideas and visions (sometimes obsessively), to help me come up with solutions, and to be my biggest cheerleader and celebrate the wins. I love you so much.

WYLDER AND INDIE: My forever inspirations and greatest purpose (you too, Theo, our little star in the sky). You are my constant reminders of what really matters in life, grounding me when I get caught up in work stress—you bring joy and lightness to my day when I need it most, just by being you. You're my most honest recipe testers (I KNOW I can count on you not to sugarcoat your feedback). Thank you for understanding when Mommy had to work on a Wy-ndie Wednesday (our special day off together each week) and for inspiring the recipes in the book that would excite adults and kids alike. You are my heart.

TO MY WONDERFUL RECIPE TESTERS: Meghan McDonald, Evelyne Diederichs, Vanessa Fabbro, and Chelsea Bewza, your input, time, and careful thought were so appreciated and integral in ensuring that the recipes, and especially the meal plans, hit the mark on flavor, ease, and efficiency! Thank you!

SUSIE SIDSWORTH: Thank you for letting us use your gorgeous home to create (beautiful?) chaos for the lifestyle images in this book. I am so lucky to have such a generous, supportive, and stylish friend like you.

JANIS NICOLAY: I'm so glad I trusted my gut. I remember our first call about potentially working together—you instantly made me feel calm, at ease, and confident that I could do this! You are so incredibly generous with your time, and your experience, eye, and incredible talent are unmatched.

SOPHIA MACKENZIE: Thank you for stepping in to uplevel the food styling. You make it look easy and made those difficult-to-style dishes come to life so beautifully!

And to the most amazing friends and family a girl could ask for, thank you for being my biggest hype people! Thank you for continuing to check in, helping me tweak recipes till they're perfect, and maintaining your excitement for the nearly five years it took this book to go from idea to publication. I could feel your support every step of the way and it truly kept me going.

Index